Nigel

Thank you so much
for all you've doing
for our Practice
+
Courtney

Very Best wishes

BEYOND TERROR

ANNE MARIE WATERS

BEYOND

TERROR

―――――

ISLAM'S SLOW EROSION
OF WESTERN DEMOCRACY

ISBN 13: 978-0-9846938-8-7

Library of Congress Control Number: 2018947633

 Printed in the United States of America

First Printing: 2018

18 17 16 15 14   5 4 3 2 1

Cover art by Judith Nicols
Cover design by Glen Edelstein
Interior design by Glen Edelstein

SOMETHING

OR OTHER

PUBLISHING

Info@SOOPLLC.com

For bulk orders e-mail: Orders@SOOPLLC.com

This book is dedicated to those who tell the truth.

FOREWORD

By Daniel Pipes

EVERY EUROPEAN COUNTRY with an advanced Islamist problem has a political party in parliament focused on dealing with this challenge – except one, the United Kingdom. This absence of what I call a *civilizationist party* (because it seeks to save Western civilization) has profound implications; it means the British have no way to enact legislation against the Islamist threat nor do the existing parties feel pressure to pay attention to it. For this reason, "Londonistan" has the bleakest prospects of any Western country.

Anne Marie Waters, author of the book in your hands or on your screen, is one of the few who can fill the gap. As *Beyond Terror: Islam's Slow Erosion of Western Democracy* amply shows, she has the biography, skills, knowledge, and will to found a civilizationist party. Indeed, she initiated the process in late 2017 by establishing For Britain, a party "for the forgotten majority."

Seen in this light, *Beyond Terror* serves the triple purpose of self-introducing Waters to the public, documenting the civilizational problem, and laying out her policies.

The self-introduction emphasizes her and the Left's mutual disaffection; it shows how criticism of Islamism rendered her longstanding political home no longer hospitable. I found her insider's views illuminating, especially how pro-Islamism has become integral to the Left's world view and program. It's reached the point, Waters explains, that "the modern political Left will turn on its comrades if they fall out of favour with Islam." Strangely, opposing "a far-Right religious extremism that openly discriminates and condones violence against women, executes homosexuals, and punishes dissenters with the sword" gets one in big trouble.

This could only happen because "the modern Left has adopted a whole new set of priorities. No longer concerned with the rights of the working classes or protecting vulnerable minorities, the new university-educated middle-class Left is an ideological beast." In other words, economics is now secondary to identity politics. Workers, make way for the academics. Goodbye Marx, hello Gramsci.

"Far Right" is what *The Economist* calls Waters and what *The Times of London* calls For Britain; but this adjective outrageously distorts both their political identities. Waters comes from a strictly leftist background, having been a member of the Labour Party for about 10 years. Her political activism began in favour of keeping the socialist National Health Service. She served as both a trade union representative and as a board member of the National Secular Society. She calls herself a second-wave feminist and a near-free-speech absolutist.

Following her clash with the Left, her outlook now contains centrist qualities: She believes in personal liberty, in limited state intrusion, government accountability, low migration, and Christian- and secular-based Western civilisation. She favours the free market along with a strong public sector. She is a nationalist who opposes mass migration. In keeping with this profile, For Britain is neither Left nor Right, much less far Right, but represents what it calls "the decent majority."

Waters is shy about providing specifics on her travails in starting the party (did you not wonder why this very British-oriented book is published in the American Midwest?) and discussing future tactics. I look forward to more information from her on these topics.

The second part surveys outrages of the Islamist scourge, knowledgeably covering twelve Western countries (with special attention to the United Kingdom and the United States) and lightly touching on several Muslim-majority countries. She documents the ravages of the combined Islamist-Leftist machine on such topics as freedom of speech, homosexuality, and school instruction.

The final part offers Waters' prescriptions. She begins by noting that, when it comes to the twin issues of immigration and Islamization, the parties which dominate the British House of Commons, four in number, "are entirely inseparable" in their agreement on a "deliberate sanitisation of Islam." She portrays this collusion as an elite arrogance that views the voting public as "completely stupid."

Fortunately, if free speech "has dramatically decreased among our leaders," it "still exists in some form among ordinary people." And so, paraphrasing George Orwell, Waters turns to those ordinary people: "Hope lies with the proles." A populist surge is needed, and now: "The only way Islamism will be defeated, or even confronted, is through the power of the people. We must use our vote and our right to stand for political office in order to unseat complicit MPs."

She outlines a program consisting of five steps:

1. Restore accountable government by returning power from international institutions (i.e., the European Union) to the nation-state.
2. Teach children positively about their country.
3. Apply one law to all, thereby ending "harmful Islamic practices."
4. Take control of immigration and deport immigrant criminals.
5. Keep a close watch on Islamic institutions for signs of Islamism.

These are unarguably sensible policy prescriptions, though I would add a #6: "Marginalize Islamism and help strengthen moderate Islam."

Waters understandably does not include such a recommendation. She writes: "I do not believe that Islam and Islamism are distinct. ... Islamism is merely the political implementation of the doctrines of Islam." In contrast, I hold the two are distinct: Islam is the entire faith, Islamism is one (extremist) interpretation of it. For Waters, Islamism represents the only true form of Islam; for me, it is just one way of implementing Islam and other, more benign interpretations exist and are equally valid.

This matter has profound importance: Waters disbelieves, and I do believe in a moderate Islam. She has no hopes for changes in Islam; I argue that radical Islam is the problem and moderate Islam is the solution. Among other benefits, my approach offers the possibility of cooperating with anti-Islamist Muslims, something I hope For Britain will make a priority.

Despite our disagreement on the nature of the enemy, Anne Marie Waters and I stand in the same trench, fighting the same opponents. I therefore hope this manifesto will contribute to creating the UK's urgently needed civilizationist party, that For Britain will soon enter parliament, and once there, it will help shape the country's future.

—DANIEL PIPES
President, Middle East Forum
Philadelphia, Pennsylvania
April 2018

CONTENTS

INTRODUCTION

THIS IS NOT a book about terrorism. Terrorism has been prevalent throughout history and throughout the world. It occurs for an assortment of reasons – political, religious, or otherwise.

This is not a book about international politics or the relationship between the so-called Islamic world and the rest. It is not about the war on terror, or the status of the USA as a global superpower. It is not about colonialism, or the past deeds of European powers.

This is a book about Islam as a political force. It is about life within Islamic societies and the beliefs that govern them. It is about Islamic attitudes to free speech, women, homosexuals, and individual freedom. It is about how these beliefs are now impacting on the democratic nations of the Western world.

For all its faults, the West is the only part of the world in which I would choose to live. This is particularly pertinent given my gender. I am a female who values my autonomy and freedom above all else. The laws of Western democracies allow me to be free, and for this reason I appreciate my good fortune in having been born into one.

The West has established many great democracies. Some

countries (such as Britain) have maintained notions of democracy for centuries. The purpose of this book is therefore to make a contribution to the defence of democracy, and to the notion that it must be protected from attack – including the attack it faces by way of mass and unconditional immigration from the undemocratic world.

What is democracy? It is governance via the will of the people. For this to be realised, there must be free speech and equal application of the laws resulting from the democratic process. Therefore all people, including minorities and women, must have their rights protected. Civil liberties and the power of the people over those they elect are essential. Without these, democracy cannot exist. The erosion of these is the erosion of democracy.

It is a simple fact that some countries in the world are not democratic. Many are ruled via religion or totalitarianism (or both). It is also a simple fact that in recent decades, migration from the undemocratic world into established democracies has occurred in numbers not previously seen in recorded history. People with undemocratic views now reside in large numbers within liberal democracies.

I am not against immigration *per se*. People have much to learn from other societies, and the exchange of experience and knowledge can help us to grow, develop and improve. However, it is my view that people have the right to maintain an identity, including a national identity.

Human beings seek identity. This we know for certain because it is what we have always done. Humans establish identities usually in solidarity with those around them. Identity means a great deal; it is deeply emotional. People will both die and kill in protection of their identity.

Immigration within numerical limits that allow newcomers to integrate and become part of a society can be a highly positive thing. When borders are open, however, migrant numbers become too high and segregation results. Ghettoised communities become the norm. This then allows for physical separation, separate social norms, and self-policing and self-regulation of minority communities. Such developments negate the identity of the host nation, and can eventually split the land mass into new nations. The original national identity is altered or demolished altogether.

If a democracy opens its borders to people who do not believe in democracy, free speech, the rights and equality of women and minorities, and allows them to enter, might this then bring about the end of democracy in the host nation?

Let us take an example. When men spend their lives in a society where women are stoned to death for adultery, or imprisoned for being victims of rape, what attitudes to adultery, rape, and women might they hold? Death by stoning and imprisonment for rape are not ideas held by the lunatic fringe that can easily be ignored; they are the laws of some lands. Isn't it possible that men who grow up in these societies will bring those attitudes to the West if they move here? What impact is that likely to have on the rights and freedoms of women in the host nation?

The answer to this question is extremely important.

In this book, I will examine the effect on the rights and freedoms of women in democratic societies that has resulted from vast migration from societies in which women do not enjoy rights and freedoms. Furthermore, I will consider the impact on freedom of speech that has resulted from mass migration from countries where free speech is not practised or valued. Indeed, in Islamic states, blasphemy (that is, any criticism of Islam) carries the death penalty. Again, this is not the ranting of an extremist fringe, but the law of the land – a law that is brutally enforced.

I am not tarring all Muslims with one brush. I'm perfectly aware that there are many Muslims who have no intention of harming anyone for insulting Islam, or of harming women. Many Muslims live with an interpretation of Islam that is private and unique to them. Many are oppressed in Islamic states for that reason, and come to the West to enjoy its democracy and freedoms. We should welcome people fleeing from oppression, but what is the point in the West being a place of refuge for the oppressed if it is also a place of refuge for the oppressor? We need to be very clear who is the oppressor and who is the oppressed. It is pertinent, therefore, to examine how widespread undemocratic beliefs are within societies from which people migrate to the West.

We are often told to believe that those who adhere to the brutal elements of Islam constitute only a tiny minority, but is this true? In Saudi Arabia, a survey in 2013 found that 87% of men believe women are to blame for sexual harassment and assault[1]. This is not a minority, and it stands to reason that when Saudi men move to the West, many will bring this belief along with them.

A Pew Research poll[2] – also in 2013 – revealed staggering results. High majorities in many countries want sharia as the law of the land. In Pakistan, for example, 85% favoured gender segregation, while 82% supported death by stoning for adultery. In Egypt, 82% support death by stoning for adultery, while 84% support the death penalty for leaving Islam. Given these statistics, is it not vital that we take care when allowing vast numbers to migrate to the West from these countries?

Currently in the West, on matters involving Islam, words have been manipulated and redefined in order to disguise unpalatable truths. An example is the word 'racist'. It is frequently alleged that objection to Islam is an act of racism, even though Islam is clearly a system of belief and has no connection whatsoever with race, ethnicity or skin colour. I am fully aware that not all Muslims in the West are immigrants. Many are fellow British citizens, so I maintain that I have every right to oppose and object to some of their beliefs and ideas, as I do those of any other British citizen, and that I have the right to do so without fearing arrest or accusations of racism. However, we frequently hear that those who object to Islam without mentioning race (i.e., the majority of critics) are merely *hiding* their racism, thus placing critics in an unwinnable position.

There are a couple of reasons that this occurs. Firstly, it is an attempt to shut down debate, and secondly, an accusation of racism deems the accused to be guilty of racism. Mere accusations – even

1 Muslim Statistics, "87% of Saudi men blame women for sexual harassment and assault – Survey," 2014, MuslimStatistics, (blog), accessed April 2, 2018. https://muslimstatistics.wordpress.com/2014/01/12/87-of-saudi-men-blame-women-for-sexual-assault-survey/
2 Pew Research Center, "Muslim Publics Divided on Hamas and Hezbollah," 2010, PewGlobal.org, accessed April 2, 2018, http://www.pewglobal.org/2010/12/02/muslims-around-the-world-divided-on-hamas-and-hezbollah/#prc-jump.

if without merit – can destroy reputations, careers, or even result in criminal charges. 'Racism' has ceased to be a word with a clear definition and has instead become a weapon used by political elites to silence the voice of opponents. This lack of clarity on the meaning of racism has resulted in many people becoming too frightened to express legitimate concerns about Islam or immigration.

ISLAM AND MUSLIMS

Unlike many others, I do not believe that Islam and Islamism are distinct and unconnected. Islamism is merely the political implementation of the doctrines of Islam. An Islamist is a person who seeks a state under Islamic law, and seeks to impose Islamic law upon all people – Muslim and non-Muslim – whether they believe in it or not, and whether they like it or not. Islamic law is sharia, and this book will make clear what sharia is, what it does, and what it means for the lives of human beings.

The fact is that Islamism derives its notions and its authority from Islamic scripture. To deny this is to deny reality. When Islamists come to power and impose death by stoning, for example, where do they get this idea? It comes from the Islamic ahadith: the example set by the Prophet Mohammed. The authority for wife beating comes from the Koran. It is a matter of fact.

The true distinction is between Islam and Muslims, because despite the best efforts of Islamists to persuade us otherwise, Islam and Muslims are not the same thing. A Muslim is a human being, endowed with rights and entirely capable of accepting, rejecting, ignoring, or re-interpreting aspects of Islam which they do not believe to be right or fair. The difference between a book and a person who reads a book is the difference between Islam and Muslims. Islam is the book, and people have every right to criticise it.

SOURCES

I believe in facts and the relevance of those facts, irrespective of who brings them to light. It is the message that matters, not the messenger. However, it is extremely difficult to find mainstream – or rather, Left-leaning publications willing to print the stories I refer to in this book. The field has been narrowed (by leftists primarily), and therefore so have my source options.

This book is written in plain English. It is not an academic exercise or an attempt at literary prowess. Nor does it provide a full measure of the scale of the problem. I have merely scratched the surface.

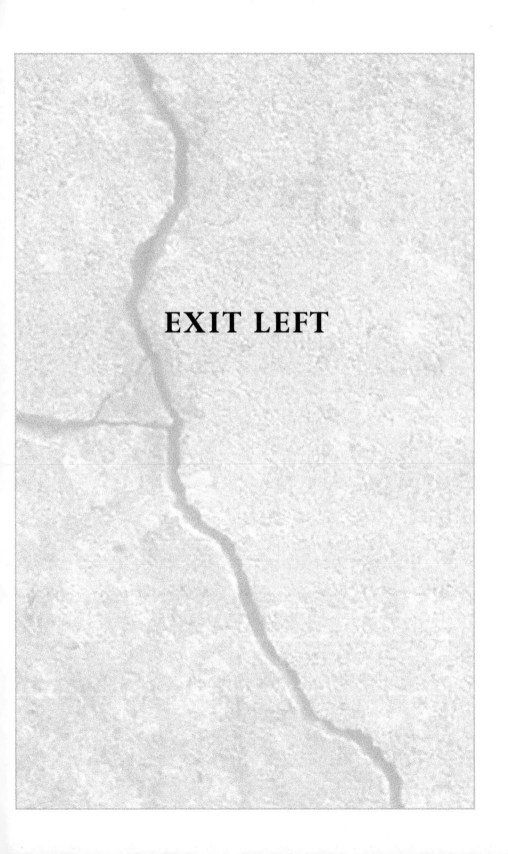

EXIT LEFT

THE BIGGEST THREAT TO THE UK SINCE THE SECOND WORLD WAR

By far the most common question I'm asked is why I stayed for so long. It's difficult to answer.

In 2013, the world I had inhabited for my entire adult life, everything I'd believed to be true and right, was turned inside-out and back-to-front. I had what I can only describe as an awakening. It is quite something to come face to face with a new reality – one which establishes not only how wrong you have been, but that the ideas you have spent years defending and propagating are the very ideas that have caused the problems you now confront.

I am referring to my complete and total departure from Left-wing politics, and my realisation that Left-wing politics had been both directly and indirectly responsible for the growth of Islamism in my country, and throughout the Western world. The Western Left is not responsible, of course, for Islam itself – Islam is responsible for that. But it is responsible for allowing Islamism to seep into democratic societies, such as the society in Britain, and alter them so they became less and less democratic and free.

My gradual departure from Left-wing politics was concluded in the city of Brighton and Hove – a seaside town in the south of

England. The reasons for my departure had begun to seep into my consciousness years before, but I failed to recognise them at the time. I had been struggling with my conscience before I realised what was causing me to do so.

Leading up to my exit, I was heavily involved in the Labour Party (Britain's major Left-of-centre political party) and was co-spokesperson of the One Law for All anti-sharia group. I was perfectly aware that many Left-wing groups were not only silent on the growth and dangers of Islamism, but actively supported Islamist campaigners and spokesmen. I failed, however, to see the intrinsic link between Left-wing thought and that of Islamists, and I believed that the Left, with persuasion, would come to its senses and realise its error.

That is the reason I held on for so long.

I had been encouraged by some active Labour Party members who told me they agreed with my position on sharia law (though I often wondered if they would be willing to say so publicly), and I was further encouraged when I put a motion to my local Labour Party constituency group asking them to support the Arbitration and Mediation Services (Equalities) Bill which Baroness Cox had placed before the House of Lords (the upper house of the UK Parliament) in 2011.

The aim of this Bill was to bring private arbitration bodies in Britain in line with laws on gender equality. For example, it would have specifically made it illegal to give the testimony of one party in arbitration more weight than the other. Under sharia law, a woman's word is worth half that of a man. This discrimination occurs, quite openly, in the network of sharia family tribunals operating with impunity in the UK. Baroness Cox wished to bring this to an end.

She also wanted to put a stop to the trickery employed by Islamists in instructing often-vulnerable women that they had no choice but to obey the rulings of their tribunals. Cox sought to make this a criminal offence. Most importantly, perhaps, the Bill aimed to limit the areas in which private tribunals could arbitrate, and remove family and criminal law matters (such as child custody and domestic violence) from their grip.

This was a controversial Bill, so I was nervous about asking my local Party to support it – but support it they did, with only one vote against. That gave me sustenance and encouraged me to think that Leftists would eventually open their eyes and robustly oppose Islamism.

These hopes were entirely dashed in July 2013 in a community centre in Brighton. Here, I learned that many (most?) activists on the political Left were in fact moving further away from opposing Islamism, and into the grip of a new Left Wing. Ideologically driven career politicians on the Left now appear to be blind to the rights of the working classes, to such a degree that they find themselves acting in opposition to Western democracy.

Brighton, as it turned out, was to prove to be my last straw.

THE BRIGHTON CAMPAIGN

In 2013, I put myself forward for Parliamentary selection in the constituency of Brighton Pavilion. Brighton is a town with a massive gay population on the south coast of England. The current MP is the only Green Party representative sitting in the House of Commons (the primary elected chamber of the UK Parliament): a popular Left Winger by the name of Caroline Lucas. I have met Lucas and she is certainly a formidable figure. However, she once came to the defence of the notorious Yusuf Al-Qaradawi (as did the former Mayor of London, Ken Livingstone of the Labour Party) when she said he had

been the victim of an Islamophobic smear campaign and most criticisms of him were based on people being ill-informed[1].

Al-Qaradawi is on record as supporting female genital mutilation[2], suicide bombings[3], and saying he longs for the day when Muslims will finish the job Hitler started[4]. Yet this man finds himself defended by many on the political Left in Britain.

1 STANDPOINT Magazine, "Overrated" (On "Caroline Lucas, Julie Bindel"), 2010, StandpointMag.co.uk, accessed April 2, 2018, http://www.standpointmag.co.uk/node/3309/full.
2 George Readings, "Female genital mutilation cannot be defended as part of Islam," 2010, The Guardian, accessed April 2.2018, http://www.theguardian.com/commentisfree/belief/2010/oct/15/female-genital-mutilation-yusuf-al-qaradawi.
3 BBC News, "Al-Qaradawi full transcript," 2004, News.bbc.co.uk, accessed April 2. 2018, http://news.bbc.co.uk/2/hi/3875119.stm.
4 "'Moderate' Qaradawi Defends Hitler and Nuclear Terror," The Investigative Project on Terrorism, accessed April 3, 2018, https://www.investigativeproject.org/2315/moderate-qaradawi-defends-hitler-and-nuclear.

During the selection campaign in Brighton, I met with several local Labour members and gained a great deal of support. Few had anything negative to say about my campaign and I spent time in many members' homes. One woman invited me to dinner and recommended other local members for me to talk to. Not long afterwards, I saw her at an event and attempted to say hello to her. Her reception, which was cold to say the least, left me wondering what on earth I had done. It turns out that my crime was to have a Union Jack on my business card. At least, this is what I was told.

Overall, I spent about a year campaigning on at least a weekly basis with Labour members in Brighton and Hove, getting to know them and working alongside them. I was, I was told, a stronger speaker than my opponent, and I'd received emails complimenting my campaign literature. I made contact with numerous local groups and charities, and was already promoting the Labour Party in the city. But none of this mattered in the end. It would be of no relevance for the sole reason that I oppose a far-Right religious extremism that openly discriminates and condones violence against women, executes homosexuals, and punishes dissenters with the sword.

(Interestingly, the Equality and Diversity Officer of the GMB Union – a major trade union in Britain – who interviewed me during the Brighton campaign asked why I was so gung-ho against sharia. I told her that it treats women as second-class citizens, to which she replied, "I'm a woman and it doesn't bother me". Solidary, eh?)

On the day of the final selection meeting, people I had known and chatted with, had a drink with, canvassed with, would not speak to me. It was my core of supporters (to whom I am extremely grateful) who enlightened me, informing me of a campaign that had been launched against me in the preceding days.

THE OXFORD UNIVERSITY DEBATE

The main cause of concern in Brighton was a debate I had taken part in at Oxford University just a couple of weeks earlier.

The motion was 'This house believes that Islam is a religion of peace'[5]. Needless to say, I was on the opposing side.

The speaker before me opened in support of the motion and suggested that the onus was on the opposition (myself and my colleagues) to prove that Islam was not a religion of peace. Here are the pertinent points of what I said in response.

The bar has been set quite high. I would suggest that the burden of proof is on the proposer, rather than us. It quite clearly says Islam is a religion of peace and I would suggest you prove it.

We've also been told here tonight, when we opened, that this debate must take place in the real world – well, absolutely. Yes it must, and I will describe what Islam is doing in the real world.

My side of the argument is that we are regularly told we are – we've heard it again tonight, it was described as 'hate' – we are told that we are demonising Islam, whipping up fear of Islam. Let me tell you what actually whips up fear of Islam.

We can take it from the top: 9/11, the London Underground bombings, Madrid, Mumbai, Mali, Bali, Northern Nigeria, Sudan, Afghanistan, Saudi Arabia, Iran, Yemen, Pakistan, death for apostasy, death for blasphemy, death for adultery, death for homosexuality, gender segregation, gender discrimination, unequal testimony between men and women in legal proceedings, child marriage, amputations, beheadings, imprisonment for being raped, anti-Semitism, burkas, execution for this, that and the other. The slaughter of Theo van Gogh on the streets of Amsterdam. Death threats on the streets of London: 'Butcher those who insult Islam'. Muslim patrols in east London telling people they are entering sharia controlled zones. Polygamous marriages. Marriage not requiring the consent of the bride. This is what causes fear of Islam. It is not me. It is not my colleagues on this side.

---

5 Anne Marie Waters and Medhi Hasan, "Islam is not a Religion of Peace/Islam is a Peaceful Religion," Debate, Oxford Union, YouTube.com, accessed April 4, 2018, http://www.youtube.com/watch?v=VQjZHFnmADQ.

All of the terrorist attacks I described, from New York to Mumbai, were carried out by Muslims and, according to them, in the name of Islam. The brutal societies that condone beheadings and amputations and imprisonment of rape victims are all real.

According to Human Rights Watch, the number of women imprisoned in Afghanistan for being raped exploded by 50% in just one year[6]. An apologist might say that Afghanistan is a tribal war-zone and this has nothing to do with Islam, but this doesn't explain the other Islamic states that have the same laws. It doesn't explain the 'modern' and 'moderate' Dubai which has imprisoned an Australian woman[7] and a Norwegian woman[8] because they reported they had been victims of rape. Both were handed prison sentences equal to or greater than their convicted rapists. In both cases, the Dubai judges were applying Islamic sharia law.

The death penalty for adultery and homosexuality is also real. Sakineh Mohammadi Ashtiani was sentenced to death by stoning for adultery, on application of sharia law, in Iran in 2007[9]. Homosexuality is a capital offence in Iran, Saudi Arabia and other Islamic states. This is the truth, but in post-modern politics, the truth is secondary to presentation and image, and whether or not it is likely to cause offence.

So, why did I speak out? I knew the response it would bring. To be fair, I have had more support for uttering these words than I've ever had before, but I've also had endless abuse. My inbox filled with delights such as "Die slut", "You'll know Islam when you're killed", and my personal favourite, "Get back to the kitchen, whore". I knew this would happen, but still I had to say it, because I strongly believe that ordinary people are sick and

---

6 "Afghanistan: Surge in Women Jailed for 'Moral Crimes'," Human Rights Watch, May 21, 2013, accessed April 3, 2018, http://www.hrw.org/news/2013/05/21/afghanistan-surge-women-jailed-moral-crimes.

7 "Woman Who Spent 8 Months In Jail After Being Raped In The UAE Breaks Silence," HuffPost, last modified May 12, 2013, http://www.huffingtonpost.com/2013/05/12/alicia-gali-raped-uae-jailed_n_3263593.html.

8 "Dubai Sentences Norwegian Woman Who Reported Rape - BBC News," BBC, July 20, 2013, accessed April 4, 2018, http://www.bbc.co.uk/news/world-middle-east-23381448.

9 Saeed Kamali Dehghan, "Iranian Facing Stoning Speaks: 'It's Because I'm a Woman'," The Guardian, August 06, 2010, accessed April 4, 2018. http://www.theguardian.com/world/2010/aug/06/sakineh-mohammadi-ashtiani-iran-interview.

tired of being told there is something wrong with *them* if they dislike or distrust Islam. Nobody speaks for such people.

I recall a Labour Party meeting where we held a discussion about people's attitudes to various ethnic minority groups in

Britain. We were shown a graph displaying lines representative of public opinion. The line was essentially flat on Hinduism (showing little-to-no dislike), Judaism, Sikhism, and others. It went off the chart, however, when Islam was mentioned. The goes-without-saying and rather tedious response focused entirely on what we (i.e., the people of Britain) are getting so wrong that we unfairly single out Islam for criticism. Ordinary people are blamed for their honest reaction to the evidence they see – and what they see is that Islam, certainly at this point in our history, is associated with violence, a disdain for democracy, and a contempt for the way of life that most people in this country hold dear.

Back in Oxford, I went on to say:

> We are told that this is just the extreme fringe of Islam. Well, let's have a look at Saudi Arabia. Saudi Arabia is the birthplace of Islam; the custodian of its holy sites. In Saudi Arabia, a woman is not allowed to drive, leave the house without a mahram, or vote – though [the government] has been incredibly generous by allowing [women] some votes in the next election. People are executed for blasphemy, executed for apostasy. This is not the extreme fringe of Islam – calling Saudi Arabia the extreme fringe of Islam is like calling the Vatican the extreme fringe of Catholicism. It just doesn't wash.

Let me list some of the countries that execute people for apostasy and blasphemy. They include: Saudi Arabia, Iran, Kuwait, Nigeria (some states), Pakistan, and Yemen. Other countries impose punishments such as lashings and imprisonment for blasphemy, and these include Indonesia, Jordan, Malaysia, and Sudan. Such punishments are imposed by these countries' state and legislature, not clergy. Can it be that all of these countries combined represent an extreme fringe only? How then do we define 'extreme fringe' if several governments can be described as such? There is something fundamentally absurd about it.

The last speaker for the proposing side at Oxford was Mehdi Hasan. Hasan was at that time a well-known journalist in Britain, a darling of the political Left, and frequent critic of the then Conservative and Liberal Democrat coalition government. (He has since moved to the United States.) He regularly appeared on TV and had a willing and keen Left-wing audience, desperate to believe every word he said.

His comebacks at the debate were pretty much what one would expect. Firstly, he told me that Saudi Arabia was only created in the 1930s, and so my point about Saudi Arabia being the birthplace of Islam was invalid (and therefore, so was everything else).

He also performed the obligatory Left-wing task on such occasions and promptly smeared me as a racist, telling me I should join the openly racist British National Party. This common tactic serves as a lesson as to the extent of the dishonesty and duplicity of some prominent Leftist commentators.

ISLAM AND STONING

I'm not going to spend much time talking about Mehdi Hasan, but I do want to cover his response to a question, raised by a woman in the audience, regarding the stoning of women in Islamic states. He told her it has no basis in Islam. Soon afterwards, I wrote on the National Secular Society's website that we must admit to, and face up to, the reality of death by stoning.[10]

It is really happening. It is happening to real people and it is happening in the name of Islam. This is the truth. Liars, apologists, the desperate to believe, and the interminably naive will deny it, or wish it not so, but no amount of wishing, denial, or apology erases objective fact, and these facts must be confronted.

10 "Stoning – the True Horror," National Secular Society, accessed April 4, 2018, http://www.secularism.org.uk/opinion/2013/08/stoning--the-true-horror.

According to the sharia laws of Iran:

1. The size of the stone is specified so that it will not be too small, or too big. Suffering is important.

2. A man is buried to his waist and a woman to her chest. If he/she can get out of the hole, they can escape the punishment, so one must make sure women cannot get out.

3. If the stoning is based on confession, the judge will throw the first stone. If it's based on witness testimony, the witness will throw the first stone.

4. Every 20 minutes or so, the stoning will stop to see if the condemned has yet died. If not, stoning continues (this is Article 23).

5. Article 16 states that the punishment should not "inflict torture, torment or mutilation of the condemned" and the stoning will be carried out "with ultimate calmness and without exercising violence".

Iran reviewed its penal code in 2013. Stoning as punishment for adultery was removed – that is, until the Guardian Council got hold of it and promptly re-inserted this religious command. The Guardian Council is a group of unelected clerics who hold supreme power in Iran, and who ensure the compatibility of all legislation with sharia law.

Saudi Arabia also stones people to death, and the barbarism is swelling as sharia law advances. In the last few years, a 13-year-old girl in Somalia, a soldier in Pakistan, and a young couple in Afghanistan have all been stoned to death. On all occasions, Islamic sharia law was cited as the justification. In fact, all of the countries which maintain stoning on their legal books are governed by sharia law.

Stoning is not mentioned in the Koran, and because of this many people deny that it stems from Islamic teaching. This is dishonest at best. Stoning is not in the Koran, but it is in the hadith, and for that reason, is part of sharia law.

So, let's clear this up – what is the basis for stoning in

Islam?
Here is the hadith:

> *A Bedouin came to Allah's Apostle and said, "O Allah's apostle! I ask you by Allah to judge My case according to Allah's Laws". His opponent, who was more learned than he, said, "Yes, judge between us according to Allah's Laws, and allow me to speak". Allah's Apostle said, "Speak". He* [i.e., the Bedouin or the other man] *said, "My son was working as a laborer for this* [man] *and he committed illegal sexual intercourse with his wife. The people told me that it was obligatory that my son should be stoned to death, so in lieu of that I ransomed my son by paying one hundred sheep and a slave girl. Then I asked the religious scholars about it, and they informed me that my son must be lashed one hundred lashes, and be exiled for one year, and the wife of this* [man] *must be stoned to death". Allah's Apostle said, "By Him in Whose Hands my soul is, I will judge between you according to Allah's Laws. The slave-girl and the sheep are to be returned to you, your son is to receive a hundred lashes and be exiled for one year. You, Unais, go to the wife of this* [man] *and if she confesses her guilt, stone her to death". Unais went to that woman next morning and she confessed. Allah's Apostle ordered that she be stoned to death.*
>
> *Sahih Bukhari 3:50:885*

As a direct result of this story (and various translations which always end the same way), stoning is a reality in Islamic states.

Lying is not the only defence against this barbarism. Apologists must also take credit.

Their arguments include:

1."There must be four witnesses, so really this is just a deterrent". Is this good enough? We don't object to a society where our sex lives are governed by the threat of a horrific punishment because it requires four witnesses for the punishment to be carried out?

2. "But it's in the Bible as well". Yes, it is in the Bible, but it's no longer carried out in the name of the Bible.

3. "This is the extreme fringe of Islam; it is a misinterpretation". It seems that all Islamic states have misinterpreted this, and so have many of Britain's mainstream and high-profile Islamists, including the moderate Muslim Council of Britain.

Inayat Bunglawala was a high-profile member of the MCB for many years. When he was the Assistant Secretary General, Bunglawala was asked by journalist Joan Smith to condemn stoning for adultery. Bunglawala refused to do so, adding, "You are asking me to condemn my prophet[11]."

Bunglawala is not alone in this regard. Suhaib Hasan is a prominent figure in the Islamic Sharia Council who blames women for the violence they face. He advocates stoning, and once said that "stoning will turn Britain into a haven of peace"[12].

The ultra-moderate Swiss academic and lecturer at Oxford University, Tariq Ramadan, debated this issue in France with Nicolas Sarkozy. Ramadan told us that his view is a minority one, which stretches as far as asking for a moratorium. In the debate, Ramadan denied there was any violence against women in Islam, having just seconds earlier called for a moratorium on stoning for adultery. This is the *Nineteen Eighty-Four*-esque doublespeak we have come to expect.

Interestingly, Ramadan also called for a "politically independent" French Muslim population[13].

The fact is that stoning is very much a part of Islamic sharia law, and very much a reality in the lives of millions of people. Whether

---

11 "Joan Smith: Islam and the Modern World Don't Mix," The Independent, November 28, 2007, Accessed April 5, 2018. https://www.independent.co.uk/voices/commentators/joan-smith/joan-smith-islam-and-the-modern-world-dont-mix-760717.html.

12 Clare Dwyer Hogg and Jonathan Wynne-Jones, "'We Want to Offer Sharia Law to Britain'," The Telegraph, January 20, 2008, accessed April 5, 2018, https://www.telegraph.co.uk/news/uknews/1576066/We-want-to-offer-sharia-law-to-Britain.html.

13 AustralianNeoCon1, "Nicolas Sarkozy Grills Tariq Ramadan over His Comments about Stoning," YouTube, December 08, 2012, accessed April 5, 2018, https://www.youtube.com/watch?v=nWaByF6xB-4.

they face the stones or the threat of them, the horror of this cannot be denied. Stoning needs to be named and shamed – there is too much at stake to run from this and bury our heads in the sand.

RELIGIOUS FUNDAMENTALISM

A further bone of contention for some in the Brighton and Hove Labour Party was a video I made for the Channel 4 series *4Thought*[14] in which I suggested that rather than turn back the clock on human rights to accommodate some immigrants who would rather not respect those rights, we should instead ask that they not live here.

Here is the transcript:

Religious fundamentalism is on the rise all over the world, and Britain is no exception to that. The problem isn't immigration; the problem is our lack of will to defend democratic principles.

My name is Anne Marie Waters, I am a secularist. I believe that Britain is a secular country and that no amount of immigration can change that. I'm not necessarily uncomfortable with high levels of immigrants, but I am troubled somewhat by the kind of religion that some are bringing with them. We've got black African churches in London performing exorcisms on people they perceive to be gay. We have sharia law which treats women appallingly. Marital rape isn't an offence under sharia, whereas in Britain, we've only just managed to achieve marital rape being a crime. So the fear is that ideas are coming back into Europe that have already been debated, and won by women and homosexuals. We shouldn't have to fight those battles again.

I'm an anti-sharia campaigner. I'm fighting a battle against a religion which is new to Europe, and it's something that I feel frightened of, and I'm not ashamed to admit that

---

14 All 4 | The On-Demand Channel from 4, accessed April 5, 2018, http://www.channel4.com/programmes/4thoughttv/ (page discontinued).

is because of how it treats women. When you talk about women, you're talking about me; you're talking about my freedom and my autonomy and my right to live in a way that makes me happy.

I don't see that everyone has a right to live in Britain; I think it's a privilege. If you come here, you must accept the rights and freedoms it has taken centuries to create. If you don't accept them, perhaps it is best you a) don't come here, or b) leave.

(I have somewhat revised my view on immigration since this interview – I believe in much stronger controls and secure borders.)

My words were to cause something of a storm. A particular source of aggravation was my statement that Islam is new to Europe. What I meant was things like sharia, the burqa, and violent threats resulting from cartoons are new to most people living in Europe today.

The first sharia tribunal opened in Britain in the early 80s, a new and extremely dangerous phenomenon. The prevalence of female genital mutilation (FGM), forced marriage, child marriage and other abhorrent practices has exploded in Europe in my life-time, and a lot of people don't like it, myself included. But this is just academic for the lofty elites of the Left. Ordinary people's everyday lives don't matter in the 21st century; what matters is political narration and lecture hall debates.

As part of the campaign against me in Brighton, a letter was sent to the Labour Party by a Mr Sunny Choudhury, General Secretary of the Sussex Bangladeshi Association[15]. Mr Choudhury was apparently "shocked" by my defence of the basic rights of women and my assertion that such rights must be respected. He declared that my selection would "destroy our party's relationship with minority ethnic communities".

I'm not sure when Mr Choudhury was elected to represent each and every ethnic minority person in Sussex, but I am fairly

15 "Labour Poised to Choose Parliamentary Candidate for Brighton Pavilion," Brighton and Hove News, September 05, 2014, accessed April 5, 2018, http://www. brightonandhovenews.org/2013/07/19/labour-poised-to-choose-parliamentary-candidate-for-brighton-pavilion/22599.

sure that is how he will have been treated. This is the racism of multiculturalism in action. A 'leader' steps forward and is treated as if he speaks for everyone who happens to share his skin colour. It doesn't seem to occur to him, or others like him, that there are thousands of ethnic minority people in this country who entirely agree with me – I know because of the messages of support I receive. It doesn't seem to occur to him that the Muslim women who are brutalised by misogynists (with free rein) in this country, or the little girls who have their genitals butchered, are ethnic minorities, nor that vast numbers of people I have worked with over the years also come under the heading of ethnic minorities – secular and former Muslims whose voices are never heard because others jump to speak on their behalf (having never actually asked for their opinion).

What my experience in Brighton revealed was the sad truth that the modern political Left will turn on its comrades if they fall out of favour with Islam, just as it turned on me. Comrades can criticise other religions by all means, but not Islam. I was completely betrayed by many on the Left Wing and the Labour movement, simply because I stand up for the rights of women, homosexuals, and others who are threatened by Islam.

THE THREATS TO
DEMOCRACY

SPEAKING OF THREATENED, I have been threatened many times by email, and on one occasion in person. I was due to give a talk on sharia law at a University of London college in Whitechapel, east London, when proceedings were interrupted by an Islamist who disapproved of my presence.

I wrote this account for the National Secular Society:

> This week I was due to give a talk to students at Queen Mary University in London on behalf of the One Law for All Campaign on sharia law and human rights. Rather fittingly – and as if to prove my point – my human rights were quashed by a person demonstrating one of the effects of sharia law: the threat of violence for criticising religion.

> Just before I was due to start, a young man entered the lecture theatre, stood at the front of the room with a camera, and proceeded to film everyone in the audience. That done, he informed us that he knew who we were, where we lived, and if he heard a single negative word about the Prophet, he would track us down.

> The organisers of the event, Queen Mary's Atheism,

Secularism and Humanism Society, called the police and the event was unfortunately cancelled.

On reflection, I am left wondering what exactly we could have done. I would love to say that we stood up to him and carried on bravely in a valiant defence of free speech, but it was a frightening experience, and I know that people felt genuinely threatened and upset. In any case, is it the role of speakers and students to face off against potentially violent Islamists in defence of our free speech, risking our safety in the process, when the state and other powers refuse to back us up?

Take the Danish cartoon affair, for example (see the section entitled 'Denmark' for more details). Look at the pathetic response of the British Government at the time:

"There is freedom of speech, we all respect that...But there is not any obligation to insult or to be gratuitously inflammatory. I believe that the republication of these cartoons has been unnecessary. It has been insensitive. It has been disrespectful and it has been wrong."

Even the UN said it would investigate whether the cartoonists were racists. How can we expect people in a university lecture hall to stand up to violent threats when this is the reaction of our leaders? The message is very clear – don't insult religion. And if you do, and you get into trouble for it, you have only yourself to blame.

Until the state speaks out and makes it clear to the likes of this guy that his behaviour is not acceptable – no excuses, no apologies – these things will continue to happen, and more and more people will be frightened into shutting up. We can then say goodbye to freedom for good.

AYAAN HIRSI ALI

Progressives and liberals all over Europe are turning against those they should support – those they would support if they believed what they say they believe. Even when a person is threatened with physical violence merely for speaking, that person will *still* be the one to come under political attack from the Left.

Condemnation of the threats is not as readily forthcoming.

Take for example Ayaan Hirsi Ali. Here is a woman who should have been the ultimate symbol of progress in the ever-so-liberal Netherlands. She was riding high until the Dutch establishment turned against her for raising her voice about Islam.

Ayaan Hirsi Ali was an asylum seeker from Somalia who arrived in the Netherlands, learned to speak Dutch, took an active role in helping other Somali asylum seekers, obtained a degree, and became a Member of Parliament for the People's Party for Freedom and Democracy in 2003. Is this not an incredible achievement? Is this not what Left-wing politics is all about? A strong woman – a black African woman, at that – standing up and expressing herself, improving her life immensely, becoming independent and educated, and then helping other women to do the same. Is this not the progressive dream?

No, it turns out it isn't – not if you criticise Islam.

Hirsi Ali wrote the script for a controversial film entitled *Submission*, made by the equally controversial Theo van Gogh. The film was critical of the treatment of women in Islamic society, and for his trouble, Van Gogh was slaughtered on the streets of Amsterdam by an extremist Muslim. Stabbed into Van Gogh's chest with a knife was a letter addressed to Ayaan Hirsi Ali, warning that she was next. She has lived with constant security ever since.

So, you would think that a black African woman who had achieved things that were nothing short of heroic would be defended by the liberal Dutch establishment in her hour of need, wouldn't you? Not a bit of it. Her neighbours said she was a security risk so she was evicted from her home, and she then found herself at risk of losing her Dutch citizenship (for admitting she'd lied on her asylum application). In the end, she moved to the United States, and one of the immigrants the Netherlands needed most has gone – and who can blame her?

THE LEFTIST-ISLAMIST ALLIANCE

Many people claim that the alliance of Leftists and Islamists is an aberration – that something has gone terribly wrong.

However, its occurrence has been no mistake. The reasons for this collusion merit a book to themselves, but my own brief opinion is that the modern Left has adopted a whole new set of priorities. No longer concerned with the rights of the working classes or protecting vulnerable minorities, the new university-educated middle-class Left is an ideological beast.

At the Passion for Freedom Festival in 2013, I was invited to take part in a discussion which followed a screening of the film *Silent Conquest*. *Silent Conquest* details the onslaught on freedom of speech in the West by Islamic states, and the aid and legitimisation of this onslaught by Western governments and Left-leaning ideologues. The women who run this festival are incredibly brave, because that is what you must be if you are to host an art exhibition highlighting the tyranny of sharia law and the threat of global Islamism. Their exhibition included a visual depiction of Mohammed with the words 'fragile' and 'handle with care' superimposed upon it.

The fact is that the political Left, both fringe and mainstream, has been successfully limiting our speech for many years, and has done so by employing a variety of tactics. The Racial and Religious Hatred Act 2006[1], for example, was introduced by a Labour government, and outlaws threatening words or behaviour, or displaying any written material intended to stir up religious hatred. Religious hatred was defined as "hatred against a group of persons defined by reference to religious belief or lack of religious belief". The 'hatred' component has been left to interpretation, and therein lies its danger.

The European Union has similar ideas. The Parliament of the EU in 2013 was presented with a proposal to force member states to monitor intolerance[2]. The proposal calls for member states to set up a National Tolerance Monitoring Commission and to outlaw "defamatory comments made in public and aimed against a group or members thereof with a view to inciting to violence, slandering the group, holding it to ridicule or subjecting

---

1 "Home Office Circulars 2012," GOV.UK, accessed April 6, 2018, https://www.gov.uk/government/publications/the-racial-and-religious-hatred-act-2006.
2 Kern, Soeren, "EU Proposal to Monitor "Intolerant" Citizens," Gatestone Institute, accessed April 6, 2018, http://www.gatestoneinstitute.org/4036/eu-intolerant-citizens.

it to false charges". This of course applies to religious intolerance, which "is understood to cover Islamophobia".

The President of the European Commission at the time was
Jose Manuel Barroso. Barroso is a Social Democrat and, as a
student, was the leader of a Maoist association[3]. He continues
to argue for greater European integration, even going so far as
to warn of a trench war if we move in any other direction[4].
Herman van Rompuy, who has been President of the European
Council, has called for "global governance"[5] and prioritises
greater European unity. This is the ideology behind the EU; an
ideology that seeks to bring an end to national governance and
to the nation-state itself. Any expression of ideas in support of
the nation-state, or in opposition to open borders, could well be
labelled 'intolerance' and thus deemed toxic and immoral.

Perhaps even more worrying is the risk to free speech in the
United States. As outlined in *Silent Conquest*, the Obama administration co-sponsored a resolution at the United Nations which
sought to outlaw defamation of Islam across the globe[6]. Obama
was unambiguous in his endorsement of such an idea.

> *"I consider it part of my responsibility as President of
> the United States to fight against negative stereotypes of
> Islam, wherever they appear[7]."*

Why he considered this his responsibility is unclear. His
actual responsibility was to defend freedom of speech – a fundamental clause in the United States Constitution.

The destruction of free speech and democracy is underway

---

3 YourTubeStop, "José Manuel Durão Barroso Maoist Days," YouTube, March 03,
2008, accessed April 6, 2018, http://www.youtube.com/watch?v=gmTOo6avlZ0.
4 "Opinion," The Telegraph, March 16, 2016, accessed April 7, 2018, http://blogs.
telegraph.co.uk/news/danielhannan/100235464/jose-manuel-barroso-the-crisis-is-over-
and-its-all-britains-fault-anyway/).
5 "Opinion," The Telegraph, March 16, 2016, accessed April 7, 2018, http://blogs.
telegraph.co.uk/news/danielhannan/100017487/.
6 "U.N. Adopts 'Religious Intolerance' Resolution Championed by Obama
Administration," CNS News, December 20, 2011, accessed April 7, 2018, http://
cnsnews.com/news/article/un-adopts-religious-intolerance-resolution-championed-obama-
administration.
7 "Text: Obama's Speech in Cairo," The New York Times, June 04, 2009, accessed
April 7, 2018, https://www.nytimes.com/2009/06/04/us/politics/04obama.text.html.

via legislative means primarily, though by no means exclusively. The propensity of Left Wingers to shout "igot" or "Extremist" at anyone who dares criticise Islam is well known and documented. As I've mentioned, I was advised to join the BNP by Mehdi Hasan in a slur during my campaign for Labour Parliamentary candidacy in Brighton. A similar tactic was employed by Labour's Sadiq Khan when he accused then Prime Minister David Cameron of writing propaganda for the English Defence League following his speech criticising multiculturalism in Germany[8].

REDEFINITION OF RACISM

The redefinition of words is auspicious, and nowhere is this more demonstrable than in the dishonest use of the word 'racist'. 'Racist' no longer involves race; it has been redefined to describe anyone who isn't Left Wing, or supportive of open borders. Ludicrous vans launched by the UK government warning illegal immigrants to "go home or face arrest" were immediately labelled the 'racist vans' in 2013[9]. Whatever one's view on immigration laws, the fact is that they have nothing to do with race. Immigration restrictions apply to all, irrespective of race, and critics know this perfectly well.

The UK Independence Party, which opposes the UK's membership of the EU, has also been labelled racist[10]. How it is racist to wish to leave a political union of nations made up of overwhelmingly white populations is not clear. It isn't racist, but many on the Left want us to believe that it is. The aim is to attack the nation-state and portray those who defend it as being on a par with the Ku Klux Klan or apartheid South Africa, and the Left has been extremely successful in this endeavour primarily

---

8 Glen Owen for The Mail on Sunday, "Fury as Labour 'smears' David Cameron after He Attacks Multiculturalism," Daily Mail Online, February 08, 2011, accessed April 8, 2018, http://www.dailymail.co.uk/news/article-1354100/David-Cameron-attacks-multiculturalism-Labour-row-Islamic-extremism.html.
9 "Racist Van," HuffPost UK, accessed April 8, 2018, http://www.huffingtonpost.co.uk/tag/racist-van.
10 "UKIP Is Not a Racist Party, Lord Heseltine Told - BBC News," BBC, October 03, 2013, accessed April 8, 2018, http://www.bbc.co.uk/news/uk-politics-24385139.

because the media is dominated by Left-wing advocates who have normalised the notion that patriotism or defence of Western democracy is an act of racial prejudice. I have a degree in journalism, and can attest to the fact that Left-wing thought on such degree courses is the default position, as it is in universities generally. The 'Westminster bubble' is an expression used in Britain to describe the enormous distance between public opinion and the main political parties in our Parliament. But politicians do not live alone in this bubble; journalists accompany them there, and it is precisely these journalists who influence them.

While free speech still exists in some form among ordinary people in the West, primarily because of the internet, it has dramatically decreased among our leaders. Take for example the burqa. Despite the fact that numerous polls in the UK show that a clear majority of people want this garment banned, no party is willing to make it a manifesto pledge (until UKIP's rather lame attempt in 2017). Offending Islam is of greater concern to our politicians than the will of the majority of the electorate, much like it was of greater concern to Obama than protecting the US constitution.

In short, by dominating academia, journalism, and law, the Left has won the battle for supreme position in political and public discourse, and our freedoms have been reduced as a result.

Islam would not be so powerful in the West if not for the complicity of the political Left – both hard-core and mainstream. What is more worrying is how little we seem to realise this. When it comes to freedom and democracy, we are not only losing the battle, in many respects it has already been lost.

RESIGNATION NUMBER ONE

As a result of my experiences in Brighton and my subsequent rethink of Left-wing politics, I decided to resign from the Labour Party. I was asked by Ingrid Carlqvist, an editor – along with Lars Hedegaard – of a Scandinavian publication *Dispatch International*, if I would allow her to publish my resignation letter.

I agreed. Here are the essential points:

Dear Mr Miliband,

While I realise that political parties rarely pay heed to the views of the voting public, or indeed their members or activists, I have decided to construct this letter anyway – I believe some people call it closure.

As I prepare to vacate your party, I would be grateful if you would – as payment for my years of loyal service – be kind enough to provide an answer to the questions I outline below.

First some background.

Just under 10 years ago, I joined the Labour Party. I immediately became active in my local constituency and spent endless hours canvassing, door-knocking, minute-taking (as constituency secretary), and I held several posts at branch, constituency, and borough level. During my years in the party, I met the most wonderful people – people who work hard and demonstrate a commitment to Labour that I am increasingly convinced it does not deserve. I wish these people well and name some of them among the finest I have known. This is not about them – this is about the Labour policies that have divided our country and filled us with fear.

I am particularly aggrieved at the racist and misogynistic arrangement known as multiculturalism.

I joined the Labour Party because I believed that all people should have equal rights, and should never be disadvantaged as a result of characteristics that they cannot change. I believed that people should have the same rights and protections irrespective of their gender or skin colour. I believed in fairness and in justice. I believed in civil liberties and a government run by the people for the people.

I still believe in those things, which is why I cannot, in any good conscience, remain a member of the Labour Party.

Let me start with multiculturalism. As a direct result of this policy, thousands of young girls have their genitals butchered every year – their clitoris removed and vagina sewn up. The purpose of this is to destroy a girl's sexuality, ensuring her virginity so that she can be offered up to a (usually) much older man to live a life as his domestic and sexual slave. Despite this abhorrent crime carrying a theoretical 14-year prison sentence in Britain, not a single prosecution has ever been brought.

When I spoke to the police about this fact, I was told (among other things) that they could not insult or offend a religion or culture. Where do you suppose they got the idea that religion and culture are more important than a young girl's bodily integrity? Could it be that they are afraid of losing their jobs if they do not show sufficient respect for religious or cultural practices – even those that constitute criminal offences?

Another of the fruits of multiculturalism is the proliferation of sharia. In Britain, we have at least 85 sharia tribunals operating a parallel system of family law. For your information, sharia law allows men to beat their wives, allows no unilateral divorce rights for women, and gives custody of children to fathers from a preset age, regardless of the circumstances. The most prominent of these sharia tribunals is the Islamic Sharia Council in east London. Despite its claim to be a party that champions women's rights, Labour said nothing about this. How can you truly be a force for gender equality if you remain silent on this deeply disturbing mistreatment of women?

It is not just the silence on these matters that is troubling. This would be unforgivable enough, but when Prime Minister David Cameron criticised the pitfalls of multiculturalism in 2011, Labour Shadow Justice Secretary Sadiq Khan accused the Prime Minister of "writing propaganda for the English Defence League". How typical this is. Instead of addressing this very important point, Labour lowered itself to mud-slinging. I know this feeling very well: when I stood for Parliamentary selection in Brighton earlier this year, exactly the same thing was directed at me...because I dared to speak out against a system that enslaves women and executes homosexuals. Of course, being described as EDL [English Defence League] (however dishonestly) is a political death-sentence; something I'm sure Mr Khan knew only too well.

Its promotion of multiculturalism is not the sole gift that Labour has offered to the advancers of Islamism. I do not have sufficient space to outline all of the appalling endorsements of Islamism by former London Mayor Ken Livingstone, but I will give it a try.

Livingstone, while Labour Mayor of London, invited to the city (at tax-payers' expense) a man by the name of Yusuf Al-Qaradawi. Qaradawi is a supporter of FGM, believes Hitler didn't quite do enough to punish the Jews, and thinks homosexuals should be punished as any other "sexual pervert". When renowned human rights campaigner Peter Tatchell criticised Livingstone for this, he was labelled Islamophobic by the Mayor.

As well as promising to turn London into a "beacon of Islam" and campaigning against his own party in Tower Hamlets with Lutfur Rahman (a man linked to the Islamic Forum of Europe, which aims to create an "Islamic social, economic and political order" in Britain), Ken Livingstone has also worked for Press TV, the media arm of the Iranian regime which stones women to death for adultery. Can you tell me how you think the selection of Livingstone by party members for the Mayoral candidacy in 2010 squares with Labour's claims to be a party of gay rights and equality?

On top of all of this, Labour presided over the introduction of insidious hate speech laws which have shut down our ability to speak our minds. We have imprisoned people for tweeting and Facebook posts. We have innumerable CCTV cameras and hold the DNA of innocent people on a database, creating a Big Brother society of fear and compliance. Is any of this compatible with democratic governance and the ability of the electorate to hold the state to account?

It is perfectly possible that Labour is not the party of equality at all. It could be the party of image-over-substance;

of snooping and speech regulation; of multicultural separation; and of appeasement of religious extremists. It could be a party of hypocrisy, presenting itself as a champion of gay rights and gender equality on the one hand, while propping up Islamists and sanitising sharia law on the other.

Tell me, Mr Miliband, what is your appraisal of your party's record on the above issues? Do you think mine is a fair assessment? If not, why not? If yes, what do you intend to do about it?

I await your reply.

Anne Marie Waters

It was my decision to publish my letter in *Dispatch International* and the subsequent fall-out that led to my second major departure of 2013: my resignation as spokesperson of One Law for All.

RESIGNATION NUMBER TWO

It began with a tweet.

In September 2013, I wrote a blog in defence of Pat Condell. Condell is a spectacular communicator who makes regular videos on YouTube criticising Islam (as well as Judeo-Christianity). In September 2013, he released a video entitled 'The Curse of Progressive Feminism'[11]. In it, he was scathing in his criticism of feminists and feminist organisations in the West who spend the bulk of their time focusing on issues such as Page Three (some tabloids in Britain feature topless women on page three of their publications) and sexist language, while turning a blind eye to what Condell repeatedly labels "Islamic misogyny".

Condell was immediately attacked as a 'racist' from many quarters, including PZ Myers on freethoughtblogs[12]. Myers,

---

11 Pat Condell, "The Curse Of "Progressive" Feminism," YouTube, September 06, 2013, accessed April 8, 2018, https://www.youtube.com/watch?v=GbmeQtGMkUU.
12 PZ Myers, "Feminism Is Not an Excuse for Your Racism, Pat Condell," Heteronormative Patriarchy for Men, Pharyngula (blog), August 02, 2014, accessed April 8, 2018, http://freethoughtblogs.com/pharyngula/2013/09/23/feminism-is-not-an-excuse-for-your-racism-pat-condell/.

who is a biologist and university lecturer in Minnesota, accused Condell of being a "racist cretin" (despite having himself previously described Islam as "a particularly vile religion")[13]. Myers did not take kindly to Condell's commentary on migration to Scandinavia in particular, nor the fact that women in Sweden are now statistically far more likely to be raped as a result.

I wrote a response, the essentials of which are below:

> While I realise that Mr Pat Condell hardly requires defending by me, I am the nosey and interfering type (apparently) so I insist on adding my tuppence worth nonetheless.
>
> Earlier this week, PZ Myers offered a rather disingenuous analysis of Pat Condell's latest video, 'The Curse of Progressive Feminism'. He began by calling Pat a "racist cretin", thereby devaluing the once-powerful word racist even further than it already has been by people like him. Much of the post was a misrepresentation and an evasion of the points Condell actually raised.
>
> Condell: "'*Progressive' feminists who confidently challenge everyday sexism but who are struck deaf and dumb by Islamic misogyny...they turn a blind eye to religiously endorsed wife-beating, forced marriage, honour killing, genital mutilation, organised rape gangs, sharia courts that treat women as less than fully human, and little girls forced to dress like nuns.*"
>
> Myers: "*I really don't know of any feminists who think anything on that list is at all acceptable. Who are these mysterious feminists who have no problem with honor killing or rape gangs?*"
>
> At no point did Condell state that progressive Western feminists have no problem with the horrors listed above, but the majority of them remain silent and do absolutely nothing about it. Simultaneously, all over Twitter you will find campaigns to stop Tesco/Asda/Whoever from stocking

---

13 PZ Myers, "Both Wrong, Both Right," Heteronormative Patriarchy for Men, Pharyngula (blog), August 02, 2014, accessed April 9, 2018, http://freethoughtblogs.com/pharyngula/2013/04/03/both-wrong-both-right/.

magazines that might contain a picture of a woman's breasts. Condell's question is a good one, and I wouldn't mind an answer either – where are all those feminists on matters concerning Islam?

I have personally sat through many meetings of feminists who spend endless hours agonising about Page Three, and I have been reprimanded by those very same feminists for raising the issue of FGM.

"We don't want to alienate the Somali community," they say.

The maiming of Somali girls doesn't seem to feature on their radar. By 'Somali community', they actually mean Somali patriarchs who (it seems) should be able to rule over their women folk and mutilate them at will. Anything else would be culturally insensitive and stir up division (that's a big favourite – it never seems to occur to these feminists that FGM itself may be stirring up division).

On another occasion, I sat with a women's forum – a body specifically set up to promote an inclusive feminism. Having suggested that the burqa and what it represents ("the covering of women prevents rape") might not be a positive step forward, I was told that the burqa "must be looked at in a cultural context" and to shut up about it. The obligatory racist implication wasn't far behind when I was asked, quite sternly, whether I condemned thongs as well. I'm still not sure quite what the two things have in common, but I had grown too weary to argue.

When Maryam Namazie and I debated with Ahmadi-yya Muslims at UCL in 2011, part of the debate centred around domestic violence. There was no dispute from the other side about whether a man may hit his wife, only how hard. This is sharia law. But do a search for sharia on the website of Refuge.org.uk and you'll find zero results.

Similarly, Women's Aid, another otherwise admirable organisation that fights domestic violence, has issued no statement, launched no campaign, and the only mentions of sharia on their website are on the forum (three examples) written by users, not the campaign group itself.

The Fawcett Society, "Working for women's rights since 1866", has zero to say about sharia either – search their site for yourself.

Other groups, and mainstream parties, are completely silent on the misogyny (and the homophobia) of Islamists. When was the last time Labour, or the Lib Dems, condemned sharia-based sexism and brutality? They haven't. They let it carry on with absolute impunity while condemning domestic violence elsewhere.

Deputy Prime Minister at the time, Nick Clegg, leader of the Liberal Democrats, was forced to issue a statement on Nigella Lawson [after her husband had gripped her by the throat in a public row] saying he condemned "all forms of domestic violence". He did so after he was criticised for his reply on a radio show when asked what he would have done if he had seen the incident involving Lawson and her husband.

"*When you see a couple having an argument...most people, you know, just assume that the couple will resolve it themselves. If of course something descends into outright violence, then that's something different.*"

Who jumped to criticise Clegg? Yvette Cooper of the Labour Party.

"*Nick Clegg revealed how little he understands violence against women this morning. Far too often violence against women is dismissed as fleeting or unimportant. Too often public institutions don't take it seriously enough. Domestic violence is still a hidden crime, and victims suffer or are ignored as a result.*"

Now, see if you can find Yvette Cooper speaking out against the Islamic Sharia Council. I've tried. I couldn't.

In his post, Myers added, "You know that backward, ugly attitude [misogyny]? Islam didn't invent it. We've got plenty of it to go around in the western world as well."

This is a gross insult to every single suffering woman in every single Islamic state on the planet. Yes, there is misogyny and violence against women in the west, but to compare it to what women face in Islamic states demonstrates total ignorance, and is a crass belittlement of the true horror of life for females under sharia law. I wonder if Mr Myers has ever tried to help a woman escape from Saudi Arabia, or find a safe place in Pakistan. I'm guessing he hasn't, but I have, and I can tell you it is nothing short of a nightmare. I wonder if he has ever had a phone call from a frightened girl escaping a forced marriage who can't turn to a woman's shelter because they might turn her over to her father. I'm guessing he hasn't, but I have.

When women in the West face violence, the law – though imperfect – tends to be on their side.

Condell is absolutely right. Most 'western progressive feminists' do ignore misogyny carried out in the name of Islam (in the case of sharia), or any misogynist practice rightly or wrongly associated with Islam. I see it over and over again. I don't know what world PZ Myers lives in, but he needs to spend more time with some progressive western feminists and see exactly what the majority of them are thinking. They're not thinking about Islam, that much I can promise him.

Having written this blog, I sent it via Twitter to Mr Condell, as well as a popular tweeter (and supporter of the English Defence League) named Queen Lareefer (now Queenie's Soapbox).

A short time later, some ludicrous lefty who called himself 'Soupy' decided to write a blog about the fact that I had sent a tweet to Unacceptable Persons. Suddenly, I found myself on the Left-wing hit list (trust me, a mere tweet will do it). Soupy bleated about how one should go through people's Twitter history and investigate every single message they've ever sent. If any should not conform to the sharia-approved criteria of Acceptable Messages, such persons must be unfollowed immediately, shunned, and if necessary, actively smeared and verbally attacked. Months later, Mr Soupy was still banging on about this.

Maryam Namazie, my co-spokesperson at One Law for All (and its founder), replied to Soupy. While I didn't wish for him to be entertained, I understood her desire to reply and didn't object.

When I read her response, however, I knew it was time to go.

She too believed that tweeting someone who supported the EDL was a crime that should not be repeated[14]. She wrote of the EDL "They hate anyone and everyone who does not look like them or agree with them". I found this rather ironic considering the attacks that these Lefties were willing to dish out just for a tweet, but I let it pass.

The problem of course with Queen Lareefer is that she is not Left Wing and therefore she should be silenced. The political Left must control all speech – that way, nothing that will challenge them or their worldview can be heard.

My letter of resignation to the Labour Party, and the fact that it was published in *Dispatch International*, led to yet more blogging and patronising emails. I could take no more.

---

14 "Ahmadi Muslims Debate Sharia Law with One Law for All (Maryam Namazie) at UCL," YouTube, last modified December 19, 2011, https://www.youtube.com/watch?v=hTYrjFE6Rcg.

EXCUSING THE
INEXCUSABLE

FOR THE SAKE of convenience, let me now provide a list of what I believe to be the ills of the Left, and why I knew I no longer belonged there.

1. Tweeting is more important than sharia

As well as Soupy, other Left Wingers took to Twitter to discuss the horrific crime I had committed in sending a tweet to Queen Lareefer. Strangely enough, I have yet to see such fury when the evils of sharia – including here in Britain – are revealed, as they frequently are. When I agreed to publish my resignation letter to Labour with *Dispatch International*, further blogs were written – this time on the farcical parody that is Islamophobia Watch. It is difficult to respond to such idiocy, but I will.

In one of the blogs, my critics did not even bother to quote me directly, but instead used some praise I had received from George Igler (a frequent critic of Islam) as evidence of my guilt. The blog also highlighted the fact that I had been published in the same place as someone who once praised Tommy Robinson (former leader of the EDL). This apparently means that everything

Tommy Robinson has ever said is now my fault. That is how it works.

Soon afterwards, I was criticised (again) for writing for *Dispatch International* – this time because it has also published somebody called Fjordman, whom I had never heard of. This critic claimed that Fjordman's writings "helped inspire a mass murderer" – Anders Breivik, who slaughtered scores of people on a Norwegian island in 2011 – simply because Fjordman had been mentioned in Breivik's notorious 'manifesto'. Breivik also mentioned many other people, of course, but uber-Leftists like Islamophobia Watch never miss an opportunity to apply collective guilt to their enemies.

To avoid confronting the verifiable facts that are some-times printed in publications like *Dispatch International*, many Left Wingers engage in disingenuous 'whataboutery'. "Women are stoned to death in Iran" – "But whatabout American drones?"; "There is violence and hatred in Islamic doctrine" – "But whatabout the Bible?"; "Islam is dangerous and threatens democracy and freedom" – "But whatabout racism?"; "Thou-sands of young girls are being forced to marry to older men in the UK" – "But whatabout Anne Marie Waters sending a Tweet to Queen Lareefer?"

2. The People's Front of Judea and the Judean People's Front

If you are wondering what on earth I am talking about here, you have probably never seen the movie *The Life of Brian*, a hilarious parody of the story of Christianity. In it, there is a famous scene featuring political activists who are approached by Brian (the 'Jesus' character)[1].

He asks if they are the Judean People's Front, and receives the reply, "Fuck off, Judean People's Front! We're the People's Front of Judea."

Personally, I find this a humorous take-down of polit-ical activism, and the fact that so many groups invariably exist even though they share almost identical aims. This seems to be particularly prevalent on the political Left. Why? Because as soon as you say something that is not approved

---

1 Layniann, "Life of Brian - The People's Front of Judea," YouTube, April 26, 2012, accessed April 8, 2018, https://www.youtube.com/watch?v=WboggjN_G-4.

by the committee-for-the-approval-of-words, you are out. You then go off and form a new group, which will last until somebody says something that is not approved by the new committee-for-the-approval-of-words.

In order for collectivism to work, there must be authoritarianism. If people begin to disagree, this dissent must be removed so that collectivism can continue. The only chance that collectivism has to survive is through authoritarian government.

On the surface, communist ideas look honourable, but they can't survive simply because – in day-to-day life – they are an affront to our sense of fairness. Take for example two workers at a factory. One of them arrives on time each day, works extremely hard, takes pride in their position and their labour. Another arrives late and is careless, does little work and leaves his/her hard-working colleague to carry the bulk of the burden. Both workers, however, take home the same salary at the end of each week.

For how long will the hard-working colleague remain content? And if there is no personal responsibility, and hence no consequence for the lazy colleague, won't the situation just continue? If input is not equal, our innate sense of fairness leads us to ask: why should output be equal? The hard-working colleague (unless they are extraordinarily patient) will become vexed and may wish to voice dissent at collectivist ideas altogether. Hearing this, other hard-workers who are forced to share their spoils with lazy colleagues may become emboldened and speak out. Soon, the collectivism collapses. Therefore, a communist state must prevent ideas from being aired which will threaten it – hence there are no opposition parties.

There are some Left-associated ideas I agree with. For example, I believe in universal healthcare. It is simply wrong to leave a person to die because they do not have enough money. I also support public healthcare because I do not believe that private insurance (motivated by profit) can be trusted to deliver the best healthcare available at no cost to the patient. But I cannot get on board with the idea that extra effort should not reap extra reward, or that there should be little to no consequence of failing to carry out one's responsibilities. This is why I believe freedom, autonomy, and responsibility are virtues. People should be held responsible for their mistakes and made to atone for them. It is, I believe, the best solution for the individual and society as a whole.

In communist societies, it is necessary to silence criticism of the government, and the same is true of the economic model. This is because communist states are not exactly known for their economic prowess – the people live in poverty and oppression, while the leaders enjoy power and luxury.

Look at most of the totalitarian societies on earth; they are either theocratic or communist. From North Korea to Saudi Arabia, the people are forced into adoration of an all-powerful leadership; their lives are dictated and their choices limited. The hard Left doesn't seem to realise that total and complete equality, including economic equality, must be manipulated and designed – it will not happen naturally, because people are different. Some work harder than others; some have greater talents in high-earning areas; some are willing to make sacrifices for financial success while others are not. This is simple truth and common sense.

In a free society, people should have equal opportunities and equal access to law, health, and education. But the outcome will not be equal because the input has not been equal. That kind of equality can only happen by force; by totalitarianism.

3. Everyone's culture is to be respected – except one

Multiculturalism is an interesting idea, and one that is frequently commented upon. Angela Merkel, currently the German Chancellor, told an audience of young members of her Christian Democratic Union party in 2010 that "the approach [to build] a multicultural [society] and to live side-by-side and to enjoy each other…has failed, utterly failed"[2]. Merkel added that immigrants needed to do more to integrate into German society, including learning the language.

Former British Prime Minister David Cameron said that the UK needed a stronger national identity, and by extension, impliethat multiculturalism is not compatible with such an

---

2 Stephen Evans, "Merkel Says German Multicultural Society Has Failed - BBC News," BBC, October 17, 2010, accessed April 8, 2018, http://www.bbc.co.uk/news/world-europe-11559451.

identity[3]. Of course he is right, in particular with reference to how multiculturalism has worked in Britain.

Multiculturalism in the UK is characterised not only by the separation of communities, subject to distinct rules, but by people who are treated by the state as part of a group rather than as individual citizens. It is also characterised by an equal respect for all cultures. To some, this can include cultural practices that constitute serious crimes (such as genital mutilation or forced marriage). While multiculturalism suggests that all cultures should be respected, there is often one exception to the rule – there is little requirement to respect British culture, or even acknowledge it. Much public discussion on British culture assumes Britain does not have a culture worthy of defence. It claims that British history is mired solely in violence and bloodshed and colonialism, and that the British should hang their heads in shame – for ever. Great British writers, poets, leaders, and musicians are ignored.

In a BBC Sunday morning TV programme[4], the following question was asked: "Should we promote a united British identity?" The British author and commentator Douglas Murray argued that there can be diversity in Britain, but it should surround a core culture and a core set of shared values. He was immediately questioned as to what that core should be, and was told that multiculturalism itself is the answer. This implies that there is no British culture *per se*, and Britain is merely a mixture of cultures brought about by migration.

An audience member said that it was "disturbing that Prime Minister David Cameron, in his Munich speech [is] trying to turn up the noise on this debate in a deliberate attempt to attract audiences...who knows what their views are?"

This statement is full of implications to pick apart. The Munich speech referred to was made by the Prime Minister in February 2005[5]. In it, he acknowledged the existence of Islamists,

---

3 Laura Kuenssberg, "State Multiculturalism Has Failed, Says David Cameron - BBC News," BBC, February 05, 2011, accessed April 8, 2018, http://www.bbc.co.uk/news/uk-politics-12371994.
4 TheAikenHead, "Should We Promote A United British Identity? (The Big Questions)," YouTube, March 05, 2012, accessed April 9, 2018, https://www.youtube.com/watch?v=HHZXEKEbLJ0.
5 "Full Transcript | David Cameron | Speech on Radicalisation and Islamic Extremism | Munich | 5 February 2011," New Statesman, accessed April 9, 2018, http://www.newstatesman.com/blogs/the-staggers/2011/02/terrorism-islam-ideology.

who may reject terrorism, but who ultimately seek an Islamic state under sharia. He said that some were drawn to Islamist ideology in Britain because:

"*...we have allowed the weakening of our collective identity...we have encouraged different cultures to live separate lives, apart from each other and the mainstream. We have even tolerated these segregated communities behaving in ways that run counter to our values.*"

He controversially added:

"*We need a lot less of the passive tolerance of recent years and much more active, muscular liberalism.*"

He is right. Liberalism and democracy must be defended. The comment made by the audience member implies that he worries the Prime Minister might attract bigots, far-Rightists, and racists, and here is the very core of the problem. A defence of British liberalism and democracy is equated with bigotry and racism, and as a result, scorn is poured on those elements of British identity.

A veiled anti-Britishness is also evident in the immigration debate. The idea that British people are too lazy to work so we need immigration is very familiar. The young are particularly vilified in this regard. I struggle to think of any other nationality who can be openly insulted in this way.

Political achievements like the Magna Carta, parliamentary democracy, trial by jury – all of which emerged from Britain and are copied all over the world – are scarcely acknowledged or celebrated in public life. Nor are the great inventions of the British – penicillin, the steam locomotive, colour photography, fingerprinting, radio, the telephone, even the flushing toilet. If you're a fan of sport, you might like to know that tennis, football (soccer), rugby, golf, cricket, badminton, darts, table-tennis, snooker, hockey, netball, and polo are all games which were devised on this tiny island. The English language is known and loved the world over.

In short, this is a country to be celebrated and it is, to my mind, high-time we did so.

4. People must pay perpetually for colonial crimes

In a debate in the Greek capital in early 2013 entitled 'Europe Should Shut the Door on Immigration', Douglas Murray, an outspoken opponent of Islamism, spoke for the motion. In the Q&A that followed[6], a young woman in the audience made the following point:

> "*The European Union was an ex-colonial power, so most of the countries of the third world were exploited from [by] us. So now we cannot say that we don't accept them because most of their riches and their wealth were taken from [by] us.*"

I will hand over to Douglas in a moment, but I do want to make a point or two myself. First of all, where would this young woman feel the need draw the line? What if a majority of immigrants supported genital mutilation and eventually voted for it to be imposed on all women? Would she happily offer up her own genitals? What if the idea of women as property, to be beaten at will, were to become the will of the majority? Would she give up her rights and submit? My worry is that she would, as would many others.

Here is Douglas:

> "*You say colonialism; I would like to return the question to you. I don't deny the crimes of colonialism, not for a moment. I'd like to ask you a question: how long do former colonial countries have to be punished for them? How long do we have to have our identity erased for? Is there any end limit to it in your argument or is it only at the point of complete negation? And finally, why is it that it is only European former colonialist countries?*"

---

6 «BBC World News Broadcast of IQ2 Greece Debate on Immigration,» YouTube, last modified March 21, 2013, accessed April 9, 2018, https://www.youtube.com/watch?v=34N-i2gjnH4.

I attended a LGBT (Lesbian, Gay, Bisexual and Transgender) Labour Party meeting one weekend where a motion was debated on whether we ought to withdraw aid from countries that impose the death penalty for homosexuality. Uganda was musing on a new law to "kill the gays" at the time. According to the speaker who presented the motion, to suggest that we should withdraw aid from Uganda would "smack of neo-colonialism". Whether it would actually save lives did not seem important.

To give an idea of how withdrawing aid could have worked, we need only look to Malawi a couple of years earlier. A gay couple had been sentenced to 14 years hard labour. Some Western countries threatened to withdraw aid, and hey presto – the two men were free. It works. And I am quite sure that neither man would have cared one iota about how neo-colonial it appeared[7].

5. All crimes are equally bad

The 'equality' obsession of lefties is often expressed through the notion that all the things they dislike are equally evil. Some believe that love of one's country (which I possess) and being opposed to mass immigration are the moral equivalent of wanting homosexuals hanged and rape victims stoned. They argue that the English Defence League and Islamists are equally dangerous, using Nazi salutes seen at EDL rallies as proof of this charge.

This is absurd. Yes, the Nazis were evil, but the EDL are not Nazis. The EDL has a stated goal which is to defeat radical Islam. Some people join the EDL for that reason and that reason alone – even if there are some bad apples. The problem is that the field of people willing to speak out about Islam has been so narrowed that those who have legitimate concerns feel that they have nowhere to go. It is the political Left that has made it nigh-on impossible to criticise Islam in the mainstream. The same people then complain when those with concerns turn to the fringe to find a voice.

But one might argue that this isn't about morality at all, or saving human lives. Instead, it is about ideology and political

---

7 "Malawi Suspends Laws against Homosexual Relationships - BBC News," BBC, November 05, 2012, accessed April 9, 2018, http://www.bbc.co.uk/news/world-africa-20209802.

point-scoring. The Left broadly disapproves of patriotism, or the concept of the nation-state itself, so insists on equating these things with violent 7th century barbarism. All of the Left's opponents are thus demonised on an equal footing, no matter how dangerous the outcome of that may be for actual living human beings.

Leftists will allow you to criticise Islam, but only if you do so in compliance with a list of rules. These are:

- Make clear that immigration to Europe is solely a positive thing
- Always aim your criticisms at Islam*ism* rather than Islam, and never suggest that Islamism is related in any way to Islam
- Precede every criticism of Islam with "all religions are equally dangerous"

The final one of those points is particularly unhelpful. I don't belong to any religion, but from observation and common sense, I can see a vast difference between religions that endorse violence and oppression and those that don't. The author and scientist Sam Harris made a brilliant speech on this in 2010[8]. In it, he distinguished between various religions.

The word 'religion', he argues, encompasses a broad range of beliefs, much like the word 'sports' encompasses such diverse activities as badminton and Thai boxing. He goes on to say that describing Islam as a religion of peace is delusional.

He names a real religion of peace as Jainism, and declares, "The crazier you get as a Jain, the less we have to worry about you." The problem is not, he adds, fundamentalism. Memorably, he makes the statement, "The only problem with Islamic fundamentalism are the fundamentals of Islam."

6. The west is to blame for everything

This one will be familiar to anyone who criticises the hard Left and its double-standards, as well as its patronising racism.

---

8 Agni Dev, "Sam Harris Real Religion of Peace Jainism Or Islam? Is Quran & Prophet Muhammad Perfect? Facts," YouTube, April 25, 2013, accessed April 9, 2018, https://www.youtube.com/watch?v=JQezdSihI-o.

Let me give you an example from an evening I spent at an event arranged to support the National Health Service (NHS) – a free health service in the UK that I support. The NHS is loved by many on the Left, which is sometimes the only good thing I can think of to say about them.

At this event, various people were distributing leaflets about the sale of arms from the UK to tyrannical regimes: governments who were using these weapons to brutalise their own people. I'm not denying there's a moral issue here, but when I asked why the governments who chose to use the weapons to abuse people were not at fault, I received a brief "*Yes, but the UK…*" style answer, and the subject was immediately changed back to bashing Britain. A few obligatory swipes at America were thrown in as well, but one thing was clear: the leaders who were using UK-made weapons to oppress and kill their own people were not to blame.

There's a powerfully patronising message here, and it goes something like this: "Those poor uncivilised folk can't help themselves. If you put powerful weapons into the hands of such people, it is inevitable that they will use those weapons to brutalise and tyrannise. It is therefore our responsibility to ensure the uncivilised do not get hold of these weapons because they are not equipped to handle them."

While holding this view, the same people will maintain that those of us who are perfectly aware that skin colour is no barrier to being a brutal tyrant are the ones who are guilty of racism.

Here's another example. At the LGBT Labour meeting I mention above, a speaker pointed out that the Ugandan proposal to 'kill the gays' was Britain's fault. Britain had brought homophobia to Uganda during colonial rule. Ugandan politicians therefore escape all responsibility, while being patronised and infantilised by a racist leftist idea that the all-powerful white man is ultimately in charge of everything.

This patronising attitude towards non-white people has enabled Islamists to promote their violent hatred for many decades. One of the most interesting interviews I carried out in research for this book illustrated how perilous this is, and how culpable Left-wing politics has been in allowing the violent abuse of women and girls to flourish, as well as the destruction of free speech.

My interviewee – let's call her Lisa – lived during the 1980s in the northern English city of Bradford. She and her female partner worked in women's shelters providing assistance to women who suffered domestic abuse, and they did this for several years. Lisa's son was a pupil at Drummond Middle School, with a headmaster by the name of Ray Honeyford, where the vast majority of pupils hailed from Pakistani or Bangladeshi backgrounds.

Honeyford shot to (undeserved) notoriety in the 1980s having been branded a racist by a clique of Left Wingers. His crime was to ask that ethnic minority children be integrated into a shared British identity.

He wrote in a magazine, *The Salisbury Review*.

> *"It is very difficult to write honestly and openly of my experiences and the reflections they evoke*[9]. *The term racism functions not as a word with which to create insight, but as a slogan designed to suppress constructive thought...decent people are not only afraid of voicing certain thoughts, they are even uncertain of their right to think those thoughts."*

The article caused an absolute storm in Bradford, and Honeyford was immediately accused of "prejudice against certain sections of our community" by a local Islamic leader. Needless to say, death threats followed and Honeyford was placed under police protection. Eventually, he was hounded from his job and never worked as a teacher again.

My interviewee Lisa told me of her own son's experiences in Honeyford's school. White children, including her son, were regularly bullied by the Pakistani/Bangladeshi children for the crime of being white. Proving that the kids had learned the

---

9 Leo Mckinstry for MailOnline, "Farewell to a Martyr to Political Correctness: Bradford Headmaster Ray Honeyford - Hounded for Warning of the Perils of Multiculturalism - Dies a Saddened but Vindicated Man," Daily Mail Online, February 10, 2012, accessed April 10, 2018, http://www.dailymail.co.uk/news/article-2099068/Bradford-headmaster-Ray-Honeyford--hounded-warning-perils-multiculturalism--dies-saddened-vindicated-man.html.

'racism' lesson well, the Pakistani/Bangladeshi children labelled the white kids racist while pushing them around. Lisa admitted she had thought of removing her son from the school, but being Left Wing herself, believed it might be racist to do so – as did many white parents.

Lisa and her partner eventually left Bradford because they no longer felt safe there. There were several reasons for this: the abuse of women; the violent intimidation of elderly white English people; and, of course, the homophobia.

In her opinion, for every white woman who came to the domestic violence shelter, there were "around six Pakistani/Bangladeshi women". These women would arrive "immersed in shame" and faced dispossession and ostracism from their communities for having sought help to escape the violence. Many were sent back to Pakistan or Bangladesh to avoid their exposure to the kind of ideas that the women's shelters might impress upon them – such as a right to live without violence, or that freedom was a possibility. Self-harm among such women was very high.

The attitudes towards women that were evident in her work did not remain within the Pakistani and Bangladeshi communities, and Bradford women more broadly began to feel unsafe. Lisa reported a high number of rapes of white English women, allegedly by Pakistani or Bangladeshi men. Often these rapes would go unreported by the media and ignored by police. A journalist I spoke to around the same time told me that she had attempted to report on the high number of rapes of white English women and girls (by 'Asian' men) in northern England in the 1980s, but no newspaper would publish her research.

This horrific neglect by police and local authorities was exposed in 2012 when reports finally emerged of organised rape gangs in numerous northern English cities. Ann Cryer, a former Labour MP in the north of England, said at the time that complaints were ignored because police and social workers were "petrified of being called racist"[10]. She added that numerous

---

10 Victoria Ward, "Members of Paedophile Gang Treated Victims as 'worthless'," The Telegraph, May 09, 2012, accessed April 10, 2018, http://www.telegraph.co.uk/news/uknews/crime/9254232/Members-of-paedophile-gang-treated-victims-as-worthless.html.

young girls had been betrayed, and therefore subjected to untold misery, by police and local authorities who "had a greater fear of being perceived in that light [as racists] than in dealing with the issues in front of them".

Back in Bradford, Lisa tells me that her lesbian relationship was also a source of ever-increasing fear, as attacks on gay people grew. Her own partner was attacked by an 'Asian' man as she was leaving a lesbian bar – she lost some teeth. Many gay people believed that they should not acknowledge the homophobic attacks, or the identifying features of their attackers, because they should *"support another minority"*.

This of course remains the case today as Left-wing gay people and groups continue to ignore homophobia coming from within mainly Muslim communities. The British journalist Johann Hari (who is gay himself) wrote a brilliant article on this in 2011[11]. In it, he mentions several incidents of homophobia in London, including stickers in the East End declaring the area a "Gay Free Zone", and the violent attack on Oliver Helmsley – a young man who ended up paralysed following an attack as he left a gay pub. This is the same East End of London that saw the emergence of Muslim patrols – groups of young Muslims roaming the streets attempting to impose sharia law. Alcohol drinkers and women were targeted[12].

There is a very real danger to women and gay people evolving throughout Britain and the West, as well as a threat to free expression, while the Left looks for anything and everything to excuse the behaviour of some Muslims. Lisa told me that it has, in her experience, been ever thus. Even when elderly white people had letters put through their doors threatening them and warning them to leave (dismissed as "kids mucking about" by police), Lisa admitted, "We made every excuse – capitalism; Thatcherism; poverty; lack of respect; patriarchy generally." Every

11 Johann Hari, "Can We Finally Talk About Muslim Homophobia in Britain?" The Huffington Post, May 25, 2011, accessed April 10, 2018, http://www.huffingtonpost.com/johann-hari/can-we-finally-talk-about_b_828037.html.
12 Ben Riley-Smith, "Islamic Converts Threatened to 'kill Non-believers' in Vigilante Patrol," The Telegraph, November 11, 2013, accessed April 11, 2018, http://www.telegraph.co.uk/news/uknews/crime/10441574/Islamic-converts-threatened-to-kill-non-believers-in-vigilante-patrol.html.

thing, in other words, to avoid facing the fact that the problem might have been with the minority, rather than the majority. As a result of this denial, this political correctness, this dominance of public and political discourse by Left-wing elites, we the public have paid, and will continue to pay, a very high price.

A NEW DIRECTION

WHEN I'D LEFT the Labour Party, things became strangely clear. I had grown more confident in my own beliefs and in what I was fighting for. As anyone for whom politics makes the heart beat faster will know, being out of the fray will never last long. I needed and wanted a new party, and I knew instinctively which one it would be.

THE UNITED KINGDOM INDEPENDENCE PARTY (UKIP)

I had always been an admirer of Nigel Farage; his frankness was jaw-dropping. He inspired and energised, and that was, I felt, exactly what politics needed.

I joined UKIP some months after leaving Labour and the differences were stark. No longer did people bully others for their opinions; open and frank discussions (even about immigration) were the norm. It was a different world, and I felt my decision had been the right one.

I decided to move out of London and settle down in the beautiful county of Essex, another of the best decisions of my life.

Essex is a part of the country where UKIP does well, and I immediately wanted to get involved. My first UKIP meetings had been in London, and I already had a UKIP candidacy (a local seat in Streatham, south London) under my belt when I arrived in Essex.

Tim Aker was the selected parliamentary candidate for UKIP in the constituency of Thurrock for the general election of 2015. I had once fought a Labour selection in Thurrock and so was invited by Tim to speak at a public meeting to promote UKIP in the area. I was very happy to accept.

It would be the meeting that announced my UKIP membership to the world, and needless to say, it changed my public life and taught me just how incredibly intolerant the Left can be. People I had worked with for years simply turned their backs on me, merely because I had switched political parties. Maryam Namazie, with whom I had worked hand-in-glove over the previous years, made no attempt to talk the issue through with me. It was done. I was now the enemy.

REPERCUSSIONS

At the time, I was sitting on the governing board of the National Secular Society (NSS). Organisations that want to fight religious influence cannot do so without recognising the dangers of immigration. Immigration is *the* issue; everything depends on it. Recognising differences is not bigotry, nor is seeking to preserve what is good. I was an admirer of the NSS, but this organisation had sold its soul to the Left, and wouldn't address the most pertinent issue of immigration. I knew that my membership of UKIP would cause problems with the NSS, so I resigned.

I didn't quite expect what would follow. The NSS continued to promote other prominent Left-wingers openly while ignoring or demonising my own efforts. An example was a conference aimed at the religious Right (not the religious Left) organised by Maryam Namazie (a communist) which enjoyed plenty of positive attention from the NSS, while it simultaneously ignored the launch of Sharia Watch UK (led by me) in Parliament. The National Secular Society also publicly disassociated itself from the

Mohammed cartoon exhibition (see 'The Mohammed Cartoons' chapter) planned for London because 'Right-wing' figures such as Holland's Geert Wilders were involved. This sent a powerful message to secularists: Left-wing secularism = good, Right-wing secularism = racism.

Back in Thurrock, Tim Aker's public meeting was a huge success – one that was reported by some local newspapers. An article on the YourThurrock website[1] described the meeting as having "unveiled the latest Labour defector" to UKIP and high-lighted my assertion that running an anti-sharia campaign within a leftist party is an impossible task to undertake.

Not long after the public meeting, I applied for, and won, the Parliamentary candidacy for the constituency of Basildon and Billericay. It would be my first experience of the job, and it did not go unnoticed.

A MATCH MADE IN HEAVEN?

Sarah Brown, a commentator on the Islam-critical Harry's Place website, wrote an article[2] asking if UKIP and I were in fact a match made in heaven. In it, she questions some of my associations and decisions, but is reassured by the fact that I had positive words to say about Quilliam – a group run primarily by former Islamists. It is interesting that she is reassured by a lack of condemnation of Quilliam, which has members who once called for brutal sharia law, but is disconcerted by my current associa-tion with people who have not. Nobody in UKIP, to my knowl-edge, has called for blasphemers to be executed, and yet they are deemed more toxic than those who once did.

Furthermore, Brown questioned how a feminist and secularist could belong in UKIP. She used as an example Nigel Farage's apparent claim that women had to choose between career and motherhood – Farage did not in fact say this. What he said was

1 «UKIP Unveil Labour Defector,» Your Thurrock, last modified April 9, 2014, accessed April 11, 2018, http://www.yourthurrock.com/2014/04/09/ukip-unveil-labour-defector/.
2 Harry›s Place, "Anne Marie Waters and UKIP: a Match Made in Heaven?," Harry's Place, last modified May 11, 2014, http://hurryupharry.org/2014/05/11/anne-marie-waters-and-ukip-a-match-made-in-heaven/.

this is how women's careers sometimes work out. Women do leave work for prolonged periods to have children, and their careers can suffer as a consequence.

It's fascinating to me that Sarah Brown, and others, could question my feminism when I joined UKIP, but not when I was a member of a party that brought multiculturalism to Britain, and thereby assured that thousands of women and girls would be subjected to brutal crimes that would go unpunished "for cultural reasons". Why would a feminist be willing to put up with that? A feminist in the Labour Party will never have her feminism questioned, and she won't have her secularism questioned, either.

When I joined UKIP, many believed I had ceased to be a secularist, as well as a feminist. The Labour Party oversaw a huge explosion in the numbers of faith schools, encouraged self-governance by Muslim community leaders, allowed sharia councils, and elevated religion in the public sector through endless accommodation of Muslim requests, but my secularism was not questioned until I joined UKIP – a party that has done none of this.

Another commentator named Alex Gabriel decided to lay out his arguments[3] as to why a secularist could not get on board with UKIP. His first question is "What will secularists do without human rights laws?" He essentially argues that we would not have human rights without the European Union. I find this argument really rather odd, and ill-informed.

The most important human rights were devised (many in England) long before the European Union. These freedoms came about as a result of revolution and political evolution in Europe. The Magna Carta, for example, helped shape the US Constitution and the UN Declaration on Human Rights, both of which precede the EU. The EU is in fact taking away our human rights, most especially our right to speak.

Gabriel's second question was, "With Ofsted [the Office for Standards in Education, Children's Services and Skills] gone,

---

3 Alex Gabriel, "4 Questions for Anne Marie Waters and Secularists Voting UKIP - Godlessness In Theory," Greta Christina's Blog, March 13, 2016, accessed April 11, 2018, http://the-orbit.net/godlessness/2014/04/29/4-questions-for-anne-marie-waters-and-secularists-voting-ukip/.

what will stop fundamentalist schools?" This made me laugh out loud. Ofsted has overseen – and continues to oversee – Islamic schools where girls are sent to the back of the room, and where libraries contain books endorsing stoning and wife-beating. Yes, Ofsted is doing a hell of a job. What would we do without it?

Gabriel then goes on to point out that UKIP opposes the disestablishment of the Church of England. Fine, I accept this is difficult if one is concerned about formal state secularism, but it's a matter of priority. Nowadays, I wouldn't disestablish the Church of England, either. It does little harm to people's everyday lives. Sharia law, on the other hand....

Gabriel finishes by doing what I'd expect: picking out tasteless comments from individuals (one of whom was thrown out of the party for what he said), demonising perfectly legitimate arguments (from a gay man) on gay marriage, and suggesting that then-deputy leader Paul Nuttall's Catholicism should prevent a secularist from voting for him. He asks what UKIP's record is on women's and LGBT rights. By opposing immigration from societies that kill women and LGBT people, UKIP's record is, I would suggest, one of the best. What has the Labour Party's elevation of Islamic clerics done for women's and LGBT rights?

PARLIAMENTARY CANDIDATE

Back in Essex, I became the candidate for UKIP in Basildon and Billericay in late 2014. It was the learning experience I'd hoped it would be. In early 2015, I stood down from that seat to fight for South Basildon and East Thurrock – a seat with a greater chance of winning. Frustratingly, as happens in politics (seat-switching is not uncommon), the popular but deselected candidate for South Basildon and East Thurrock was placed back on the candidate list just in time for the hustings (a meeting at which political candidates address the electorate). I had no option but to declare my own support for Kerry Smith, to whom the seat rightly belonged. But it meant I found myself without a seat, temporarily.

When I was then selected for the London seat of East Lewisham, the fun really began.

The run-up to the general election in 2015 was a time I'll never forget. Being a Parliamentary candidate for the first time was an incredible honour. It's a very difficult job, but if you make the most of it, it can be a life-changing experience.

The two months prior to election day are the busiest, and I was thrown in at the deep end. I had to take part in my first Parliamentary hustings. As the UKIP candidate, I was of course the enemy of all other candidates, and often of the audience.

There is no way of knowing what the members of the audience are going to ask, so I had to be clued up on current affairs and know my party's policy on each issue. It was a lot to remember, especially in front of an often hostile audience, but it went well. I enjoyed every hustings, and got better at every one, but there is one that deserves a stand-out mention.

This hustings was organised by a women's group in Lewisham called 'Mummy's Gin Fund'. 'Anti-fascists' attended this event and, I am told, made themselves known to some audience members to request politely that they not applaud me. I was accompanied into the venue by the police, who waited around to accompany me back out again.

A local paper reported[4] the matter like this:

> *Members of South London Anti-Fascists gathered to protest the presence of UKIP candidate Anne Marie Waters at a hustings at The Good Shepherd church in Hither Green on Thursday evening.*

The *East London Times* thereby implied that I am a fascist, and that those opposing me oppose fascism. Matter of fact. No questions asked. No definitions or evidence needed.

This article directed the reader to another one published in *The Mirror* only days before.

---

4 Tom Harrisson, Matty Edwards, Emma Henderson, Hajera Blagg, and Majd Bouchto, "'People Will Call Me Islamophobic': UKIP's Waters," Eastlondonlines, May 01, 2015, accessed April 11, 2018, http://www.eastlondonlines.co.uk/2015/05/people-will-call-me-islamophobic-ukips-waters/.

> *"Lewisham East UKIP candidate Anne Marie Waters*
> *has strong links to street fascists, in particular her work*
> *with prominent English Defence League figure Tommy*
> *Robinson in establishing Islamophobic 'think tank'*
> *Victims of Islamic Cultural Extremism. For this reason,*
> *South London Anti-Fascists called a mobilisation at the*
> *hustings in Lee on April 30."*

My favourite part is the "strong links to street fascists" allegation, when the only street fascists I have ever encountered are those on the Left.

The Mirror article is an interesting one, because it came about as a result of my first encounter with a journalist who attempted to befriend me in order to ruin me. He wasn't very good at it, fortunately, and only managed to 'expose' something I'd already said in public many times. But it was a lesson in media spin.

Myself and fellow UKIP Parliamentary candidate Magnus Neilsen had both spoken at an event at Parliament in London organised by the group Mothers Against Radical Islam and Sharia (or MARIAS). I'd highlighted how prior to the Suffragettes, many of the restrictions Muslim women face today under sharia were also faced by British women. Then, a British woman didn't have divorce rights or rights over her children, and a good slap from her husband was simply a righteous assertion of his authority.

Let us remind ourselves that the Suffragettes are now deemed heroines by the entire political class (one of the few things they get right). There is a statue of Suffragette leader Emmeline Pankhurst standing tall right outside the Houses of Parliament. And yet, the same political establishment sees no problem in allowing sharia to bring back to Britain the very things that the Suffragettes defeated.

Speaking out for the rights of women matters nothing to *The Mirror*, though not when Islam is involved. I have no doubt that *The Mirror* would happily shine its feminist halo on safe white-man-bashing issues, but when the misogyny at the heart of Islam is discussed, I become the hater and the misogynist becomes the victim.

The article[5] begins by telling the reader that I am "far-Right" and guilty of "hate". It doesn't bother to offer a definition of 'far-Right', let alone examine whether anything I've said actually fits it; the label is enough and the job of demonising me is done.

---

5 Colin Cortbus and Russel Myers, "Watch Ukip Candidates Spouting Vile Anti-Islamic Hate at a Far-right Rally," Mirror, April 16, 2015, accessed April 12, 2018, http://www. mirror.co.uk/news/uk-news/watch-ukip-candidates-spouting-vile-5526503.

THE MOHAMMED CARTOONS

THIS WAS ONE of the worst periods of my life, and it really brought home to me the terrible situation we find ourselves in: Britain is terrified of Islam.

It started with a phone call from Tommy Robinson – founder of the notorious English Defence League (EDL). Following his resignation from the EDL, Tommy and I had agreed to work together. Try as I might, I cannot remember the first time I met Tommy, but I do know that he's a man I greatly admire. We took part in an event together while I was a UKIP candidate, when I interviewed Tommy on stage to raise money for Victims of Islamic Cultural Extremism in London. My local paper[1] found this worthy of reporting and couldn't resist a quick mention of Tommy's criminal record, while putting "Islamic cultural extremism" in quote marks.

The initial idea had been that Tommy would work with me in Sharia Watch. He phoned me one day to ask whether, theoretically, I would be willing to put together an exhibition of

1 "Basildon Election Candidate to Launch Group Opposing 'Islamic Cultural Extremism' with Former EDL Leader," Echo, accessed April 11, 2018, http://www.echo-news.co.uk/ news/local_news/12916707.Basildon_election_candidate_to_launch_group_opposing__ Islamic_cultural_extremism__with_former_EDL_leader/?ref=rss.

Mohammed cartoons in London. I said that I would. The *Charlie Hebdo* massacre (cartoonists slaughtered in their office for drawing pictures of Mohammed) had had a profound effect on me; it completely altered my thinking. The gloves came off. This was an attack on freedom, secularism, and on Europeans and our way of life, so I decided that post *Charlie Hebdo*, I would say whatever I liked. I cared nothing about causing offence. I concluded that Islam offends me every day of my life, and I will apologise for the offence I've caused only when I receive an apology for the content of the Koran.

ORGANISING THE MO CARTOONS EXHIBITION

My first task in organising the Mo cartoons was to get in touch with Geert Wilders, who I wanted as our special guest. To my very pleasant surprise, Mr Wilders' assistant responded to me almost immediately. He agreed to attend, and now I found myself with the task of trying to find a venue that would host something that could get us all killed.

Tricky.

The time I had was very short. Mr Wilders's appointment book is packed, and in order to raise funds, I was obliged to give notice pretty much immediately. I contacted those who set up *Vive Charlie*, a free speech publication that lampoons Islam and others, in response to the *Charlie Hebdo* murders. They had run an online cartoon contest, and were willing to let us use the prints for the exhibition.

When I announced the exhibition on my website, messages of support immediately came in. One message in particular would change the course of the event – I was contacted by Jack Buckby of Liberty GB. I was happy to work with Jack and his party. This was about freedom, and all who believe in it are free to fight for it. But even while we were organising an event for freedom, very many people objected to Mr Buckby's freedom, and that of Liberty GB leader Paul Weston. Why? Because Paul Weston dares to talk about race and the future of the white one.

Meanwhile, news of the cartoons was having a wider effect.

An event that had been planned for Tommy and me at the House of Lords was no longer allowed to go ahead, effectively scuppering our plans for Sharia Watch. I found this extraordinary. The Houses of Parliament were no longer open to us because we were organising an unrelated cartoon exhibition elsewhere. Speaking out for freedom is too big a risk, while plenty of Muslim Brotherhood[2] types manage perfectly well to have events at the mother of all Parliaments. Love Britain and its freedoms? Too controversial. Hate Britain and want it destroyed? Welcome to the Houses of Parliament.

As our plans for Sharia Watch drifted away, so did Tommy's association with the cartoons. This was early on, so most of the run-up to the cartoons did not involve him. However, never missing an opportunity to stir up confusion and lies, the far-Left hate-mongers of the ironically named Hope Not Hate decided to write a piece of fiction about it.

Apparently, Tommy Robinson and I were going to start a civil war in England. Just the two of us. The whole thing was based on one meeting we had had with Jim Dowson (whom I had no previous knowledge of) to redesign the Sharia Watch website. That was it – that was the point of the meeting.

It was held in a pub somewhere in Bedfordshire and we sat for a couple of hours discussing all kinds of issues. Our conversation involved speculation about the possibility of civil war further down the line if issues with Islam continued as they were, but according to Hope Not Hate, merely discussing the possibility meant we were guilty of plotting it.

Here's the essence of what I wrote at the time:

> The entire Hope Not Hate report is a self-declared *"exposé"* of something that never happened. I was not *"involved in discussions"* about civil war; I was going to work with Tommy Robinson on Sharia Watch, because he represents a large voice that is ignored by the state, usually at the insistence of groups like Hope Not Hate. If we can agonise over what drives people to join ISIS, why can't we

2 "Muslim Brotherhood," Wikipedia, May 24, 2018, accessed May 28, 2018. https://en.wikipedia.org/wiki/Muslim_Brotherhood.

talk about why people join the EDL? Why don't we discuss their legitimate and sincerely-held concerns?

Hope Not Hate has called for the Mohammed cartoon exhibition to be banned. Extreme leftists despise democracy and routinely interrupt the democratic process. They cannot allow voices like mine to be heard (just in case people agree with us), so instead of facing up to the points we've raised, or the facts we've stated, they attack speakers and intimidate people into not listening.

My own thought is that the best way to deal with groups like Hope Not Hate is to make sure they have no bearing on my decisions whatsoever. I won't let them dictate whom I can speak to about a website, or whom I can work with on Sharia Watch. In the face of their lies, there is only one thing that I, and all who agree with me, can do – carry on.

Along with *Vive Charlie* and Liberty GB, the Lawyers' Secular Society (LSS) was on board with the Mohammed cartoons. The LSS was one of the few organisations with the guts to stand up for real freedom of expression – overwhelmingly due to its leader at the time, Charlie Klendjian. Charlie is a very good friend of mine, and was nigh-on unique on the mainstream secularism circuit. He was willing to be shunned in order to stand up for what he believed in. Most activists, even when they agree – or especially when they agree – are far too frightened of losing the party invites and the cosy metropolitan wine-bar scene to risk getting involved with the wrong kind of people. They don't want to be outcasts, so they'll accept all kinds of hypocrisy if it keeps them at the heart of the in-group.

Sadly, however, Charlie found himself in a tricky spot when some 'secularists' of the Lawyers' Secular Society began to object to the presence of Liberty GB and Geert Wilders. That was the level of commitment to free expression from some – this far and no further. Bullying by the leftist chatterati had the desired effect and people began to pull away. It is simply an unpleasant fact – bullying works.

At this point, I essentially found myself alone – I was the figurehead of this thing; the little support I'd had drifted away.

Not one single secular or free speech group, apart from the LSS, had the guts to make a stand.

It was then that I had my first visit from the police. They wanted to warn me of the risks, that could well include me having to leave my home, and to check whether I was secure. I wasn't. How could I be? My home life was temporarily turned upside down, and I got a glimpse of what Tommy Robinson had been living with for some years.

It isn't pleasant.

I searched through countless options for a venue. When I asked them if they were free to host an exhibition on a particular date, most venue owners said yes. Then I would tell them what it was for, and would not hear from them again. Finally, I found a woman brave enough to take the exhibition on. With her venue, I told her what the exhibition included, and didn't hear back for a few days. She then told she had thought it through and was willing, for the sake of free speech, to take it on.

I was delighted – it was a beautiful place.

Not long after the second police visit to my house, however, she wrote to me again to apologise, and say she couldn't go ahead. The risk was simply too high. She was worried about violence, relations with her neighbours, and insurance. I completely understood and thanked her.

This had to be the last nail in the coffin. There was no choice but to cancel – no choice for me, at least.

MEDIA INTEREST

Suddenly, the media became far more interested in the Mohammed cartoons than it had been before. Not interested in highlighting people standing up to Islam, they are very happy to show the world our defeat. I was even invited on to prime weekend BBC television – a rare treat[3].

The question asked by the BBC, "Is cancelling the Mohammed

3 "Anne Marie Waters - Episode 10 Photo Gallery - Episode 10, Series 6, Sunday Morning Live One," BBC, accessed April 14, 2018, https://www.bbc.co.uk/programmes/p030vryt/p030vrgk.

cartoons bad for free speech?", placed the blame firmly on me. The BBC didn't ask whether Islamic censorship is bad for free speech. The BBC didn't ask whether murder in France by Muslims upset about the depiction of Mohammed is bad for free speech. The BBC asked only whether I, fearing for my loved ones' safety primarily, am bad for free speech.

One of my fellow guests that morning was Remona Aly of the Exploring Islam Foundation. I had said in my opening comments that everyone gets offended and people should get over it. Sian Williams, the presenter, put this to Aly: everyone gets offended, right?

Aly not only didn't recognise the exhibition as a legitimate thing to do, but she decided that I was insincere in my motivations. I had clearly stated that my motivation was defence of free speech, but she appeared to believe she knew better and told the view that "this isn't really about offending sensibilities; this is about inciting hatred". I and others like me all have a sinister hidden agenda is the implication, and therefore none of what we state about Islam is observably true. Instead of addressing the death and misery, she deflected the issue by insisting that I am guilty of some never-defined hate.

Aly then went on to say that she was "relieved" the event had been cancelled, and that this was why we have incitement laws in Britain. But this cartoon exhibition did not breach any incitement laws. It was not cancelled by the police.

Her response to this was effectively nothing.

> "As I've said, I support freedom of speech, but inciting violence and causing conflict is never going to be a very good thing. This exhibition, if it had been held, wouldn't have been good for the message of Britain which should be about unity and co-existence. Really we need more positive messages out there rather than ones that are divisive."

'Divisive' is the PC word *du jour*; the new 'racist'. What it actually means is daring to be awkward and insisting on truth in a world appeased by lies. The one who ruins the lie with the truth is 'unhelpful' (another favourite). We are expected to stay quiet while our society is Islamised, because objecting is 'divisive' and 'unhelpful'.

PEGIDA UK

Things were quiet after the cartoons episode, and I wanted them to be so. I wanted to get on with Sharia Watch and publish this book. I also wanted to get on with things in UKIP – I had a wonderful local party in a fantastically strong UKIP area, so that was where I wanted to focus.

But it would not last long. I was soon working with Tommy Robinson and Paul Weston again, founding Pegida UK. Pegida is a group, born in Germany, which holds regular street protests against mass migration and Islamisation. The English translation of its acronym is 'Patriotic Europeans Against the Islamisation of the West'.

It started with a press conference in Bedfordshire, followed by a mini tour to Europe. We went to Copenhagen[4] first, then Prague, then to the birthplace of Pegida in 2014, Dresden[5]. It was a fantastic few days and we met like-minded people from across Europe. It was also an extraordinary honour for me to address the people of Dresden, who gather weekly in large crowds to demonstrate peacefully against their Chancellor's disastrous open border and the obvious dismantling of the country they know.

The trip to Copenhagen was one of the great eye-openers of my experience in anti-Islam activism. The behaviour of the 'anti-fascists' was extraordinary.

I wrote upon my return:

> Behind a banner reading 'For Freedom', we set out on a short walk through Copenhagen's city centre. It was not an all-white affair, and it

---

4 "Ann Marie Waters Speech in Copenhagen," YouTube, January 24, 2016, accessed April 11, 2018, https://www.youtube.com/watch?v=z-k3lCmJJJc.

5 "Ann-Marie Waters Von Pegida UK, PEGIDA Dresden, 25.01.2016," YouTube, January 25, 2016, accessed April 11, 2018, https://www.youtube.com/watch?v=kzO3LXgIisk.

certainly wasn't a group of football hooligans or neo-Nazis. These were ordinary people who are desperately concerned, as I am, about the changing face of this continent – change that is likely to be irrevocable and to make us significantly less safe and free.

While we walked through Copenhagen, we were heavily guarded by an excellent Danish police force. It was perfectly clear from the outset what the role of the police was to be – to protect us from violent attack by anti-fascists. There wasn't a single act of aggression from Pegida marchers. There was no shouting or baiting; all of this came exclusively from the black-clad leftists lining the streets. If Angela Merkel really wants to see people with "hate in their hearts", she ought to join a Pegida rally and see just what brutes we are up against.

Chancellor Angela Merkel referred to Pegida as people with "hate in their hearts" when she urged Germans not to join them. Similarly, the iconic Cologne Cathedral switched off its lights in protest when Pegida marched there following the notorious sexual assaults of 2015 (see 'Germany' for details). I was therefore stunned when I arrived in Dresden and saw the thousands of decent, ordinary men, women and children, of all ages, standing in peaceful defence of the country they love, singing German folk songs. I saw not a single person who made me feel intimidated or worried that I was in the company of Nazis, apart from the leftist protestors, who looked like a rather nasty bunch to me.

I recall being asked by Adrian Kennedy, a Dublin radio presenter, when he interviewed me in January 2016, if I was concerned about a Muslim woman who had told him she was terrified at the presence of Pegida in that city. Did Kennedy assume that I would agree with him that the fear this Muslim woman was experiencing was of the utmost importance? I don't. Why should she fear Pegida? There is no evidence it would do her any harm. There is no evidence Pegida has done harm to anyone. Quite frankly, if I were a Muslim woman in the West, I'd be far more afraid of the millions of men making their way across the sea who might think rather differently about the freedom she presumably enjoys in Ireland.

Back in London, I had been selected as a candidate for the May 2016 London Assembly elections by UKIP. Standing with Paul and Tommy to form Pegida UK, I knew there would be consequences, so when I received a phone call, I knew exactly what it was about.

I was to have a brief meeting near Westminster to discuss my shenanigans. I was the first to speak at this meeting and asked whether, if I stood down from the candidacy for London, I could remain a member of the party. This was accepted. The only guilt I felt was the difficulty I might have caused to other candidates.

My UKIP career wasn't exactly going smoothly, but I didn't know then what was still to come.

THE UKIP LEADERSHIP CAMPAIGN

Fast forward to 2017. Prime Minister Theresa May announced a snap general election in April, and I applied for a candidacy. Having come third there in 2015, defeating all but the two main parties (Labour and Conservative), I returned to the London seat of Lewisham East. Selected again with some enthusiasm by local party members, I set out my stall.

But it wasn't to last. I was soon summoned to UKIP head office to account for myself and explain my views on Islam. At a meeting of the party's National Executive Committee, attended by then-party leader Paul Nuttall, I said I would not apologise for telling the truth and there is nothing outrageous about criticising a religion. Some at the meeting certainly appeared to agree with me, but it was not enough.

Nuttall repeatedly made it clear he was not willing to deal with the tough questions from the media that my candidacy would elicit. Despite the fact that UKIP were running an 'integration agenda' that included banning the burqa and sharia councils, its leader was not willing (or able) to explain why we should ban these, or indeed criticise the religion behind them. It was another case of so far and no further. Nuttall did not seem to realise that the voting public largely agreed with UKIP on the burqa and sharia law, which are Islamic. As such, Islam itself is the problem.

The following day, I found out that I had been deselected and could not stand in the 2017 election. I was not told this by anyone in the party; instead, I read about it in the newspapers. To this day, nobody in UKIP has contacted me to inform me of this decision. Inadvertently, however, the deselection increased my profile in the party, and indeed my support, so when UKIP was trounced at the election that followed, and Paul Nuttall announced he was to stand down from the leadership, I knew what I must do.

By this point, I had begun a speaking tour of UKIP branches around the country. Following my latest deselection, I set about attempting to convince party members of the need to confront Islam, and many of them agreed. When I put myself forward for the leadership, I already had branch meetings booked up, but now the purpose of them had changed – I was trying to convince members to allow me to talk openly about Islam as leader of the party.

The level of support I received was enormous. While I was not surprised, I suspect many in the party's higher levels were, and so came the newspaper articles aimed at bringing me down. The first was from a really rather unpleasant MEP (Member of European Parliament) named Bill Etheridge[6].

Entitled 'Neo-fascist Entryists Want to Take Over UKIP. We Must Save our Freedom Loving Party', the article could have been written by a leftist – a clueless leftist with no idea of the meaning of fascism, or freedom. Having spent years fending off accusations of fascism, many in the party had learned to use these dishonest tactics themselves.

I was compared to a Nazi, as if it were me spreading poisonous anti-Semitism across Europe and attacking Jews. The description of UKIP as 'our freedom loving party' was particularly amusing. This freedom obviously did not include the freedom to speak observable, verifiable truths about a religion.

People like Etheridge truly don't understand this issue. I

---

6 Bill Etheridge, "Neo-fascist Entryists Want to Take over Ukip. We Must save Our Freedom Loving Party," The Telegraph, June 22, 2017, accessed April 12, 2018, http://www.telegraph.co.uk/news/2017/06/22/neo-fascist-entryists-want-take-ukip-must-save-freedom-loving/.

have forever made it clear that I am a pro-Britain democrat who believes in the primacy of the will of the British people. Some UKIP MEPs, however, were now willing to ignore the will of millions of British people on Islam, because they simply didn't have the knowledge or courage to tell the uncomfortable truth.

A second MEP did a similar thing when he denounced me as a racist on radio[7]. This MEP was Mike Hookem, MEP for Yorkshire and the Humber. This is a part of northern England where only a couple of years before, it was discovered that gangs of Muslim men had been routinely raping white English girls (primarily) for decades, and had got away with it partly because politicians feared being called racists if they spoke out or took any action against it. Similarly, Jane Collins, who is also MEP for the same region, attempted to persuade party members not to attend my campaign launch in the town of Rotherham, where at least 1,400 girls had been raped by Muslim gangs[8].

The hustings held throughout the leadership campaign were close to laughable. My fellow candidates implied frequently that I was a 'single issue' candidate, despite the fact that I had presented by far the widest range of policy proposals.

Henry Bolton was a really rather dull entry to the contest, who came in later than the rest of us. Bolton presented himself as the favourite of former leader (and, to some, messiah), Nigel Farage, and was every bit the establishment candidate. His initial speeches were a lesson in how not to make a political speech: "me, me, me – I've done this, I've done that". He didn't mention the country or the British people until later; he certainly didn't mention Islam until he saw the support I was receiving.

This was something of a pattern. The country rarely got a mention; most candidates seemed content with boasting about themselves or focusing solely on the inner machinations of the party. It was incredibly boring and the public didn't care, as I continually pointed out.

---

7 "Ukip Isn't Racist, Which Is Why Anne Marie Waters Shouldn't Be Leader: Ex-Party Whip," LBC, August 12, 2017, accessed April 11, 2018, http://www.lbc.co.uk/radio/presenters/ian-payne/ukip-isnt-racist-which-is-why-anne-marie-waters-sh/.
8 Brian Wheeler, "Anti-Islam Campaigner Anne Marie Waters Launches UKIP Bid - BBC News," BBC, June 30, 2017, accessed April 13, 2018, http://www.bbc.co.uk/news/uk-politics-40442878.

Bolton showed the true cut of his jib, and the kind of leader he would be, when he attempted to have me removed from the ballot paper altogether, while saying he would listen to members and openly discuss all issues.

One notable event was the official party hustings in London, attended by Nigel Farage. Once again I stood my ground against baseless implications and slurs by other candidates, and once again, I won the approval of much of the audience. Afterwards, along with Peter Whittle, a well-known figure in the party and member of London's governing assembly) was taken to the BBC studios to appear on a flagship current affairs programme, *Newsnight*[9].

It was fascinating to watch Whittle's performance. He switched from denouncing my approach to Islam (I called it evil because that is what it is) to again implying I'm a single issue candidate, all in one sentence. Whittle confirmed his opposition to sharia law, but wasn't able to say why. What is it about sharia law that is problematic and where exactly does it derive from? These answers are rarely forthcoming, because when they are, even UKIP will denounce the speaker as racist.

I really believe that many in UKIP enjoyed their reprieve from being on the receiving end of media bias and lies when I was a leadership candidate. Suddenly they were almost being praised, essentially for not being me. They could finally present themselves as 'moderates' and send the press venom in my direction. In other words, UKIP had proven to be no better than the rest, and the public got a strong indication of that during this long and fractious leadership election.

The result of the contest was to be announced in September at the party conference in Torquay, a seaside town on the south coast of England. Though I arrived in Torquay the night before, I did not attend the conference until just before the announcement as I knew exactly what it would be like, and I was right. The moment I arrived, I was flanked by the press. They followed me around like vultures. Though I'd expected it, it was still

---

9 BBCNewsnight, "UKIP Leadership Candidates on Brexit, Islam and the EDL – BBC Newsnight," YouTube, September 05, 2017, accessed April 13, 2018, https://www. youtube.com/watch?v=nGLvUR5Erkc.

unbelievable. I was the lowest of the low to the media, as hated by the Right Wing as I was by the Left.

During the campaign, some in the alternative Right-wing media had attempted to portray me as a leftist, while to the Left-wing media, I was on the far Right. This is what happens when a person refuses to fall into neat little categories and has the courage to have clear beliefs and defend them. I won't sidle up to anyone; I will stand my own ground. Politics is not used to this, so I was deemed an enemy all round.

Eventually, the candidates were gathered in a small room to await the result, the press rattling around outside, smelling blood. If I won, it was going to be an impossible task. Most of the party's MEPs had already threatened to resign from the party[10], and I was aware that the dishonest tactics of many senior party members during the campaign would continue until I was driven out. As the names of the defeated were read out, I desperately wanted to hear my own, and at last it came. I was in second place, and Henry Bolton was the victor.

In hindsight, the UKIP leadership election could not have gone better. The primary reason was the exposure of UKIP's leaders for what they really are: professional politicians more concerned about negative press attention than telling the truth and standing up to the greatest threat to Britain since the Second World War. The public now knew for certain that UKIP did not have the courage or principles to defend the country against any and all enemies. It was an important lesson for them to learn.

Following the result, even the messiah Farage made known his capitulation to the mainstream press[11]. After years of being called a racist for wanting out of the European Union, Farage would then imply that others are racist for opposing an incredibly dangerous religion which, at that time, had prompted the murder of scores of Britons and the rape of thousands.

10 Owen Bennett, "Ukip MEPs Will Quit En Masse If Anti-Islam Candidate Becomes New Leader," HuffPost UK, July 03, 2017, accessed April 13, 2018, http://www.huffingtonpost.co.uk/entry/ukip-islam-farage-anne-marie-waters_uk_595a4ae7e4b0da2c7324aac0.
11 Nigel Farage, "Racists Nearly Killed Ukip This Week, but We Live to Fight Our Most Important Battle," The Telegraph, September 30, 2017, accessed April 13, 2018, http://www.telegraph.co.uk/news/2 017/09/30/racists-nearly-killed-ukip-week-live-fight-important-battle/.

For his part, Bolton immediately took the opportunity to denounce myself and my supporters as "national socialists"[12]. The damage this does is incalculable. UKIP had told the country that if they have concerns about Islam, they are racists and fascists. In doing this, they set back public confidence and trust by years. Having seen what UKIP had become, I did the only thing I could: I left the party and said good riddance. While some had urged me to stay (using the argument that Bolton wouldn't last long), I simply could not stomach being in a party that would stoop so low. I decided to form my own party, and I'm glad that I did.

We are still in the very early stages of getting For Britain off the ground, and it is indeed a mammoth task to undertake. The press immediately denounced us as far Right (of course), but the truth is that For Britain is a party for those who can't find honesty and truth anywhere else in politics.

I am by nature an optimist. I have taken pretty much every punch the lying establishment press can throw at me, and I'm still standing. At the beginning of 2018, following the most incredibly intense year of my life, I took 10 days in the remote countryside – no internet; no TV; no contact with the outside world – and it completely revived me. Now I'm ready to carry on with the battle of all battles: the battle to save the country I love from a tyrannical Left-wing/Islamist alliance that aims to enslave future generations of Brits.

Indeed, it is already happening, and in the following chapters, I'll explain exactly how and why.

---

12 Peter Walker, "Ukip Risks Becoming 'UK Nazi Party' If It Selects Wrong Leader," The Guardian, September 11, 2017, accessed April 13, 2018, https://www.theguardian.com/politics/2017/sep/11/leadership-hopeful-warns-wrong-leader-could-turn-ukip-into-uks-nazi-party-henry-bolton.

THE UNITED KINGDOM

EDUCATION IN THE UK

THE UK IS changing, fast. Massive migration over recent decades has altered the national demographic immeasurably. Religious and social ideas, many of which are incompatible with the rights and freedoms that have been established in Britain over centuries, are now both commonplace and accommodated. The UK has adopted a multicultural approach to mass immigration and encouraged its newcomers to bring with them the social norms of their homeland.

The education system is particularly fertile ground for sowing Islamist seeds. The UK's schools have provided, and are providing, a highly useful tool for the expansion and cultivation of Islamist thought – and regulators do not prevent it.

Britain's school system is monitored by an organisation called Ofsted – the Office for Standards in Education, Children's Services and Skills. It reports to Parliament, and part of its role is to inspect schools and regulate what goes on within them. There is one type of school, however, which Ofsted does not monitor – the madrassa (Islamic school).

It was revealed in 2011 that teachers in UK madrassas are imparting on to young children extreme Islamic ideas – a major feature of which is isolation from, and hatred of, non-Muslims or

Muslims of a different sect or interpretation. More than 100,000 children are attending madrassas in Britain.

In Keighley, Yorkshire, a film of a Koran-reading class in 2011 showed teachers and leaders kicking and punching the children in their charge[1]. One man was arrested following this specific incident, but madrassas remain unregulated despite the fact that more than 400 allegations of physical abuse (and 30 of sexual abuse) have been made.

'LESSONS IN HATE AND VIOLENCE'

Madrassas are far from the only institutions of concern. Faith schools (state funded but run with a religious character) are increasing sources of unease, particularly as government after government enthusiastically promotes them. In a documentary entitled 'Lessons in Hate and Violence'[2] in 2011, British broadcaster Channel 4 revealed disturbing messages being taught to young children in Islamic faith schools. Not only is violence being used against children, hatred is encouraged by teachers and clerics. Quotes include: "The disbelievers, they are the worst of all creatures" and "A person who has less than a fistful of beard, you should stay away from him, the same way you would stay away from a serpent or a snake".

There are 2,000 or so Islamic faith schools in Britain – including full- and part-time, primary and secondary. Darul Uloom is a secondary faith school in Birmingham that had been given the green light by Ofsted, despite being one of the schools investigated by the *Dispatches* 'Lessons in Hate and Violence' documentary. In it, a speaker was heard telling a room full of children that Hinduism is a "ridiculous" belief system, as well as lying about a number of Hindu practices ("the Hindus drink the piss of a cow"). At the same school, pupils were checked for Islamic haircuts following their summer break, and those not deemed Islamic enough were

1 Riazat Butt, "Mosque School Arrest following Channel 4 Documentary," The Guardian, February 14, 2011, accessed April 13, 2018, http://www.guardian.co.uk/uk/2011/feb/14/mosque-schools-arrest-channel-4
2 "Islam, Lessons in Hate and Violence - 1 of 4," LiveLeak.com - Redefining the Media, accessed April 14, 2018, http://www.liveleak.com/view?i=826_1297870709.

sent to stand by a wall.

Also given the green light by Ofsted was Mandani Girls' School in east London. The school forces its students to wear the full Islamic niqab – the face veil. An Ofsted report of this school made no mention of its strict uniform policy. In fact, it was praised for its contribution to "community cohesion". Mandani demonstrates its commitment to community cohesion by discussing "The most important factors which protect Muslim children from the onslaught of Euro-centrism, homosexuality, racism, and secular traditions".

Andrew Gilligan, in his article 'Ofsted Praises Islamic Schools Which Oppose Western Lifestyle'[3], claimed that the Ofsted inspector responsible for many of the reports, Michele Messoudi, had been accused of links with Islamist organisations. Another Ofsted inspector, Akram Khan-Cheema, was Chief Executive of IBERR, which has links to the Muslim Brotherhood[4].

There is little interest in any of this from the powers-that-be. Indeed, criticisms from leading figures following the screening of 'Lessons in Hate and Violence' appeared reserved for the programme makers rather than those filmed. For example, the Liberal Democrat MP, John Hemming, is reported to have said:

> "This kind of documentary is ideal fodder for the EDL [English Defence League]. Channel 4 is putting the safety of children at risk by criticising a school which is doing its job properly"[5].

---

3 Andrew Gilligan, "Ofsted Praises Islamic Schools Which Oppose Western Lifestyle," The Telegraph, November 06, 2010, accessed April 14, 2018, http://www.telegraph.co.uk/education/educationnews/8114452/Ofsted-praises-Islamic-schools-which-oppose-Western-lifestyle.html.

4 GlobalMB, "Islamic Educational Organization Tied To Muslim Brotherhood Announces Forum," The Global Muslim Brotherhood Daily Watch, March 15, 2008, accessed April 15, 2018, http://globalmbreport.com/?p=619.

5 Reporter, Daily Mail, "'Muslim Eton' at Centre of Channel 4 Hate-preaching Allegations Is Forced to Shut over Far-Right Safety Fears," Daily Mail Online, February 14, 2011, accessed April 15, 2018. http://www.dailymail.co.uk/news/article-1356854/Dispatches-Muslim-Eton-centre-Channel-4-hate-preaching-allegations-forced-shut-far-Right-safety-fears.html.

Denis MacEoin, author of *Sharia Law or One Law for All?*[6] wrote a report on the issue in 2009. He posted a comment on the website of One Law for All (www.onelawforall.org.uk) claiming that he had given a report on Muslim schools to Ofsted, but they were more concerned about shielding Islam from criticism than any information contained in the report[7].

'UNDERCOVER MOSQUE'

This is not uncommon. Similar occurred following the Channel 4 broadcast of its *Dispatches* documentary, 'Undercover Mosque'[8], in 2007, revealing secret recordings made in some of Britain's largest mainstream mosques. Representative of these mosques often claim dedication to interfaith dialogue and respect, but when they think nobody is listening, their tone changes somewhat. Children were present during all of the speeches recorded.

On the arrest of terrorism suspects:

"I don't believe them because they are kuffaar and lying is part of their religion."

On women:

"Allah has created the woman, even if she has a PhD, deficient. Her intellect is incomplete."

(Broadcast to the mosque from Saudi Arabia): *"Men are in charge of women. Wherever he goes she should follow him. She shouldn't be allowed to leave the house without his permission."*

"It becomes an obligation on us to force her to wear hijab, and if she doesn't wear the hijab, we hit her."

"Mohammad practically outlined the rules regarding marriage prior to puberty with his practice. He clarified what is

---

6 "Sharia Law or 'One Law For All?'" Civitas: Institute for the Study of Civil Society, January 27, 2016, accessed May 15, 2018, http://www.civitas.org.uk/publications/sharia-law-or-one-law-for-all/.

7 "On Channel 4's Dispatches: Lessons in Hate and Violence," One Law for All, accessed May 15, 2018, http://www.onelawforall.org.uk/on-channel-4's-dispatches-lessons-in-hate-and-violence/.

8 "Dispatches - Undercover Mosque," Vimeo, May 25, 2018, accessed May 25, 2018, http://vimeo.com/19598947.

permissible and that is why we shouldn't have any issues about an older man marrying a younger woman."

On non-believers:

"We love the people of Islam, we hate the kuffaar"

On different Islamic practices:

"If you leave off the prayers out of negligence, then you are a kaffir."

On apostasy:

"Whoever changes his religion to anything else, kill him in the Islamic state."

On children:

"What is sad to see is that, for many parents, they send their children to the kuffaar school. They allow them to mix with the kuffaar."

'Undercover Mosque' also shined a light on the Saudi Arabian establishment. The Saudi Arabian form of Islam – known as Wahhabism – is being propagated across the Western world with the use of Saudi funds. Wahhabism is here described by Dr Arfan Al-Alawi on 'Undercover Mosque':

> *"Wahhabis believe you cannot show tolerance to other religions, so the religion of Islam has to rule the world. Green Lane in Birmingham, that mosque is one of the most extreme Wahhabi centres in the UK."*

Abdal-Hakim Murad explained further:

> *"It's [sic] principle is totalitarian. It is highly judgmental. It has no track record of dealing with other sorts of Islam, or with unbelievers with any kind of respect."*

Following the broadcast, the Crown Prosecution Service

(CPS), which is responsible for prosecuting criminal cases on behalf of the Crown (state), determined that there was not enough evidence to initiate any criminal charges against those filmed. However, a spokeswoman said: "The CPS has demonstrated that it will not hesitate to prosecute those responsible for criminal incitement[9]." This comment was aimed at the film's producers, not its on-screen stars. West Midlands Police investigated the film and subsequently reported the makers to Ofcom, the responsible regulatory body. Ofcom rejected complaints that the film had misrepresented the speakers.

It concluded:

> *"'Undercover Mosque' was a legitimate investigation, uncovering matters of important public interest...On the evidence (including untransmitted footage and scripts), Ofcom found that the broadcaster had accurately represented the material it had gathered and dealt with the subject matter responsibly and in context[10]."*

The makers of the documentary launched a libel action against West Midlands Police, who apologised, along with the CPS, for accusing them of misrepresentation.

In a second film 'Undercover Mosque: The Return' a year later, Channel 4 went back to some of the same mosques and found that nothing had changed. Hate and intolerance was still being preached – including at the famous Regent's Park mosque in London (which had promised to change its ways following the initial broadcast). Again, people were being taught to reject non-Muslims and kill apostates and homosexuals, all of it emanating from Saudi textbooks.

In a further documentary, this time broadcast by the BBC, the influence of Saudi Arabian Islam on British children was again highlighted. This film explained that the demand for

9 UK | England | West Midlands | "C4 'distorted' Mosque Programme," BBC News, August 08, 2007, accessed May 16, 2018, http://news.bbc.co.uk/1/hi/england/west_midlands/6936681.stm.

10 John Plunkett, "Ofcom Rejects Police Complaints over Channel 4's Undercover Mosque," The Guardian, November 19, 2007, accessed April 16, 2018, http://www.theguardian.com/media/2007/nov/19/channel4.ofcom.

Islam-centred state education is growing. Entitled 'British Schools, Islamic Rules'[11], the investigation looked specifically at the Jame'ah Mosque in Leicester – a mosque with an associated girls' school close by. Here, from the age of 11, all girls must cover their faces entirely with the niqab. The mosque also runs a fatwa service advising Muslims on what is and is not permissible. Advice includes that a female should remain in the home unless she must leave by necessity, and that music is a deliberate ploy by Western kuffaar to undermine Islam. An Ofsted report on this school declared that it teaches children to value diversity and to respect other ideas and traditions. Links between the mosque, school, and fatwa service were denied.

The BBC reporter on 'British Schools, Islamic Rules' carried out an internet investigation of various Muslim schools across the country and found the following statements expressed on their websites: "We need to defend our children from the forces of evil"; "Our children are exposed to a culture that is in opposition to almost everything Islam stands for"; "The curriculum must be kept within the bounds of sharia"; "Birthdays, it should be remembered, are the practices of disbelievers and immoral people".

At the Tooting Islamic Centre in south London, pupils from a nearby private secondary school were invited to listen to Riyadh ul Haq. Ul Haq is an Indian born Islamic scholar who helped to found the Al Kawthar Academy schools in the English Midlands[12].

Here is a statement from ul Haq:

> *"Allah has warned us in the Koran, do not befriend the kuffaar, do not align yourself with the kuffaar – the verses are so many and so numerous, I can't recite every one of them."*

The Tooting school insisted that Mr ul Haq had not made any statements of this kind when he spoke to local schoolchildren.

---

11 "BBC Panorama: British Schools, Islamic Rules (Part 1 of 2) HQ," YouTube, last modified November 23, 2010, http://www.youtube.com/watch?v=uRH6EV5rRMU.
12 Al Kawthar Academy website, accessed April 16, 2018, https://akacademy.org/.

However, his views had been exposed by a newspaper reporter just prior to his visit to the Tooting Islamic Centre.

Perhaps the most disturbing discovery was the textbooks, obtained by the BBC, containing lessons on how to amputate the limbs of thieves, describing Jews as cursed, attempting to control the world, and looking like monkeys and pigs (the book also asks children to list the "reprehensible qualities of the Jews"), and arguing that homosexuals must be killed. The building in London from which the books were distributed was revealed as being owned by the Saudi government.

SCHOOL DINNERS

Madrassas and Islamic faith schools are serious sources of alarm, due mainly to their teachings and messages, but many people in Britain are also worried about Islamic principles being mainstreamed and applied throughout the education system more generally. This is particularly the case in relation to food.

In April 2013, the Larkswood Primary School in Chingford, Essex, altered its lunch menu[13]. The school has pupils from a diversity of backgrounds and around 10% of them come from Muslim families. Despite the small number of Muslims, the school informed parents that it would only be serving halal meat (meat from animals slaughtered in accordance with Islamic ritual) in the future. A report the same month revealed that three quarters of state funded schools in an east London borough were serving halal meat only[14]. Halal is also routinely served in hospitals and sporting venues in Britain, without the knowledge of the consumer[15].

---

13 "Row over Halal Meat at School," East London and West Essex Guardian Series, accessed May 7, 2018, http://www.guardian-series.co.uk/news/10308743.Row_over_ Halal_meat_at_school.

14 "Halal Meat Served in Three-quarters of Council-supported Schools," East London and West Essex Guardian Series, accessed April 17, 2018, http://www.guardian-series. co.uk/news/10334813.Halal_meat_served_in_three_quarters_of_council_supported_ schools.

15 "Halal Meat Served to Patients, Staff & Students Within All of Your Establishments - a Freedom of Information Request to University Hospitals of Leicester NHS Trust," WhatDoTheyKnow, last modified February 16, 2015, https://www.whatdotheyknow.com/ request/halal_meat_served_to_patients_st_3.

Ramadan is an important month in the Islamic calendar. It is a time when observant Muslims, among other acts, forego food from morning until sunset every day. In 2013, a parent in Portsmouth complained to the Charles Dickens Primary School when her son, who is not Muslim, was prevented from drinking water during class lest it upset children who were fasting[16]. Indeed, the imposition of fasting upon children in schools is an issue that has been raised with me on several occasions.

In 2010, local government councils throughout the country issued guidance to schools on how to observe Ramadan. Teachers were instructed not to hold exams or parents' meetings, that there should be no swimming, no sex or relationship classes, and extra prayer time should be accommodated during this time [17]. The instructions mirror some of the demands made in a document issued by the Muslim Council of Britain entitled 'Meeting the Needs of Muslim Pupils in State Schools'[18]. This document instructs that girls should be covered entirely except for their faces and hands. It also calls for the accommodation of prayers and the collective celebration of both annual Eid festivals.

(You can read a full Sharia Watch report on this document here http://www.shariawatch.org.uk/?q=content islam-and-british-schools-what-s-going)

Schools in Britain are taking these Islamic instructions increasingly seriously, and it seems that even employment rights are now subject to Islamic sensitivity. A woman who had worked as a dinner lady in a school in Staffordshire for 11 years was sacked in the summer of 2013 for accidentally (she claimed) almost serving pork to a "Muslim child"[19]. The media reporting

---

16 Jessica Elgot, HuffPost UK, July 12, 2013, accessed April 17, 2018, http://www.huffingtonpost.co.uk/2013/07/12/pupil-school-water-ramada_n_3588106.html.
17 "Council tells schools to rearrange exams and cancel swimming for Ramadan," The Telegraph, July 11, 2010, accessed April 17, 2018, http://www.telegraph.co.uk/education/educationnews/7884040/Council-tells-schools-to-rearrange-exams-and-cancel-swimming-for-Ramadan.html.
18 "MCB launches "Toward Greater Understanding – 'Meeting the Needs of Muslim Pupils in State Schools'," The Muslim Council of Britain, February 20, 2007, accessed April 17, 2018, http://www.mcb.org.uk/mcb-launches-towards-greater-understanding-meeting-the-needs-of-muslim-pupils-in-state-schools/.
19 Mehdi Hasan, "Gammongate: The Truth?," HuffPost UK, last modified August 2, 2013, http://www.huffingtonpost.co.uk/2013/08/02/alison-waldock-row-muslim-parents-speak_n_3694477.html.

of this was beyond parody. Some mentioned what a relief it was that the school's headmaster had swooped in and whipped away the pork just in the nick of time so that catastrophe was averted. But despite the quick action of the headmaster, the woman was fired anyway.

Mehdi Hasan wrote in the *Huffington Post* soon afterwards that the school's decision to fire the dinner lady was not based solely on her erroneous serving of pork[20]. In his article, he wrote that the parents of the child claimed to have approached the school on previous occasions about Alison Waldock, the dinner lady in question, serving non-halal meat to Muslims. According to Hasan, the school had confirmed that this incident was not unique. The school's head teacher is reported to have said, "We understand from Lunchtime UK [the catering company] that this was not a one-off event, and due to the significant number of children involved, the company treated the issue with the seriousness it deserved". The seriousness it deserved? Why is this so serious, when the unlabelled and compulsory feeding of halal to non-Muslims is not deemed serious at all[21]?

There have been countless 'scandals' involving halal meat. Take this example from Leicester[22]. A company, based in Doncaster, was supplying Leicester schools with meat. A burger was found to have contained pork. And then the sky fell in. Leicester City Council deemed such an abhorrence to be "unacceptable" and ceased to do business with the supplier. A spokeswoman said, "The council's view is that whether it's [the level of "contamination"] 1% or 99%, it's still impure and unacceptable".

Suleman Nagdi, from the Federation of Muslim Organisations, said, "For people, this is touching at the very tenet of their faith, the very heart of their faith. There needs to be a criminal procedure against the company." It wasn't enough that it had lost a major contract; it had to be prosecuted, too.

---

20 Ibid.

21 Nick Fagge, "Halal Britain: Schools and Institutions Serving Up Ritually Slaughtered Meat," Mail Online, last modified January 25, 2011, http://www.dailymail.co.uk/news/article-1313458/Halal-Britain-Famous-institutions-routinely-serve-public-ritually-slaughtered-meat.html.

22 «Halal School Burger ‹up to 50% Pork›,» BBC News, last modified May 10, 2013, http://www.bbc.co.uk/news/uk-england-leicestershire-22479712.

When Lancashire County Council attempted to stop un-stunned meat (it would still be halal, but stunned halal) being served in its schools, the Lancashire Council of Mosques (LCM) made it clear that this would not suffice. Despite clear assurances from the Food Standards Agency that most halal meat is stunned[23], LCM did not agree and insisted on un-stunned slaughter.

The county council voted in favour of banning un-stunned meat from its schools in October 2017[24]. Needless to say, Muslim councillors (from the Labour Party) objected, with one saying he was "very unhappy" as the proposal caused "offence to him and his faith". The LCM even argued that stunning was inhumane, in spite of both common sense and overwhelming evidence to the contrary. The Royal Society for the Prevention of Cruelty to Animals (RSPCA) and other animal groups in Britain agree that stunning should be carried out for the benefit of the animal, but in the end, it made no difference. Lancashire County Council backtracked in early 2018 and agreed to consult with Muslim groups[25].

This is standard in the UK – any concerns about Islamic practices must be approved by Islamic groups, and any action taken to prevent cruelty in the name of Islam will therefore be prevented by such groups.

FREE SCHOOLS

Free schools – a new type of school funded but not controlled by local government – are also aiding the advancement of Islam. In Derby in 2013, Al-Madinah school was accused of forcing its female teachers to wear the hijab, regardless of their religion.

---

23 James Meikle, "What Exactly Does the Halal Method of Animal Slaughter Involve?," The Guardian, last modified December 22, 2017, https://www.theguardian.com/lifeandstyle/2014/may/08/what-does-halal-method-animal-slaughter-involve.

24 "Unstunned Halal School Meals Banned," BBC News, last modified October 26, 2017, http://www.bbc.co.uk/news/uk-england-lancashire-41765927.

25 "County Council Backs Down over Decision to Ban Unstunned Halal Meat in Schools," Lancashire Telegraph, accessed June 2, 2018, http://www.lancashiretelegraph.co.uk/news/15893032.County_council_backs_down_over_decision_to_ban_unstunned_halal_meat_in_schools.

According to the *Derby Telegraph*, female teachers had been required to sign contracts obliging them to wear the Islamic headscarf. The school was also accused of making girls sit at the back of the classroom[26].

Following these reports, the school was temporarily closed by the governing body Ofsted. Confusion over the reason for the closure subsequently followed, with the school insisting that it had nothing to do with an Ofsted inspection, but undisclosed safety concerns. It opened again only days later.

Soon after it reopened, it was threatened with closure again. According to the BBC, the school's principal, deputy principal, and head of administration all resigned. The government had, the BBC claimed, told the school to write to its female staff and inform them that they did not have to wear the headscarf if it conflicted with their religious beliefs.

Three governors of Al-Madinah were interviewed by the BBC's Zoe Conway on 11 October 2013. Here is the transcript of that interview[27]:

> Abdullah Shahjan: *"The very first question we ask, to everybody, Muslim and non-Muslim, is would you be prepared to cover your hair if you came in to the school, as part of the uniform? To this date, all those who have come to interview point, none of them have ever refused, those who have succeeded and got a job as well as those who haven't."*
>
> Zoe Conway: *"Why should they have to wear a headscarf if they're not Muslim?"*
> Abdullah Shahjan: *"Let's just talk about uniform. You don't expect a surgeon not to wear his surgeon gear at the point he's doing surgery. You don't expect a dentist not to wear his overalls when he's doing his dentistry."*

26 Hayley Dixon, "Non-Muslim Teachers 'forced to Wear Veil' at Faith School," Telegraph.co.uk, last modified September 20, 2013, https://www.telegraph.co.uk/education/educationnews/10322872/Non-Muslim-teachers-forced-to-wear-veil-at-faith-school.html.
27 "Three Al-Madinah governors defend school's policies," BBC, October 11, 2013, accessed April 18, 2018, http://www.bbc.co.uk/news/uk-24502536.

Zoe Conway: *"You're not saying to me that you can't teach maths unless you've got a headscarf on?"*

Abdullah Shahjan: *"We're not saying that at all. What we're saying is we're proud of the uniform that we have in terms of what we want for our children."*

Zoe Conway: *"How do you know that there aren't women who are brilliant teachers who are not going to come and teach at your school because you require them to wear a headscarf and they don't want to wear a headscarf?"*

Mohammed Burhaan: *"As an organisation, do we not have the right to stipulate our code of dress? We have chosen, we have sat down, and this is the code of dress that we have adopted. If you look at an air hostess, for example, they may be required to wear certain headgear. The female air hostesses wear a different code of dress to the male ones. Now, we're not saying that they're discriminated against – that's a choice, and that's a decision made by the business...This is the corporate image that we would like our female staff to present. That's a decision that we made. We're not saying that by wearing the headscarf, you are changing your religious identity at all. What we're purely, sincerely and clearly saying is this is the code of dress that we would like our female members of staff to adopt and that's the decision, as an organisation, we have made. Is it possible to review that? Yes, it is."*

On the allegations of girls sitting at the back of the class:

Fasal Hussain: *"Nobody is forced to do anything in this school. The allegations are unfortunate. When it comes to the seating arrangements in the class, what we don't do, we don't have a boy-girl, boy-girl seating arrangement. The way the classroom is designed, all of our children are treated equally – we have girls sitting at the front and at the back, we have boys sitting at the front and at the back. There is no discrimination going on in this school whatsoever."*

On reports that only one pupil in the school was non-Muslim, despite its obligations to honour all faiths, Hussain said:

"We are on a journey. There are things that yeah – by all means – we have to improve, we know that. But, like everything else, it takes time. It takes time to nurture a flower. We are just coming out of a seedling point. We have to ensure that the right practices and the right teaching and learning [are] effective...for people to come automatically to us and say, 'Actually, I'm going to that school, not because it's a Muslim faith school, [but] because it's an excellent school'."

By the looks of things, the school has a long way to go. In a letter to Al Madinah[28] dated 8 October 2013, Lord Nash – Parliamentary Under Secretary of State for Schools – threatened to terminate the school's funding if certain breaches were not remedied. He accused the school of "failing to ensure the safety of the children in the school; delivering an unacceptably poor standard of education; discriminating in its policies and procedures towards female staff; and failing to discharge its duties and responsibilities in respect of the governing body."

In February 2014, it was announced that the school was to close – its secondary section at least[29].

'RACIST' KIDS AND TROJAN HORSES

There are innumerable problems concerning Islam and schools in Britain. In Scotland, a plan to immunise children against flu was put on hold (for all children) because of protests that the

28 GOV.UK, accessed April 18, 2018, https://www.gov.uk/government/publications/letter-from-lord-nash-to-al-madinah-education-trust.
29 Shiv Malik, "Al-Madinah Free School Ordered to Shut Down Secondary Wing," The Guardian, last modified November 30, 2017, https://www.theguardian.com/education/2014/feb/07/al-madinah-free-school-secondary.

vaccine contained pork derivatives and was thus unacceptable to Muslims[30]. In November 2013, parents in the mid-England county of Staffordshire received a rather alarming letter from a head teacher[31] informing them that their children were to be taken to visit Staffordshire University as part of their cultural education. The school's head warned in the letter that if any child failed to attend, a "racial discrimination note" would be made on the child's school record, and would remain there for the duration of their schooling careers.

Some parents did not know how to react. One mother said, "I feel my child will be racist if I don't allow her to go."

Others were somewhat angrier, with one stating, "I was shocked by the letter. To be told my kids have got to attend this workshop is disgusting." She added, "I don't want a stain on my kids' record as a result. They are not old enough to be called racist."

Though the school later apologised (following media coverage and condemnation from a local MP), the explanation of the head teacher is worth considering: "We are a mainly Christian school, but we have to cover at least one other religion as part of the national curriculum. This visit is part of that."

One other religion? Which one, I wonder.

What was also interesting was the response of the County Council, which deemed it "a school matter", adding, "We believe it is important for children to find out more about different cultures." They conceded, however, that talk of racial discrimination was "not appropriate" and that parents should be able to withdraw their children if they wished.

A 'Trojan Horse' campaign was brought to light in early 2014[32]. A leaked letter between Islamists revealed that a plan was afoot in Birmingham to drive out school head teachers. The idea was to stir up trouble for head teachers (make false accusations

30 «Concerns Delay Schools› Flu Vaccine,» BBC News, last modified October 4, 2013, http://www.bbc.co.uk/news/uk-scotland-24394844.
31 News agencies, "School Children As Young As 8 Told They Would Be Labelled 'racist' for Missing School Trip," Telegraph.co.uk, last modified November 22, 2013, https://www.telegraph.co.uk/education/educationnews/10468353/School-children-as-young-as-8-told-they-would-be-labelled-racist-for-missing-school-trip.html.
32 Andrew Gilligan, "Extremists and the 'Trojan Horse' Approach in State Schools," The Telegraph, Telegraph.co.uk, last modified March 9, 2014, http://www.telegraph.

against them, for example). They would then be replaced with teachers more likely to ensure that schools were "run on Islamic principles".

According to Andrew Gilligan in the *Telegraph*:

> "...*the leaked documents describe how the alleged plotters stir up 'hard-line' parents to attack head teachers with allegations that they are 'corrupting their children with sex education, teaching about homosexuals, making their children pray Christian prayers and* [carrying out] *mixed swimming and sport'.*"

The letter is reported to have included the statement "Whilst sometimes the practices we use may not seem the correct way to do things, you must remember that this is jihad, and as such using all measures possible to win the war is acceptable."

Eventually, several schools across the country were investigated, particularly in Birmingham. Findings confirmed that some head teachers had been forced from their jobs and "a culture of fear and intimidation had taken grip"[33].

A report, ordered by the government, stated that there was:

> "...*very clear evidence that young people are being encouraged to accept unquestionably a particular hard-line strand of Sunni Islam that raises concerns about their vulnerability to radicalisation in the future. Essentially the ideology revealed by this investigation is an intolerant and politicised form of extreme social conservatism that ultimately seeks to control all Muslims. In its separatist assertions and attempts to subvert normal processes, it amounts to what is often described as Islamism. The agenda, but not the tactics, involved stems from an international movement to increase the role of Islam in education.*"

co.uk/news/uknews/terrorism-in-the-uk/10685418/Extremists-and-the-Trojan-Horse-approach-in-state-schools.html.
33 Sean Coughlan, "Ofsted Says Schools Were Targeted," BBC News, last modified June 9, 2014, http://www.bbc.co.uk/news/education-27763113.

Two organisations identified by the report's author as being behind the movement were the Muslim Council of Britain and the Association of Muslim Schools – UK[34].

Finally, the report revealed that there was "incontrovertible evidence that both senior officials and elected members of Birmingham council were aware of activities that bear a striking resemblance to those described in the Trojan Horse letter many months before it surfaced."

The then-Prime Minister David Cameron and Education Secretary Michael Gove announced new plans to ensure that children were taught British values in schools, and that there would be unannounced inspections to ensure this teaching was carried out. Needless to say, the Muslim Council of Britain dismissed the whole thing as a "witch hunt"[35], and their public sector allies as usual had their back.

The most striking example was the response of then-Chief Executive of Birmingham City Council, Mark Rogers. He launched an attack on Michael Gove (and his wife), and the Chief Inspector of schools, Sir Michael Wilshaw[36], while attempting to downplay the homophobic, misogynistic, anti-Semitic hatred that had been imparted on to young and vulnerable minds throughout several of his city's schools. According to the *Telegraph*, Mr Rogers insisted there was no Trojan Horse plot, merely "new communities" raising "legitimate questions and challenges" to the "liberal education system". Well, well, well, I wonder if he would say the same to a room full of feminists or gay rights campaigners.

'EDUCATION AGAINST HATE'

In 2015, three schoolgirls from Bethnal Green Academy in east London made headlines when they flew to Syria to become

34 Patrick Wintour, "Trojan Horse inquiry...," The Guardian, July 17, 2014, accessed April 18, 2018, http://www.theguardian.com/uk-news/2014/jul/17/birmingham-schools-inquiry-hardline-sunni-islam-trojan-horse.

35 "Education and Muslims: End this Witch-Hunt of British Muslims," The Muslim Council of Britain, April 16, 2014, WebCite Query Result, accessed April 18, 2018, http://www.webcitation.org/6OxaIrr9E.

36 Andrew Gilligan, "Council expects 'firestorm' over Trojan Horse schools plot," The Telegraph, May 10, 2014, accessed April 19, 2018, http://www.telegraph.co.uk/education/educationnews/10822259/Council-expects-firestorm-over-Trojan-Horse-schools-plot.html.

'jihadi brides'[37]. The Metropolitan Police then informed us that Shamima Begum, Amira Abase, and Kadiza Sultana would not face terrorism charges if they returned 'home'. It soon emerged that Abase Hussen, father of Amira Abase, had taken his daughter to anti-Western rallies organised and attended by some of the most extreme Islamic voices in the country[38]. Also in 2015, a schoolboy from Blackburn in the north of England became Britain's hitherto youngest terror suspect when the 14-year-old was arrested for taking part in a 'credible' terror plot in Australia[39].

In an extraordinary article published in November 2015 in a major British newspaper, *The Independent*[40], Sadja Khan wrote, "Simply put, the way to combat Islamic extremism is to invest in teaching Islamic theology in British schools". One wonders what kind of Islamic theology she had in mind. Perhaps she was referring to the theology found in Jamiatul Ummah School in east London where, in 2016, books promoting the stoning of women were discovered in its library[41].

The Education Secretary in 2016 was Conservative Nicky Morgan. She launched a website that year entitled 'Educate Against Hate'[42], which was aimed primarily at teachers and offered guidance on how to teach British values to children. Interestingly (and revealingly), respect for the equal rights of women was not mentioned. This, and other toothless measures

37 David Barrett and Martin Evans, «Three ‹Jihadi Brides› from London Who Travelled to Syria Will Not Face Terrorism Charges if They Return,» Telegraph.co.uk, last modified March 10, 2015, accessed April 19, 2018, http://www.telegraph.co.uk/news/uknews/11461693/Sisters-of-the-missing-jihadi-brides-to-face-radicalisation-tests.html.
38 Sam Greenhill for the Daily Mail, "Runaway Jihadi Schoolgirl Attended Rally with Her Father Aged Just 13," Daily Mail Online, April 07, 2015, accessed April 19, 2018, http://www.dailymail.co.uk/news/article-3027035/Father-runaway-jihadi-schoolgirl-filmed-burning-flag-protest-admits-attending-says-took-daughter-demonstration-just-13.html.
39 "Boy, 14, Held over Australia 'plot'," BBC News, last modified April 20, 2015, http://www.bbc.co.uk/news/uk-32379812.
40 Sajda Khan, "The Prophet Mohammed Had British Values," The Independent, last modified November 1, 2015, accessed April 19, 2018, http://www.independent.co.uk/voices/the-prophet-mohammed-had-british-values-so-the-only-way-to-combat-extremism-is-to-teach-more-islam-a6717066.html.
41 Steven Hopkins, "Muslim School In East London Had Books 'Promoting Stoning People To Death'," HuffPost UK, last modified January 20, 2016, https://www.huffingtonpost.co.uk/2016/01/20/muslim-school-fails-inspection-over-books-promoting-stoning-people-to-death_n_9029780.html.
42 Educate Against Hate, accessed April 20, 2018, https://www.educateagainsthate.com/.

initiated by the government, appear not to be having the desired effect. By 2017, Ofsted continued to find schools teaching anti-Western propaganda. Darul Hadis Latifiah, an all-boys school in east London, was producing pupils who were "not prepared for life in modern Britain"[43]. The *Daily Mail* reported that "Inspectors also found a book which 'promoted inappropriate views' on how girls and women should behave".

Meanwhile, a Catholic girls' school in Birmingham found itself in the headlines when it refused to allow a four-year-old pupil to wear the Islamic hijab in its classes[44]. According to the *Birmingham Mail*, "St Clare's School in Robert Road, Handsworth, has a strict uniform policy, including no headwear or scarf, and asked parents of the girl to respect it." But that would never do.

A Birmingham City Councillor named Waseem Zaffar (Labour) was in charge of equalities, and he made it clear to the school who was the more equal. He told the head teacher that the policy contravened the Equalities Act. One can't help but wonder why the Equalities Act is so rarely invoked when girls are made to sit at the back of the classroom, but in any case, he was wrong. The policy did not contravene the Equalities Act.

It was later revealed that the pupil in question was a relative of Councillor Zaffar, who resigned from the City Council cabinet in March 2017[45]. Dame Louise Casey, the government's integration tsar, condemned his behaviour.

The case was described as having 'echoes of the Trojan Horse scandal' – a scandal that would go on to reach far beyond Birmingham.

Clarksfield Primary School in Oldham, Greater Manchester, also experienced a 'Trojan Horse-style plot' in early 2017.

43 "Islamic School Slammed by Ofsted After They Found CCTV in Toilets," Mail Online, last modified January 9, 2017, http://www.dailymail.co.uk/news/article-4101968/Islamic-school-pupils-t-PM-boys-independent-slammed-Ofsted-inspectors-CCTV-cameras-TOILETS-said-students-unprepared-life-UK.html.

44 Neil Elkes, "Row breaks out after four-year-old told not to wear jidab to Catholic school," Birminghammail, January 24, 2017, accessed April 20, 2018, https://www.birminghammail.co.uk/news/midlands-news/row-breaks-out-after-four-12493960.

45 Jeanette Oldham, "Senior councilor Waseem Jaffar quits cabinet role over hijab ban furore," Birminghammail, March 03, 2017, accessed April 20, 2018, https://www.birminghampost.co.uk/news/regional-affairs/senior-councillor-waseem-zaffar-quits-12684991.

Counter-terror police investigated the school amid claims that the head teacher had received death threats from Muslim parents opposed to Western lifestyle. The *Daily Mail* reported that she had "endured 'harassment and intimidation' in the form of 'aggressive verbal abuse' and 'threats to blow up her car' from parents pushing conservative Muslim ideals"[46]. The MP for the area, Debbie Abrahams, jumped straight to political correctness:

> "*We must, of course, be vigilant to any issues that could inflate community tensions. This is why, along with the council, other Oldham MPs, organisations and leaders, we continually work across our diverse communities whilst tackling underlying inequalities which ultimately fuel these tensions.*"

The MP had decided – it was underlying equalities that were the problem.

In 2018, the story is the same. The year opened with yet another Islamic primary school found with 'unsuitable books'. The Olive Tree Primary School in Luton claimed it had removed the unsuitable books, but the same books were found again during its latest inspection[47].

And it doesn't get any better as you climb the educational ladder.

UNIVERSITY IN THE UK

British universities were described as "hotbeds of Islamic extremism"[48] by MPs and Peers (members of the House of Lords)

---

46 Daily Mail Online, accessed May 26, 2018, http://www.dailymail.co.uk/news/article-4239352/Muslim-parents-sent-school-headteacher-death-threats.html (page discontinued).

47 Camilla Turner, "Islamic Primary School Had Books Written by Banned Extremist, Ofsted Report Finds," The Telegraph, January 16, 2018, accessed May 7, 2018, http://www.telegraph.co.uk/education/2018/01/16/islamic-primary-school-had-books-written-banned-extremist-ofsted.

48 "University Campuses Are 'hotbeds of Islamic Extremism'," Telegraph.co.uk, last modified April 27, 2011, accessed May 26, 2018, http://www.telegraph.co.uk/news/religion/8478975/University-campuses-are-hotbeds-of-Islamic-extremism.html.

in 2011. In a report by an All-Party Parliamentary Group on Homeland Security, concern was expressed about members of extremist groups running Islamic societies at universities, as well as overseas funding for such societies. The Quilliam Foundation[49], an anti-extremism think-tank, produced a report in 2010 warning of the radicalisation of students in universities in Britain, and said that such radicalisation, while not always resulting in terrorism, can "generate intolerance towards others and encourage the denying of basic freedoms such as freedom of speech...religion and...expression"[50].

The Centre for Social Cohesion has produced a list of UK students involved in or convicted of terrorist offences[51]. It lists 17 students, including the 'underwear bomber' Umar Farouk Abdulmutallab and the Glasgow airport suicide attacker Kafeel Ahmed. The report also provided a detailed list of radical Islamist speakers attending British universities on a regular basis. These include:

Riyadh ul Haq: *"They're all the same. The Jews don't have to be in Israel to be like this. It doesn't matter whether they're in New York, Houston, St Louis, London, Birmingham, Bradford, Manchester. They're all the same."*

Murtaza Khan (aka Abu Hasnayn Murtaza Khan): *"For how long do we have to see our mothers, sisters and daughters having to uncover themselves before these filthy non-Muslim doctors? We should have a sense of shame."*

Khalid Yasin: *"This whole delusion of the equality of women is a bunch of foolishness. There's no such thing."*

---

49 Website of The Quilliam Foundation, accessed May 26, 2018, https://www.quilliaminternational.com/.
50 "Quilliam Briefing Paper Radicalisation on British University Campuses: a case study October 2010", accessed May 26, 2018. Available as download from http://www.safecampuscommunities.ac.uk/resources/quilliam-foundation-radicalisation-on-university-campuses.
51 "Most Islamist Terrorists in UK Are Born Here," The Independent, last modified July 5, 2010, accessed May 26, 2018, https://www.independent.co.uk/news/uk/home-news/most-islamist-terrorists-in-uk-are-born-here-2018507.html.

Abdur Raheem Green: *"The truth is that Islam teaches its followers to seek death on the battlefield; that dying while fighting jihad is one of the surest ways to paradise and Allah's good pleasure."*

GENDER SEGREGATION

Just as worryingly, it has been discovered that gender segregation is both widespread and increasing in the UK's universities. Student Rights, a group which works to combat extremism on campus, produced a report in 2012 detailing instances of gender segregation at university events[52]. Its investigation found that 25% of the events it observed had "either explicitly promoted segregation by gender, or implied that this would be the case". In one incident, University College London barred the Islamic Education and Research Academy from its campus following complaints that men and women had been forced to sit separately at an event involving one of the Academy's speakers.

In 2013, the issue of gender segregation at UK universities exploded on to the national scene. Universities UK, a group which describes itself as the "voice of Britain's universities", issued guidance stating that gender segregation was permissible if requested by the speaker, because to do otherwise would be to deny the free speech rights of the speaker. The group claimed that as long as women and men were segregated side-by-side, as opposed to women sitting at the back, there would be no disadvantage and therefore no problem. Soon afterwards, a protest was organised outside the group's headquarters (where I spoke), and there was broad condemnation of the guidance. It was even condemned by the Prime Minister, who "does not believe that guest speakers should be allowed to address segregated audiences, so he believes that Universities UK should urgently review its guidance"[53].

It did, and the guidance has since been withdrawn. It may

---

52 «Segregation on Campus Briefing,» Scribd, accessed June 2, 2018, http://www.scribd.com/doc/141019975/Segregation-on-Campus-Briefing.

53 David Barrett, "Gender Segregation Guidelines to Be Reviewed as David Cameron Steps into Row for the First Time," The Telegraph, December 13, 2013, accessed April 13, 2018, http://www.telegraph.co.uk/news/religion/10515651/Gender-segregation-guidelines-to-be-reviewed-as-David-Cameron-steps-into-row-for-the-first-time.html.

well reappear, however.

At the time of this scandal, a report appeared in the *Daily Mail* showing photographs of women sitting at the back of lecture theatres, with seats reserved for men at the front, at British universities[54]. More shocking was the revelation that women were not allowed to speak[55] and had to write their questions down. This happened at Queen Mary University in London, and one attendee described the experience as "degrading".

A spokesman for the university said:

> "*Segregated events are not in line with Queen Mary's values or equality policy. We will be raising this with our students' union as this should extend to student society-organised events with external speakers such as this one.*"

What was interesting during this whole debacle was the response of the media. I've said there was widespread condemnation of gender segregation, and there was – but it was far from unanimous. Unsurprisingly, some sanitised the notion of gender segregation and called those of us who oppose it Islamophobic. Equally unsurprisingly, the bulk of this came from those on the political Left. So-called feminist Laurie Penny, writing in the *Guardian*, argued that the whole issue was "vastly" exaggerated, and those of us who opposed segregation were (of course) Islamophobic in intent[56].

The *Huffington Post* reported the matter using male and female toilet signs in its accompanying visual[57], the idea being that if we can have separate toilet facilities for men and women, we can also have women and men sitting separately at universities – what's the big deal? Shohana Khan, a freelance

---

54 "Inside the British University Where Muslims Were Segregated by Sex," Mail Online, last modified January 15, 2014, http://www.dailymail.co.uk/news/article-2523787/Inside-British-university-Muslims-segregated-sex-Shocking-picture-shows-men-reserved-row-seats-women-sit-back.html.

55 "Female Students Banned from Speaking at Islam Seminar," Mail Online, last modified December 16, 2013, http://www.dailymail.co.uk/news/article-2524183/Female-students-banned-speaking-Islam-seminar-University-Leicester.html.

56 Laurie Penny, «This Isn›t ‹feminism›. It›s Islamophobia | Laurie Penny,» The Guardian, last modified November 30, 2017, http://www.theguardian.com/commentisfree/2013/dec/22/this-isnt-feminism-its-islamophobia.

57 "Topless Protest Planned Against 'Forced' Gender Segregation Guidelines," HuffPost UK, last modified January 25, 2014, http://www.huffingtonpost.co.uk/2013/12/09/topless-protest-forced-gender-segregation-university_n_4411449.html.

writer, asked "why the uproar?", arguing that the segregation was voluntary and moves to oppose it represented "yet again another Muslim practice...in the firing line"[58]. Why Khan thinks she has a right to define what is or isn't a Muslim practice, only she can answer.

There is an important point to be made here about Khan's use of the word 'voluntary'. Imagine this scenario: there is a room full of 100 people. The likelihood that all of them will want segregation is small. If a woman wants to sit in an area designated for men and is denied that right, then the segregation is not voluntary. If she is not denied that right, then the room is not segregated. In short, voluntary segregation is nigh-on impossible.

The Federation of Student Islamic Societies (FOSIS) is an organisation which describes itself as "a body that caters for the needs of Muslim students in further and higher education across the UK and Ireland"[59]. FOSIS, in its guidance on how to run an Islamic society, requires that the executive committee "maintain segregation between brothers and sisters, keeping interactions between them at a minimum". The language of 'voluntary' and 'freedom' does not appear here.

Islamists know perfectly well that they are winning over many, particularly on the Left, and one of their most effective tactics is exploiting the language of rights and freedoms with the hidden aim of destroying just those freedoms. We need to wake up to this tactic very quickly.

In mid-2014, the Equality and Human Rights Commission (EHRC) – a public body with responsibility for the promotion and enforcement of equality and non-discrimination laws – issued advice on gender segregation, and said that it was:

> "...*not permitted in any academic meetings or at events, lectures or meetings provided for students, or at events attended by members of the public or employees of the university or the students' union. Any claim of religious discrimination on the basis of a refusal to permit gender-segregated seating would not succeed as the*

58 "Gender Segregated Seating: Why the Uproar?," HuffPost UK, last modified February 11, 2014, http://www.huffingtonpost.co.uk/shohana-khan/gender-segregated-seating_b_4433393.html.
59 Website, FOSIS, accessed May 26, 2018. http://www.fosis.org.uk/about.

prohibition would be justified in order to prevent unlawful sex discrimination."

This is welcome, isn't it? Well no, it makes little difference because it "does not apply to religious worship" and "a religious student society or association may organise a gender segregated event, for the duration of any religious service"[60].

Great. We all know what this will mean in practice.

So despite condemnation from the Prime Minister, the withdrawal of guidance from Universities UK, and advice from EHRC, segregation has carried on unabated. In March 2014, a report[61] showed the extent of gender segregation in Britain, and the extent to which it is tolerated by the Left. The article, by Chris Moos, alleged that extremist Islamic organisations continued to preach in UK universities, and that this happened largely without interference or criticism.

'NO TO RACISM – NO TO ISLAMOPHOBIA'

In the London School of Economics (LSE), a major international university in central London, the Students' Union passed a resolution in early 2012 entitled 'No to racism – No to Islamophobia'[62]. Immediately, racism was equated with Islamophobia in the title of the resolution, but it gets worse than that. The justification for the resolution, which was debated at a specially convened Extraordinary General Meeting, was that "Many Muslim students were offended by the LSE Students' Union Atheist, Secularist, and Humanist (ASH) Society's publication of a 'Jesus and Mo' cartoon, in which the two are portrayed having

60 "Gender Segregation at Events and Meetings: Guidance for Universities and Students' Unions | Equality and Human Rights Commission," Home Page | Equality and Human Rights Commission, last modified 17, 2014, https://www.equalityhumanrights.com/en/publication-download/gender-segregation-events-and-meetings-guidance-universities-and-students.
61 Chris Moos, "Institutionalising Gender Segregation: the Role of Universities and Students' Unions," HuffPost UK, May 26, 2014, accessed April 21, 2018, http://www.huffingtonpost.co.uk/chris-moos/gender-segregation_b_5035964.html.
62 "LSE Students say 'No to Islamophobia," Mend - Muslim Engagement and Development, February 2, 2012, accessed April 21, 2018, https://mend.org.uk/news/lse-students-say-no-to-islamophobia/.

a pint [of beer]"[63].

Jesus and Mo is a satirical website (www.jesusandmo.net) which runs a regular series of cartoons featuring Jesus and Mohammed in various scenarios. They often feature the two figures sitting in a bar drinking alcohol and discussing religion. Prior to the LSE resolution, another London university, University College London (UCL), had ordered its Atheist, Secularist and Humanist Society (ASH) to remove a Jesus and Mo cartoon from its Facebook page. The LSE ASH society then posted its own Jesus and Mo sketch in solidarity with the UCL group.

As a precursor to the resolution, the LSE Union listed the reasons the motion should pass. These included:

> "*The rise of Islamophobia in the UK; the rise of the extreme Right in Europe; the 762 Islamophobic offenses in London alone between April 2009 and June 2011 as confirmed by the Metropolitan Police; ethnic minorities are 42 times as likely to be targeted under the Terrorism Act; and recent Islamophobic incidents at LSE.*"

The "recent Islamophobic incidents"? The Jesus and Mo cartoon.

LSE Students' Union representatives reassured us that they believe in free speech and the right to criticise religion, but with the proviso that freedom of speech does not include hate speech. Apparently, they get to decide what constitutes hate speech.

Helpfully, they provided a definition of 'Islamophobia' within the motion. Here it is in full:

1. **To define Islamophobia as "a form of racism expressed through the hatred or fear of Islam, Muslims, or Islamic culture, and the stereotyping, demonization or harassment of Muslims, including but not limited to portraying Muslims as barbarians or terrorists, or attacking the Qur'an as a manual of hatred**

2. **To take a firm stance against all Islamophobic**

---

63 Ibid.

incidents at LSE and conduct internal investigations if
and when they occur

3. To publicly oppose actions on campus that are
   Islamophobic based on the aforementioned definition

4. To ensure that all Islamophobic incidents aimed at or
   perpetrated by LSE students either verbal, physical
   or online are dealt with swiftly and effectively in
   conjunction with the School

5. To work with the Pro-Director for Teaching and
   Learning and Deans to address Islamophobia and
   other forms of racism on campus and methods to
   alleviate it

6. To ensure that this definition is used to promote and
   enhance legitimate debate regarding the morality
   and legitimacy of international conflicts and oppose
   illegitimate acts of Islamophobia on campus

How about that for an all-encompassing edict? According to
the LSE Union, we're not allowed to fear Islamic culture, which
no doubt includes sharia law. It matters not that there is every
reason to fear it.

A few years later, the London School of Economics conceded
that at least some extreme Islamic practices could be mildly
criticised. The University's Islamic Society had organised an
event where men and women were separated by a large screen.
Following a letter of complaint by some students, the LSE authorities acknowledged that there "might have been an obligation
on the School to investigate this matter more thoroughly at the
outset"[64]. Carola Frenge, head of Equality, Diversity and Inclusion, wrote "I have therefore conducted an investigation into
this matter and accept that there is a likelihood that the Annual
Dinner was unlawfully gender segregated."

The Independent reports, however, that the LSE authorities "did not act on all of the concerns the students had raised
and, according to the students, refused to take pertinent

---

64 May Bulman, "Top University accepts Islamic Society's gender-segregated event was
'unlawful'," The Independent, September 28, 2017, accessed April 19, 2018, http://
www.independent.co.uk/news/uk/home-news/london-university-islamic-society-gender-
segregated-event-unlawful-london-school-economics-lse-a7972311.html.

action to ensure that gender segregation would not reoccur".

My group, Sharia Watch UK, would in 2014 come face to face with the extraordinary contradiction of allowing jihadists free rein in universities while banning those who are critical. Sharia Watch produced a report giving evidence of the high number of jihadists and Islamists who had spoken at British universities over a six month period[65]. I had spent time looking through the activities of university Islamic societies' social media pages to ascertain what speakers had been invited. Some of the most notorious jihadists in the country were on the list.

I was booked to talk about the report by a student at the University of West London, but that student soon found himself in hot water as university authorities stepped in and demanded I be denied a platform. The event was cancelled[66]. Here was another nail in the coffin of British free speech and another boost for jihadists in the UK. Muslims would continue to preach contempt for the West, Britain, women, gays, Jews, and liberty. I, however, would be prevented from discussing this, as to do so may cause offence.

---

65 Sharia Watch, "LEARNING JIHAD: ISLAMISTS IN BRITISH UNIVERSITIES," Sharia Family Law and Women | Sharia Watch UK Ltd, accessed April 14, 2018, http:// www.shariawatch.org.uk/?q=content/learning-jihad-islamists-british-universities&.
66 Graeme Paton, "Anger over University's Decision to Cancel Islamic Extremism Report Launch," The Telegraph, November 11, 2014, accessed April 14, 2018, http://www. telegraph.co.uk/education/educationnews/11223990/Anger-over-universitys-decision-to-cancel-Islamic-extremism-report-launch.html.

THE LAW IN THE UK

FREE SPEECH

IT IS A common theme across Western democracies that criticism of Islam or Islamic ideals or practices amounts to intolerance, or even racism. As a result of this, freedom of speech has been, and continues to be, seriously compromised in Britain and throughout the democratic world. Any criticism can result in violence, riots, illegal threats, and calls for speech restrictions. This has given licence to Islamic activists to advance their cause.

I've said that free speech is our most important freedom, and this is precisely why it is under such sustained attack. If freedom of speech is destroyed, democracy itself will follow. Democracy, in its literal meaning, denotes the will of the people. But how can we know the will of the people if the people are not permitted to speak freely? Without the ability to speak our minds, debate, question, and express ourselves, there is no democracy.

To say that free speech is restricted in Islamic states – that is, states governed by sharia law – is something of an understatement. Several Islamic states apply the death penalty, while other more secular-leaning Muslim-majority nations impose less severe sentences. Countries that impose the death penalty include Saudi Arabia, Iran, and Pakistan. These laws are not just on the books, which would be terrible enough, but actual punishments are a regular occurrence.

In 2012, a young journalist was extradited from Malaysia to Saudi Arabia to face a probable death sentence for tweeting about Mohammed[1], and from Iran over the years several fatwas (religious rulings) have been issued for blasphemy, including one which resulted in one of the most notorious blasphemy controversies ever to occur in the UK.

In the late 1980s, the author Salman Rushdie published a book called *The Satanic Verses*. In it, Rushdie was alleged to have insulted the Prophet Mohammed. The Ayatollah Khomeini, Iran's Supreme Leader, issued a fatwa calling for his murder, and Rushdie was forced into hiding for over a decade. Two bookshops were bombed in London and a Japanese translator was murdered. The fatwa was re-issued from Iran in 2012, and again in 2014.

The eyes of the UK had been opened to the sharia demand that Islam not be criticised. We had seen book-burnings on the streets and calls for an author to be killed. The Rushdie Affair implanted fear into the mind of the West, and a new kind of censorship and self-censorship was born.

Iqbal Sacranie was a leading protagonist who argued that death was "too easy" for Rushdie[2]. Sacranie was knighted in 2005 and served as Secretary General of the apparently moderate Muslim Council of Britain[3].

While the Rushdie Affair brought new censorship to British shores, the Danish cartoon controversy delivered ever more. Following the publication in a Danish magazine of caricatures of the Islamic Prophet Mohammed, violent protests erupted around

---

1 Kathy Marks, "Saudi Journalist Left Facing the Death Penalty over Twitter Posts," The Independent, February 13, 2012, accessed April 15, 2018, http://www.independent. co.uk/news/world/middle-east/saudi-journalist-left-facing-the-death-penalty-over-twitter-posts-6804831.html.
2 Peter Murtagh, The Guardian, February 18, 1989, accessed April 21, 2018, http://www. theguardian.com/books/1989/feb/18/fiction.salmanrushdie.
3 BBC News, June 10, 2005, accessed April 21, 2018, http://news.bbc.co.uk/1/hi/ uk/4081208.stm.

the world and hundreds of people were killed. In London, protestors took to the streets, waving placards declaring: "Freedom go to hell"; "Europe you will pay, your 9/11 is on its way"; and "Butcher those who insult Islam". Despite calls from various Members of Parliament for the protestors to be prosecuted for incitement to murder, the response of the then British Home Secretary Jack Straw was to argue that there is no obligation to "insult or be gratuitously inflammatory"[4]. He did not, in other words, unequivocally defend freedom of speech as he should have done, and hinted that those who speak out of turn, are the real troublemakers.

This response undoubtedly gave succour to the protestors who had had their grievances legitimised. Free speech had been undermined by the UK government – precisely, no doubt, the response the protestors had hoped for. According to a BBC report at the time, police arrested two people for carrying copies of the pictures of Mohammed, while making no arrests for the calls for violent retribution. The report mentions a speaker at a rally against the cartoons who had called upon governments across the Muslim world to sever links with Europe until it "controlled the media"[5].

In 2012, the London headquarters of the internet search engine Google were picketed by a group of Muslims calling for censorship and restrictions on freedom of speech. This was a protest in response to Google's refusal to remove the video 'Innocence of Muslims'[6] from YouTube.

At Google headquarters, protesters said, "This is not freedom of expression, there is a limit for that. This insult of the Prophet will not be allowed."

---

4 "Irate Muslims Stage New Protests," Washington Post: Breaking News, World, US, DC News & Analysis - The Washington Post, last modified February 3, 2006, accessed April 21, 2018, http://www.washingtonpost.com/wp-dyn/content/article/2006/02/03/AR2006020302604.html.

5 "Profile: Iqbal Sacranie," BBC News, last updated February 05, 2006, accessed April 21, 2018. http://news.bbc.co.uk/1/hi/uk/4682262.stm.

6 "10,000 Muslim Protesters Demonstrate At Google UK HQ Over YouTube Film," TechCrunch, last modified October 15, 2012, accessed April 21, 2018, https://techcrunch.com/2012/10/15/10000-muslim-protesters-demonstrate-at-google-uk-hq-over-youtube-film/.

Another said, "If you push people too far, you will turn the peaceful elements into violence[7]."

One of the most remarkable recent examples of Islamic censorship was the barring of Dutch Parliamentarian Geert Wilders from entering the UK. Wilders openly opposes Islam and Islamism, and campaigns for an end to Muslim immigration to the Netherlands. He is a provocative figure.

Wilders challenged his barring and eventually came to Britain in 2010. He screened his controversial film *Fitna*[8] at the House of Lords and gave a press conference in the company of two members of the House. *Fitna* is a short film which places passages from the Koran next to images of terrorist attacks, the idea being that the Koran verses prompted the attacks. Though this film was condemned by many, and is undoubtedly contentious, it does not at any time call for violence against Muslims, or anyone else.

The same cannot be said for the protestors at Britain's Parliament during Mr Wilders's visit. Outside, people were calling for his head[9]. One 'protestor' sought to remind Wilders that "in Islam, the punishment for the one who insults the prophet is capital punishment, and he should take lessons from people like Theo van Gogh and others, who've faced the punishment". By any standards, this is a threat of violence aimed at an elected politician for speaking his mind.

Free speech in Britain has undergone a strange transformation. Hate speech laws have been introduced and causing offence has become, at least socially, an unacceptable transgression. But only for some. Many Muslims have free rein to be as hateful as they like, but hitting back at them can land you in serious trouble. We have witnessed glaring inconsistencies in the application of hate speech laws, and such inconsistency has created fear, confusion, and anger.

I have referred to some instances of incitement to violence against women and homosexuals which were captured by

7 Jennifer OMahony, The Telegraph, October 14, 2012, accessed May 26, 2018, http:// www.telegraph.co.uk/news/9607763/Muslims-protest-age-of-mockery-as-thousands-descend-on-Google-HQ.html.
8 "Fitna - Geert Wilders [Full Movie with English Subtitles]," YouTube, last modified March 30, 2013, https://www.youtube.com/watch?v=2HlptyGvlIY.
9 Chefkaffee, YouTube, October 17, 2009, accessed May 26, 2018, http://www.youtube.com/watch?v=4N7bwEqFPGI.

Channel 4 on 'Undercover Mosque'. No action was taken against the individuals responsible. Here are a couple of other examples.

US authors Pamela Geller and Robert Spencer were barred from entering the UK. Both are high-profile critics of Islam (who have not called for violence). In the same week, Saudi preacher Muhammad al-Arefe came to Britain for a speaking tour. He promotes the beating of disobedient women[10].

An Islamic TV station, DM Digital, which is based in Manchester, was fined in July 2013 for broadcasting comments by Abdul Qadir Jilani. Mr Jilani stated on air:

> "It is your duty, the duty of those who recite the holy verse, to kill those who insult Prophet Mohammed. Under the guidance from Islamic texts, it is evident that if a Muslim apostatises, then it is not right to wait for the authorised courts. Anyone may kill him. An apostate deserves to be killed and any man may kill him"[11].

However, no arrests were made. By contrast, a couple of weeks earlier, an 85-year-old woman was arrested, handcuffed, and held in police custody for shouting at worshippers outside a mosque in Kent[12]. According to some reports, the woman had demanded they "go back to [their] own country".

This is not a recent phenomenon. Further back in time, prominent human rights campaigner Peter Tatchell was arrested for protesting at a rally by the Islamist group Hizb-ut-Tahrir in 1994. This is despite the fact that Hizb-ut-Tahrir openly calls for Britain to be an Islamic state in which Mr Tatchell, a gay man, would face execution.

These instances are not insignificant. They embolden the notion of a two-tier system of justice in Britain which provides Islam with a distinct and unique privilege. On a social level, it

10 "Preacher Who Backs Wife-Beating Let Into UK," Sky News, accessed April 22, 2018, https://news.sky.com/search?q=preacher-who-backs-wife-beatings-let-into-uk&sortby=relevance.

11 "Muslim TV Station Fined for Allowing Contributor to Incite Murder," National Secular Society, accessed April 22, 2018, http://www.secularism.org.uk/news/2013/07/muslim-tv-station-fined-for-allowing-contributor-to-incite-murder.

12 "Woman, 85, on Race Charge over Mosque 'abuse'," Kent Online, May 24, 2013, accessed April 22, 2018, http://www.kentonline.co.uk/medway/news/friday-prayers-patrol-1128/.

is somewhat acceptable to criticise Islamism, but you must be extremely careful, because if you veer off into criticising Islam itself, you will soon find yourself labelled an 'Islamophobe'. I myself have experienced this on innumerable occasions; I have been shunned by colleagues, lost friends, and been threatened. This does not happen with Judeo-Christianity or other belief systems. An unwillingness to criticise Islam has become anchored in the collective British mind. When such criticism is considered toxic, the masses will turn a blind eye to the actions of Islamists, and it is this, in part, which has facilitated the relentless advance of sharia tribunals and councils across the UK.

SHARIA LAW

Sharia law is without doubt the most useful weapon employed by Islamic activists in imposing their will upon others. Sharia forms the legal code in Islamic states, including Saudi Arabia and Iran, and its implementation in those countries is barbaric. Stoning, amputation, capital punishment and brutal oppression are commonplace. It is through the oppression of women, however, that sharia is expressing its power in the UK. It does so via a network of family tribunals and councils which now operate openly across the country.

It's important to talk about the law and clarify what we mean. If we say "the law", we tend to mean the law of the land. So if I'm in Britain, I mean the law that governs Britain.

When questioned about the presence of sharia law in the UK, the government responds that essentially there is no sharia law in the UK. Because sharia law does not have the weight of state behind it, and the state does not enforce sharia law, there is no sharia law.

But there is.

Sharia is a set of laws. It exists in an objective form, often imposed by Islamic nation states, and is adhered to across the world. Just like an association obliges its members to obey the laws of that association, sharia law, for many, must be obeyed in order to be a devout Muslim. Vast numbers of Muslims take that requirement very seriously.

It's unfair to claim that sharia law is always a choice. For many, it isn't. Apostasy is widely condemned in even the most moderate Muslim communities, and people take great risks if they question Islam. But even if sharia was a choice, should an individual be able to choose sharia law in the UK?

The answer has to be no. Sharia, or any other set of laws, should not be available for use if it runs contrary to the law of the land. The law governs our practical daily life in areas such as driving or taxes, but it is also a reflection of our morals as a nation. One of its primary functions is to protect. Who it protects, and from what, is derived from our common morals and values. The law prohibits violent physical assault as a criminal offence because we believe violent physical assault is wrong. The Law prohibits sexual engagement with minors because we believe that sex with minors is wrong.

The law of the land is built on several foundational and fixed principles that don't change as new laws are introduced. Fundamental principles in criminal law, for example, include the standard of proof being beyond reasonable doubt; the burden of proof being on the state; etc.

Family law, the area of law most pertinent when we're discussing sharia law in the UK, is of the utmost importance. Like criminal law, there are fundamental principles in family law. For example, the equal rights of the parties to a family law dispute don't change. A husband and a wife have the same status in law; their word carries the same weight. Also fundamental is the status of children in disputes, the principle being that the best interests of the child are paramount in any decision involving that child.

Under sharia family law, a wife cannot divorce of her volition, even if she is subjected to violence and abuse. Her testimony in a family law dispute is worth only half of her husband's, to make it as difficult as possible for women to win in any family law dispute. The reason for this is simply because the Koran deems women to be worth less than men.

Furthermore, in sharia family law, the best interests of the child do not come first because Islam deems that children are the property of their fathers. Men have sole power over their lives. Mothers have no input and no rights.

In the practice of sharia law here in Britain, decisions as to child custody are being made. This inevitably means that children will be placed with their fathers, irrespective of circumstances, including if he is violent. Because mothers have no rights, they can't stop this.

Sharia law practice takes on different guises in Britain, including under powers of the Arbitration Act. The Arbitration Act allows parties to a dispute to agree to appoint a 'judge' and be bound by the judge's decision. Arbitration *per se* is not a problem. In principle, it is a legitimate way for free people to conduct their affairs. But the law itself, i.e., the Arbitration Act itself, places restrictions on this practice that ensure it adheres to the principles of British Law. For example, the Arbitration Act requires that arbitration be fair, impartial, and in the public interest.

Sharia law is not fair, nor impartial, and given its terrible treatment of women and children, it is hardly in the public interest.

For the most part, however, sharia councils operate as charities. The problem here is that charity laws tend to view religion as a force for good, without examining the detail of what the religion teaches. Across the board in public life, religions are deemed to be essentially the same and encourage moral behaviour.

If we are going to oppose sharia law, and we should, we must stop designating unquestioning privilege to religion. We must look at what the religion teaches and the impact these teachings can have on its followers. We must also stop pretending that there is nothing specific to sharia that should worry us. There is. It is a system predicated on female subservience, violent punishment, oppression, arbitrary whims of clerics, and complete disregard for the rights of children. Sharia is not compatible with British social values, legal principles, or who we are as a nation. Its practice should therefore not be permitted. The fundamental principles of British Law should instead be upheld as supreme.

Repeated statements from successive governments insist that British law is available to all. This is indeed correct from a legal standpoint, but it is entirely removed from the reality of many people's lives – people who are coerced or forced by threat of violence to use sharia councils.

Crucially, no British government has addressed whether or not the use of sharia, given its flagrant disregard for the basic civil rights of women, *ought* to be a choice. Should we have the choice to operate a legal code which was declared "wholly incompatible" with human rights (including the UK's human rights laws) by our own Supreme Court equivalent in 2008[13]?

The House of Lords, in the case involving a Lebanese woman who sought to remain in the UK because her return to Lebanon would have meant that, under sharia law, custody of her children would automatically be awarded to her husband, ruled that she should not be returned to Lebanon for this reason. Lord Hope, in the judgment, stated, "It is discriminatory...because it denies women custody of their children after they have reached the age of custodial transfer simply because they are women."

Lord Bingham acknowledged the automatic award of child custody to fathers under sharia, even when "a father ... has inflicted physical violence and psychological injury on the mother". Taking this into account, the British government simply must answer this question: Should sharia law be a choice at all, given that it is entirely at odds with our mainstream legal system? When responding, the government must take into account the declared intentions of the men who run sharia law in Britain: to expand sharia further and further into the lives of British Muslims, and to create mini jurisdictions within Britain under full sharia law.

> "Sharia is knocking at the door of Britain. If sharia law is implemented, then you can turn this country into a haven of peace, because once a thief's hand is cut off, nobody is going to steal. Once, just only once, if an adulterer is stoned, nobody is going to commit this crime at all. We want to offer it to the British society. If they accept it, it is for their good, and if they don't accept it they'll need more and more prisons.

13 Afua Hirsh, "Sharia Law Incompatible with Human Rights Legislation, Lords Say," The Guardian, October 23, 2008, accessed April 23, 2018, http://www.theguardian.com/world/2008/oct/23/religion-islam.

"Allah has decreed this thing that I am going to be dominant. The dominance, of course, is a political dominance.... [This political dominance would include] *... the chopping of the hands of the thieves, the flogging of the adulterers and flogging of the drunkards...* [and would lead to] *jihad against the non-Muslims, against the people who are the oppressors*[14].*"*

Suhaib Hasan, Islamic Sharia Council

"We do not get involved in criminal cases, but only the sort of remit we are looking at at the moment, and we are discussing it with the authorities like the CPS and the police... we desire to give – in the case of domestic violence – the opportunity to look at an alternative form of resolution[15].*"*

Faiz Ul-Aqtab Siddiqi, Muslim Arbitration Tribunal

"A man should not be questioned why he hit his wife because this is something between them. Leave them alone. They can sort out their matters among themselves. Even the father of the daughter who is married to the man, he should not ask his daughter, "Why have you been beaten or hit by your husband[16]?*"*

Haitham al-Haddad, Islamic Sharia Council

"Clearly there cannot be any rape within the marriage. Maybe aggression, maybe indecent activity...Because when they got married, the understanding was that sexual intercourse was part of the marriage, so there cannot be anything against sex in marriage[17].*"*

14 Anne Marie Waters, "Sharia Law: Extremism the Government Ignores," HuffPost UK, April 14, 2013, accessed April 23, 2018, https://www.huffingtonpost.co.uk/anne-marie-waters/sharia-law-extremism-the-_b_2668212.html.
15 Richard Edwards, "Sharia Courts Operating in Britain," The Telegraph, September 14, 2008, accessed April 23, 2018, https://www.telegraph.co.uk/news/uknews/2957428/Sharia-law-courts-operating-in-Britain.html.
16 Channel4News, "Does Sharia Law Allow a Man to Beat His Wife? | Channel 4 News," YouTube, July 14, 2014, accessed April 23, 2018, https://www.youtube.com/watch?v=Cd4A4fPejXE.
17 Mark Hughes and Jerome Taylor, "Rape 'impossible' in Marriage, Says Muslim Cleric," The Independent, October 13, 2010, accessed April 23, 2018, http://www.independent.co.uk/news/uk/home-news/rape-impossible-in-marriage-says-muslim-cleric-2106161.html.

Maulana Abu Sayeed, Islamic Sharia Council
"In Britain, the ultimate authority is the Prime Minister. In an army, it is the Commander-in-Chief. On the bus, it is the bus driver. And in the house, the smallest unit of society, sharia says authority must be with the man to maintain the house[18]*."*

Suhaib Hasan, Islamic Sharia Council

On underage sex in the UK:

"You won't like it. But sharia says if they're caught doing it, you stone the woman[19]*."*

Sarfraz Sarwar, Basildon Islamic Centre

The above quotes from senior figures in the sharia movement in Britain display an unashamed desire for sharia law to grow and expand here, and extreme hostility to Britain and its values.

THE 'ISLAMIC REPUBLIC OF TOWER HAMLETS'

Muslims Against Crusades (formerly Al-Mujahiroon) displayed posters across east London declaring certain areas Sharia Controlled Zones[20] in which there was to be no alcohol, music, drugs or smoking, gambling, or porn or prostitution. The group promised a team of vigilantes on the streets of London to enforce sharia rules. Local authorities quickly took down these posters, and three vigilantes were arrested and jailed.

Dubbed the 'Islamic Republic of Tower Hamlets', this east London borough is a well-known British hub of Islamism and Islamic intimidation. In 2009, the journalist Andrew Gilligan

---

18 Edna Fernandes, "Sharia Law UK: Mail on Sunday Gets Exclusive Access to a British Muslim Court," Daily Mail Online, July 04, 2009, accessed April 23, 2018, http://www.dailymail.co.uk/news/article-1197478/Sharia-law-UK--How-Islam-dispensing-justice-side-British-courts.html.
19 Ibid.
20 Rebecca Camber for the Daily Mail, "'No Porn or Prostitution': Islamic Extremists Set up Sharia Law Controlled Zones in British Cities," Daily Mail Online, July 28, 2011, accessed April 23, 2018, http://www.dailymail.co.uk/news/article-2019547/Anjem-Choudary-Islamic-extremists-set-Sharia-law-zones-UK-cities.html.

documented incidents in Tower Hamlets involving Muslims that had either been ignored or glossed over by police. These include[21]:

A man attacked for smoking during the month of Ramadan. Mohammed Monzur Rahman claims he was left partially blind following a street attack by a mob warning him against smoking during the Muslim holy month. He reported the incident to the police who, he claims, said there was no way of tracking down the attackers.

However, Ansar Ahmed Ullah, a local anti-extremism campaigner, said, "There is CCTV in that street and it is lined with shops and people."

Campaigning for the compulsory veiling of girls in schools. Various teachers have reported feeling "under pressure" to enforce the veiling of girls. One teacher is reported to have said, "The atmosphere became extremely unpleasant for a while, with constant verbal aggression from both the children and some parents against the head [teacher] over this issue."

The storming of a gay pub and attacks on patrons inside, including one young man who was left paralysed following the attack. Despite claims that a mob of over 30 people stormed the bar in 2008, only one person was arrested and prosecuted.

'Gay-free Zone' stickers placed around the borough. A routine stop-and-search by police is reported to have found a young man with the stickers in his possession, but he was released without charge.

At the time, Peter Tatchell, the gay human rights campaigner, said, "The police said no-one was allowed to talk publicly about this because they didn't want to upset the Muslim community."

A second person, Mohammed Hasnath, was caught on CCTV posting the stickers at a local train station. He pleaded guilty and was fined £100.

---

21 Andrew Gilligan, "Police 'covered Up' Violent Campaign to Turn London Area 'Islamic'," The Telegraph, June 12, 2011, accessed April 23, 2018, http://www.telegraph. co.uk/news/uknews/law-and-order/8570506/Police-covered-up-violent-campaign-to-turn-London-area-Islamic.html.

Even the borough's council has been the scene of controversy as elected officials were heckled with homophobic remarks when rising to speak. The Labour leader, Josh Peck, heard cries of "Unnatural acts! Unnatural acts!" when he spoke in the council chamber, while the Conservative leader, Peter Golds, was repeatedly heckled as "Mrs Golds" and a "poofter".

> *"If that happened in a football stadium, arrests would have taken place. I have complained, twice, to the police, and have heard nothing. A Labour colleague waited three hours at the police station before being told that nothing would be done. The police are afraid of being accused of Islamophobia".*
>
> Peter Golds

Furthermore, it has been alleged that Islamists have infiltrated the Labour Party in Tower Hamlets and placed sharia advocates at the highest levels. The Islamic Forum of Europe, which believes in transforming the "very infrastructure of society, its institutions, its culture, its political order and its creed...from ignorance to Islam", was accused in 2010 of acting as an entryist organisation to the Labour Party to "get one of our brothers" into the newly created mayoralty in Tower Hamlets.

> *"People were being signed up to be members and then told to turn up at the meetings, where candidates were being selected [from] a list of those who [we] should be voting for, and who we had never seen before and have never seen afterwards".*
>
> Local MP Jim Fitzpatrick

East London is also home to the Leyton Sharia Council, which was investigated by the BBC in its flagship show *Panorama*. The programme featured Dr Suhaib Hasan and an undercover reporter, who posed as an abused wife and attended the council to seek advice on the violence she had suffered.

Here is part of the conversation that took place:

Hasan: *"So he actually beats you?"*
Reporter: *"He hits me. He does hit me."*
Hasan: *"Severely or just?"*
Reporter: *"What do you mean severely?"*
Hasan: *"It leaves some bruises on your body?"*
Reporter: *"He has hit me at times and it hurts. Do you think I should go to the police? Do you think I should leave the house? What do you suggest?"*
Hasan: *"The police, that is the very, very last resort."*
Hasan later goes on to say:
"I think you should be courageous enough to ask this question to him: 'Just tell me why you are upset, huh? Is it because of my cooking? Is it because I see my friends? So I can correct myself'."

The reporter in question was then referred for 'counselling' with Hasan's wife. Mrs Hasan asked the reporter, "Did you, before he come, did you try to dress up and have makeup and get ready or not?" She also asked if "the food is ready, the house is clean and you are ready as well? You did not ignore yourself?"

Not only is sharia rarely condemned in Britain, it has been defended and encouraged by public figures such as the former Archbishop of Canterbury, Rowan Williams, and the former Lord Chief Justice, Lord Phillips. Both have spoken of the integration of sharia law into the UK, with Williams describing this as "unavoidable"[22].

FEMALE GENITAL MUTILATION

Parallel sharia legal systems aside, Britain is fundamentally divided at various levels. Different groups of people have different laws applied, and those paying the highest price are almost always female. Take, for example, female genital mutilation (FGM). FGM, at its most basic, is the removal of a girl's clitoris, the aim being to deprive her of sexual pleasure. Under

---

22 "UK | Sharia Law in UK Is 'unavoidable'," BBC News, February 07, 2008, accessed April 23, 2018, http://news.bbc.co.uk/1/hi/7232661.stm.

British law, FGM carries a 14-year prison sentence. Despite statistics showing that well over 100,000 women in Britain have undergone FGM, with thousands more at risk, there has never been a conviction for this crime.[23].

British MPs have admitted, in a report in 2000, that the primary reason for the lack of punishment for this serious crime is political correctness and cultural sensitivity[24]. A report from a committee of MPs stated:

> *"The UK's international leadership is weakened by its failure to address violence against women and girls within its own borders, particularly female genital mutilation from which 20,000 girls within the UK are at risk. Robust action should be taken to counter political correctness and address culturally sensitive practices such as female genital mutilation within the UK."*

When I interviewed a detective and asked her why this crime was carrying on unhindered, she very matter-of-factly told me, "We cannot attack anyone's culture or faith."

The police often insist that evidence is the problem when they're dealing with FGM. If evidence, and the oft-mentioned problem of having to ask a young child to testify against her parents, were indeed the issue, this would still not explain quite a few things. Why do local authorities not step in to prevent FGM, or investigate further when they know of a mother or sisters who have been mutilated? Why was dentist Omar Addow[25], who was reportedly recorded offering to carry out the mutilation on young girls, and was struck off (barred from practice) by the General

23 Sandra Laille, "Doctor Found Not Guilty of FGM on Patient at London Hospital," The Guardian, February 04, 2015, accessed April 23, 2018, https://www.theguardian.com/society/2015/feb/04/doctor-not-guilty-fgm-dhanuson-dharmasena.

24 Nigel Morris, "Political Correctness Resulting in Female Circumcision Being Ignored in UK, Say MPs," The Independent, June 12, 2013, accessed April 24, 2018, http://www.independent.co.uk/news/uk/politics/political-correctness-resulting-in-female-circumcision-being-ignored-in-uk-say-mps-8656224.html.

25 Reporter, Daily Mail, "Dentist Struck off for Offering to Perform Female Genital Mutilation on Girls as Young as 10 in Birmingham," Daily Mail Online, September 09, 2013, accessed April 24, 2018, http://www.dailymail.co.uk/news/article-2415492/Dentist-Omar-Addow-struck-offering-perform-female-genital-mutilation-girls.html.

Dental Council for doing so, not investigated by police? Lack of evidence doesn't explain why a doctor, who appeared in front of Manchester medical malpractice tribunal accused of mutilating baby girls, had no charges brought against him[26]. Is lack of evidence really a problem when we take into account that over half of London's GPs (general practitioners) have treated victims of FGM[27]? What about the fact that we have specialist FGM treatment centres across the country, as advertised on National Health Service websites[28]?

In December 2013, Jemima Thackray wrote in the *Telegraph* of an anti-FGM campaigner who, on her way to a meeting to discuss the issue, asked a policeman for directions.

He replied, "It [FGM] is a cultural practice and none of our business. I don't believe we should take a stance on this[29]."

A tweet from West Midlands Police was reported by the *Telegraph*. The West Midlands force had said that making arrests for FGM was unlikely to be of benefit to the children.

DOMESTIC VIOLENCE

Another 'culturally sensitive' issue in the UK, and another field where the law seems rather inconsistently applied, is in the area of domestic violence. I've highlighted the disgusting attitudes to violence against women at the heart of sharia tribunals that operate in the open, but it is even more serious than that.

---

26 John Lichfield, "The French Way: A Better Approach to Fighting FGM?" The Independent, December 15, 2013, accessed April 24, 2018, http://www.independent. co.uk/news/world/europe/the-french-way-a-better-approach-to-fighting-fgm-9006369. html?origin=internalSearch.
27 "'More than Half of London GPs Have Treated an FGM Victim'," Evening Standard, December 23, 2013, accessed April 24, 2018, http://www.standard.co.uk/news/health/ more-than-half-of-london-gps-have-treated-an-fgm-victim-9022280.html.
28 "Guide to Sexual Health Services - The NHS in England," NHS Choices, accessed April 24, 2018, http://www.nhs.uk/NHSEngland/AboutNHSservices/sexual-health-services/Pages/fgm-health-services-for-women.aspx.
29 Jemima Thackray, "Human Rights Day: Is the UK's Cultural Freedom Stopping It from Tackling FGM?" The Telegraph, December 10, 2013, accessed April 24, 2018, http://www.telegraph.co.uk/women/womens-life/10508177/Human-Rights-Day-Female-Genital-Mutilation-is-the-language-of-rights-stopping-the-UK-tackling-FGM.html.

Banaz Mahmod[30] was a young Iraqi Kurd who, on five occasions, told police that she was being beaten and raped by her husband, and threatened by her family for having the audacity to leave him. On all five occasions, the police did not follow up on her complaints. Banaz had said of her family, "If something happens to me, it's them." She was later found dead and buried in a suitcase in Birmingham in 2006.

Nazir Afzal of the Crown Prosecution Service gave his opinion as to why the police look away and allow appalling crimes against women to continue:

> *"There are plenty of people around the country who tell me that they are actually wary of stepping into this minefield, because…the moment that they start talking about this issue, they will be branded racists."*

I don't condemn individual police officers for this. They are in an impossible position because they have been politicised to the point where if they make a 'politically incorrect' decision, they risk their jobs and livelihoods. Accusations of racism against police are quite common, and an accusation of racism is a very dangerous thing.

RAPE AND SEXUAL ABUSE

The desire to avoid being called a racist is strong in Britain – so strong that local councils stay silent while thousands of young girls (many in their care) are raped and pimped by Muslim gangs.

On 26 August 2014, a report was published in Britain revealing that around 1,400 (a conservative estimate) young girls in the town of Rotherham had been sexually abused, raped, and pimped by Pakistani Muslims. Rotherham has a population of around 250,000, approximately 10,000 of whom are Muslims. An investigation by the *Times* newspaper in 2012

---

30 Tracy McVeigh, "'They're following Me': Chilling Words of Girl Who Was 'honour Killing' Victim," The Guardian, September 22, 2012, accessed April 24, 2018, https://www.theguardian.com/world/2012/sep/22/banaz-mahmod-honour-killing.

alleged widespread abuse of young girls in the town and related that a confidential 2010 report by the Police Intelligence Bureau detailed "a significant problem with networks of Asian males exploiting young white females, particularly in Rotherham and Sheffield[31]."

We soon learned that this was happening all over the country as gangs were prosecuted in Rochdale, Oxford, Birmingham and Newcastle.

In August 2017, the *Express* reported that, despite criminal prosecutions, government reports, and promises of action, rape by Muslim gangs in Rotherham was still happening on an "industrial scale"[32].

CLOTHING

Can a person in Britain wear a balaclava in a bank? No. Such a thing would undoubtedly cause alarm, and I suspect if a person refused to remove their balaclava upon entry to a bank, they would get their collar felt by the local Bobby[33]. We often see signs in shops, for example, which ask motorbike riders to remove their helmets before entering. If a biker refuses, again, I strongly suspect they would find themselves in hot water. What about a defendant who insists on wearing a mask throughout a criminal trial process? Do you think it would be allowed? No, neither do I.

But there is one exception to all of the above. In Britain, it is perfectly acceptable for a person to cover their face in a bank, a shop, even when standing trial, provided that face-covering is an Islamic burqa/niqab.

In 2013, a judge in London allowed a woman standing trial for a criminal offence to cover her face with a black cloth throughout the trial – the only exception being when she herself

31 "South Yorkshire Police Deny Hiding Girls' Sex Abuse - BBC News," BBC, September 24, 2012, accessed April 24, 2018, http://www.bbc.co.uk/news/uk-england-south-yorkshire-19701760.
32 Nick Gutteridge, "ROTHERHAM ABUSE SCANDAL: Horrific Reality of 'industrial Scale' Child Grooming Revealed," Express.co.uk, August 09, 2016, accessed April 24, 2018, https://www.express.co.uk/news/uk/697583/Rotherham-abuse-scandal-child-grooming-gangs-industrial-scale-victims-CSE.
33 Bobby is a commonly-used word in England for police constable.

gave evidence. This was the first time such a thing had been permitted in British judicial history[34], but it won't be the last. Supreme Court President Lord Neuberger said that courts should show *"respect"* and allow women to wear the full niqab[35].

One of the most remarkable stories I've read in relation to the burqa, and the appalling double-standards applied to face-covering and identity-hiding, was that of David Jones. Jones arrived at the security gates of Gatwick Airport in 2012 and promptly found himself accused of racism when he commented on the fact that a woman, wearing the niqab, had passed through security without showing her face, despite everyone else having to undergo rigorous checks.

Jones, the creator of the popular children's TV show *Fireman Sam*, commented to officers, "If I was wearing this scarf over my face, I wonder what would happen." After being told he wasn't "allowed to say that", Jones very astutely stated, "George Orwell's *1984* now seems to have arrived in Gatwick airport[36]."

In the UK, we have a duality of regulation. Muslims are allowed to cover their faces in court, in banks, on public transport, but other people are not. Muslims can commit FGM, a crime that carries a 14-year prison sentence, without any interference from police. We have sharia tribunals operating a de facto parallel system of family law which permits domestic violence, marital rape, and treats a woman's word as being worth half of a man's. This carries on in the open, despite a ruling from the House of Lords that it is "wholly incompatible" with basic human rights. Our authorities turned a blind eye to the organised gang rape of thousands of white English girls across the country

---

34 Rebecca Camber for the Daily Mail, "You Must Take off Your Veil: Judge Rules That Muslim Defendant Can Wear Niqab during Trial but NOT When Giving Evidence," Daily Mail Online, September 17, 2013, accessed April 24, 2018, http://www.dailymail.co.uk/news/article-2421893/Judge-Peter-Murphy-rules-Muslim-woman-REMOVE-face-veil-evidence.html.

35 Jake Burman, "Britain's Top Judge Says Muslim Women should Be Allowed to Wear veil in Court," Express.co.uk, April 17, 2015, accessed April 24, 2018, https://www.express.co.uk/news/uk/571042/Muslim-niqab-Supreme-Court-Neuberger-court-full-face-veil.

36 Jason Lewis, "Fireman Sam Creator Detained at Airport for Veil Comment at Security Gate," The Telegraph, February 26, 2012, accessed April 25, 2018, http://www.telegraph.co.uk/news/uknews/law-and-order/9105788/Fireman-Sam-creator-detained-at-airport-for-veil-comment-at-security-gate.html.

for decades, because the men committing these rapes were overwhelmingly Muslim. Despite all this, we remain impeccably polite
in our public discussions of Islam, so as not to cause offence.

FIGHTING BACK?

Communities Secretary Eric Pickles[37] wrote to over 1,000
imams, asking for help with the fight against radicalisation. The
letter could not have been more obliging or polite. It named
Islam as a "great faith" with a "message of peace" in the opening
paragraph.

Despite this, the Muslim Council of Britain was displeased[38].
Harun Khan, Deputy Secretary General of the MCB, said:

*"Is Mr Pickles seriously suggesting, as do members of
the far-Right, that Muslims and Islam are inherently apart
from British society?"*

No, the Muslim Council of Britain is seriously suggesting it.
It consistently advocates for sharia and separate standards for
Muslims, then claims exclusion when its demands are unmet.

Prior to becoming Prime Minister in 2016, Theresa May held
the post of Home Secretary – a brief which includes law and
order. When Home Secretary, May ordered a review into the use
of sharia councils in Britain. Immediately there was difficulty, as
with anything involving Islam.

From the get-go, it was clear that the underlying aim of the
review was to find best practice for sharia. Those who want sharia
councils abolished were scarcely involved in the review, and there
was certainly no room for anyone critical of Islam itself. Ridicu-
lously, the chair of the review board would be an Islamic scholar,

---

37 Eric Pickle and Tariq Ahmad, "Final Draft Letter to Mosques," Https://docs.
publishing.service.gov.uk. Accessed April 25, 2018, https://assets.publishing.service.gov.
uk/government/uploads/system/uploads/attachment_data/file/396312/160115_Final_
Draft_Letter_to_Mosques_PDF.pdf.
38 Patrick Wintour, "Muslim Council of Britain Objects to Pickles Letter to Islamic
Leaders," The Guardian, January 19, 2015, accessed April 25, 2018, https://www.
theguardian.com/politics/2015/jan/19/uk-muslim-council-objections-eric-pickles-letter.

and two imams would be along to assist[39].

I've written elsewhere in this book about the denigration of white people that is occurring in the West alongside the appeasement and accommodation of Islam, and the two are not unrelated. "White people should stay out of it" is a common theme, and it was repeated some months later when the sharia reviews (May's review had since been joined by another one, held by a Home Affairs Committee in the House of Commons) hit the headlines again.

In November 2016, the Muslim Women's Network wrote an open letter complaining about the sharia review process. Their grievance was essentially that Muslim women were not being sufficiently consulted. Fair enough. But while complaining of being excluded, the network's chair Shaista Gohir hinted at others who ought to be excluded. She told the BBC, "I do feel that there are people who are anti-faith, particularly anti-Islam, who are using women's rights as a guise, wanting to abolish Sharia councils[40]."

Two issues here:

1) Does Gohir have the ability to know what other people are thinking?

2) Why does she have the right to determine that "anti-faith, particularly anti-Islam" views have no place in this debate?

The National Secular Society, to its credit, criticised the lack of secular voices in the sharia debate. Was it finally realising what some of us had been saying all along?

Here is part of a statement from Benjamin Jones, then-communications officer of the society:

> *"If sharia councils operated fully within UK law, they would still pose a profound cultural challenge, and even if they made no pretence at legal power, non-Muslims would still have every right to object to their malign influence."*

39 Hannah Summers, "Sharia Courts Review Branded a 'whitewash' over Appointment 'bias' Concerns," The Independent, July 09, 2016, accessed April 25, 2018, http://www.independent.co.uk/news/uk/home-news/sharia-courts-review-branded-a-whitewash-over-appointment-bias-concerns-a7128706.html.
40 Martin Bashir, "Muslim Women Complain about Sharia Inquiries - BBC News," BBC, November 01, 2016, accessed April 25, 2018, http://www.bbc.co.uk/news/uk-37830589.

Naz Shah is a Labour MP for the northern English constituency of Bradford West. Bradford is a city with an enormous Muslim population, and the constituency's previous MP had been George Galloway, a firebrand Left Winger and staunch ally of Islam. Shah unseated Galloway in the 2015 general election – a victory which was itself mired in controversy. Shah claimed to have been a victim of a forced marriage in her teens, while Galloway accused her of lying about this, claiming she was whipping up hate against the Pakistani community with stereotypes about forced marriage. Her own life experience didn't appear to be significant for Mr Galloway[41].

In any case, following a bitter campaign, she won by a significant margin.

When the sharia inquiries began, Shah had plenty to say, including commenting that the inquiries were "Islamophobic and racist".

Shah went on to say:

> *"There are issues with Sharia councils. Usually they're under-resourced, there's not that professional standard. What we need to be doing is supporting the Sharia councils[42]."*

This is the very same Naz Shah MP who later shared social media messages sarcastically suggesting that white rape victims of Muslim gangs should "shut their mouths for the good of diversity"[43]. She claimed the retweet was a genuine accident rectified within minutes, but this came on top of another controversy only days earlier, when Shah had condemned Sarah Champion,

41 Helen Pidd,"George Galloway Accuses Naz Shah of Lying about Her Forced Marriage," The Guardian, April 09, 2015, accessed April 25, 2018, https://www.theguardian.com/politics/2015/apr/09/george-galloway-naz-shah-forced-marriage-nikah-bradford-hustings.
42 Ajay Nair, "'Sharia Councils Need SUPPORT' Labour MP Says Muslims See Inquiry as 'Islamophobic'," Express.co.uk, November 01, 2016, accessed April 25, 2018, http://www.express.co.uk/news/uk/727432/naz-shah-support-sharia-councils-inquiry.
43 Joseph Curtis for Mailonline, "Labour MP and Key Corbyn Ally Shares Twitter Message Telling Rotherham Sex Abuse Victims to 'shut Their Mouths for the Good of Diversity' - ...", Daily Mail Online, August 23, 2017, accessed April 25, 2018, http://www.dailymail.co.uk/news/article-4813870/MP-shares-Twitter-post-telling-abuse-victims-shut-up.html.

Labour MP for Rotherham, for her article headlined, "Britain has a problem with British Pakistani men raping and exploiting white girls". Champion had finally said something that resonated with the truth, but as is so often the case, she soon retracted it, saying it "should not have gone out in my name"[44].

This didn't stop the outrage, though, and Champion resigned from the shadow cabinet. However, when Naz Shah faced calls to resign for her Twitter endorsements[45], these were ignored.

Another Labour MP, Yasmin Qureshi, accused fellow MP Philip Davies of picking on religions when he proposed that halal meat ought to be labelled to allow the consumer to make an informed choice. Qureshi said: "I am a bit concerned about the way this debate on halal and kosher has been taking place in the country and also some of the things said in the chamber as well[46]."

When former Justice Secretary Sadiq Khan ran for the office of Mayor of London in 2015, his Conservative opponent merely questioned his previous associations with jihad-sympathetic groups like the Muslim Council of Britain. Zac Goldsmith was quickly dismissed as a racist and the Left went for him hammer and tong. His questions went unanswered.

Here is part of an article I wrote in *Breitbart London* at the time:

> The election of Labour's Sadiq Khan to the office of Mayor of London should come as no surprise. Labour selected well. It's the perfect time for it – Khan is a Muslim and so Labour can do what it does best: play the champions of 'tolerance' and 'equality', all the while cloaking real intolerance and inequality and protecting it from public scrutiny.
>
> To listen to the BBC, one would think that Khan had been subjected to a terrible racist smear campaign orchestrated

44 Jessica Elgot and Graham Ruddick, "Sarah Champion Distances Herself from Sun Article on British Pakistani Men," The Guardian, August 16, 2017, accessed April 25, 2018, https://www.theguardian.com/politics/2017/aug/16/sarah-champion-complaint-sun-article-british-pakistani-men.

45 Ben Lazarus, "42,000 Sign Petition for MP to Resign after Tweet Sex Victims Should Be Quiet," The Sun, August 31, 2017, accessed April 25, 2018, https://www.thesun.co.uk/news/4358394/labour-mp-rotherham-abuse-tweet-petition/.

46 "Halal Meat Labelling Plan Rejected by MPs - BBC News," BBC, May 13, 2014, Accessed April 25, 2018. http://www.bbc.co.uk/news/uk-politics-27402428.

by his Conservative opponent Zac Goldsmith. But it was Goldsmith who had been subjected to a smear campaign, by a Labour Party using one of the great weapons of modern British politics – the word 'racist'. Reality is irrelevant; it is speaking of reality that causes problems.

Goldsmith wrote[47] in the *Daily Mail* that Khan, and others in the higher echelons of the Labour Party, had "repeatedly legitimised those with extremist views". He's right, they have.

We all know that the Labour leader Jeremy Corbyn has described the anti-Semitic terror group Hamas as his "friends". This is the same Hamas that has a founding charter calling for the religiously-motivated annihilation of Jews. Khan himself has referred[48] to moderate Muslims as "Uncle Toms" – a derogatory term describing non-white people who act subserviently to white rule. This alone would be considered unforgivable for most candidates, but with Khan, it actually gets much worse.

Throughout his career, he has mingled with and repre-sented Muslim extremists, and according to Daniel Johnson in *Standpoint*, has supported[49] incorporating sharia law into the British legal system. He has argued that there are uncontroversial aspects of sharia that we ought to permit. Needless to say, these are highly likely to be the exact same 'uncontroversial' bits of sharia that Islamists and jihadis are constantly clamouring for – family law.

Furthermore, the new London Mayor has given 'three cheers' to the Islam Channel. This TV channel has been

---

47 Zac Goldsmith for The Mail On Sunday, "On Thursday, Are We Really Going to Hand the World's Greatest City to a Labour Party That Thinks Terrorists Is Its Friends? A Passionate Plea from ZAC GOLDSMITH Four Days before Mayoral Election," Daily Mail Online, May 01, 2016, accessed April 25, 2018, http://www.dailymail.co.uk/debate/article-3567537/On-Thursday-really-going-hand-world-s-greatest-city-Labour-party-thinks-terrorists-friends-passionate-plea-ZAC-GOLDSMITH-four-days-Mayoral-electi-on.html.
48 David Maddox, "Sadiq Khan Apologises after Using 'Uncle Tom' Racial Slur against Moderate Muslim Groups," Express.co.uk, May 05, 2016, accessed April 25, 2018, http://www.express.co.uk/news/politics/667294/Sadiq-Khan-apologises-Uncle-Tom-racial-slur-moderate-Muslim-groups.
49 Daniel Johnson, "The Spectre Of Mayor Khan's Islamist London | Standpoint," Sentimental Nihilism And Popular Culture | Standpoint, Accessed April 25, 2018, http://www.standpointmag.co.uk/node/6482/full.

censured by Ofcom for advocating[50] violence against women. Nevertheless, Khan praised it at a conference while the black flag of jihad flew freely[51] in his audience.

In response to all of this, Goldsmith was, if anything, too timid. It is important if a Mayor of London holds these views about sharia, and it is serious if he mixes among Islamists and jihadis. Merely for politely mentioning this, Zac Goldsmith became a villain, and the very real concerns about Khan's associations were forgotten, buried under an avalanche of Left-wing halos and sanctimonious slime.

Let us imagine a scenario. Imagine that Zac Goldsmith had once spoken to an EDL rally and had shared a platform with Tommy Robinson. Would he even be a member of the Conservative Party today, much less its candidate for Mayor of London? Keep in mind that Tommy Robinson has never called for brutal theocracy, the killing of homosexuals or Jews, or the subjugation of women, and yet he is deemed to be morally inferior to those who do. Why? Because Tommy opposes Islam. He questions Islam. He tells the truth about Islam. He tells the truth about jihad. Goldsmith went nowhere near as far as Robinson, but he now finds himself equally maligned, merely for telling the truth.

The Loony Left in London is congratulating itself on its tolerance and is bleating on about hope. What it's actually done is remind every jihadi in Britain that the deception still works. They can continue to be as anti-Semitic, homophobic, and misogynistic as they like, and if anyone complains, or even points it out, the Left will immediately spring into action and silence awkward questions. They have made absolutely sure that more and more jihad is coming our way.

50 Neil Midgley, "Islamic TV Channel Rapped for Advocating Marital Rape," The Telegraph, November 08, 2010, accessed April 25, 2018, http://www.telegraph.co.uk/news/uknews/8108132/Islamic-TV-channel-rapped-for-advocating-marital-rape.html.
51 Jake Wallis Simons for Mailonline, "EXCLUSIVE: Sadiq Khan, Labour Candidate for London Mayor, Made a Speech While the 'black Flag of Jihad' Was Flying and Gave His Support to Groups Linked to Extremism," Daily Mail Online, last modified February 16, 2016, http://www.dailymail.co.uk/news/article-3270034/Sadiq-Khan-Labour-s-candidate-London-mayor-filmed-praising-Islamic-TV-station-advocated-marital-rape-violence-against-women.html.

IN CONCLUSION

BEFORE I MOVE on from this section on the UK, I must mention some of the lowlights of the Islamisation of Britain over the past few years. Most are copied from lists compiled by the Gatestone Institute[1].

- The Department of Theology of the Blackburn Muslim Association ruled that it is "not permissible" for a woman to travel more than 48 miles – deemed to be the equivalent of three days' walk – without her husband or a close male relative. The group also ruled that men must grow beards and women must cover their faces. The rulings were accompanied by the catchphrase "Allah knows best."
- The Greater Manchester Police (GMP) apologised for a counter-terrorism exercise in which a mock suicide bomber shouted "*Allahu Akbar*" (Allah is the Greatest). Eight hundred volunteers took part in the overnight drill to make it as realistic as possible.

---

1 Gatestone Institute International Policy Council, accessed April 25, 2018, https://www. gatestoneinstitute.org

Manchester peace activist Erinma Bell criticised the use
of the words "Muslim terrorist". She said, "A terrorist can be anyone" and "We need to move away from
stereotypes". Islamists went on to murder 22 people in
Manchester at a pop concert in 2017.

- Former Prime Minister David Cameron apologised to
  Suliman Gani, a Muslim extremist, for saying he is a
  supporter of the Islamic State. Gani said accusations that
  he backs the Islamic State are defamatory and must be
  retracted. In a statement, Cameron said he was referring
  to reports that Gani supports *an* Islamic state rather than
  the Islamic State. The Muslim Council of Britain called on
  Cameron to repeat his apology in Parliament, and for an
  urgent review of Islamophobia in the Conservative party.
- Belmarsh, a maximum-security prison in London, has
  become "like a jihadi training camp", according to testimony from a former inmate.
- Azad Chaiwala, a Muslim entrepreneur in Manchester,
  launched a campaign to "remove the taboo" of polygamy by starting two polygamy matchmaking sites:
  secondwife.com, exclusive to Muslims, and polygamy.
  com. Polygamy is illegal in Britain.
- Sir Michael Wilshaw, the head of Ofsted, warned that
  the Trojan Horse campaign to impose radical Islamic
  ideas on Birmingham schools has "gone underground"
  but has not gone away. He warned that Birmingham was failing to ensure that "children are not being
  exposed to harm, exploitation or the risk of falling
  under the influence of extremist views".
- Residents in Manchester received leaflets in their mail
  boxes calling for a public ban on dogs. The leaflets,
  distributed by a group called Public Purity, stated: "This
  area is home to a large Muslim community. Please have
  respect for us and for our children and limit the presence
  of dogs in the public sphere. As citizens of a multicultural nation, those who live in the UK must learn
  to understand and respect the legacy and lifestyle of
  Muslims who live alongside them. Help us make this a

reality. Let your local MP know how you feel about this. Make Muslims feel like they live in a safe and accepting space, welcoming them and respecting their beliefs."

- Nearly 900 Syrians in Britain were arrested in 2015 for crimes including rape and child abuse, police statistics revealed.
- A public swimming pool in Luton announced gender-segregated sessions for cultural reasons. The move will give men exclusive access to the larger 50-metre pool, while women will have to use the smaller 20-metre pool. The gender-segregated sessions are named 'Alhamdulillah (an Arabic phrase which means 'praise be to Allah') Swimming'.
- Stephen Bennett, a 39-year-old father of seven from Manchester, was sentenced to 180 hours of community service for posting "grossly offensive" anti-Muslim comments on Facebook.
- Chief Constable David Thompson, head of West Midlands Police, one of the largest police forces in Britain, said he would consider allowing Muslim officers to wear the burka while on duty in a bid to boost diversity.
- Reverend Giles Goddard, vicar of St John's in Waterloo, central London, allowed a full Muslim prayer service to be held in his church. He also asked his congregation to praise "the God that we love, Allah".
- Reports of alleged links between Islamic charities and terrorism or extremism surged to a record high, according to the Charity Commission, a charity watchdog. The number of times the Commission shared concerns about links between charities and extremism with police and other agencies nearly tripled, from 234 to 630, in just three years.
- St. Mary's Episcopal Cathedral in Glasgow featured a reading from the Koran which denied the divinity of Jesus Christ. The Koran reading, aimed at "reaching out to Muslims", was held on Epiphany, a festival which celebrates the incarnation of God in the person of Jesus Christ.
- Gloucester Cathedral invited Imam Hassan of the local

Masjid-e-Noor mosque to perform the traditional
Muslim invocation to worship at the launch of a multicultural Faith Exhibition. A video of the call to prayer
was posted on the cathedral's Facebook page.

- The City of Edinburgh invited citizens to vote
  for projects designed to create a city free from
  Islamophobia.
- Changing of the Guard ceremonies at Windsor Castle
  were cancelled amid fears of jihadist attacks.
- Six Muslim men shouted *"Allahu Akbar"* as they were
  sentenced at Sheffield Crown Court for a total of 81
  years for sexually abusing two girls – including one who
  became pregnant at the age of 12 – in Rotherham.
- A National Health Service (NHS) project based on research
  by Leeds University claimed that Muslims with mental
  health issues could be helped by re-embracing Islam.
- Mohammed Aslam, an independent candidate for
  Mayor of Greater Manchester, caused controversy after
  he delivered his election manifesto completely in Urdu
  on the BBC.
- The Church of England said that British children should
  be required to learn about Islam. Derek Holloway
  of the Church of England's education office said that
  Judeo-Christian parents who do not want their children
  to learn about Islam should not be allowed to withdraw
  their children from religious education lessons.
- Robbie Travers, a 21-year-old law student at Edinburgh
  University, was investigated for a hate crime after he
  allegedly mocked the Islamic State on social media.
- TheCityUK, London's top lobby group, urged the British
  government to prioritise Islamic finance to retain its
  status as Europe's financial hub ahead of Brexit negotia-
  tions to exit the country from the European Union.
- The All Saints Church in Kingston upon Thames held a
  joint birthday celebration for Jesus and Mohammed in
  December 2017.
- The British government refused to say whether telling
  people about Judeo-Christianity could be considered a

hate crime. Lord Pearson of Rannoch said that when he raised a question on the issue in the House of Lords, the government failed to state clearly whether Judeo-Christians can be prosecuted just for stating their beliefs.

Three terror attacks in quick succession took place in the UK in 2017: five people died when a jihadist terrorist drove a van into crowds on Westminster Bridge in London; 22 died in a bomb attack at a pop concert in Manchester; and eight people died during an attack weeks later at London Bridge when knife-wielding jihadis went on the rampage. After each attack, senior politicians reminded the British public that they were not related to Islam. Prime Minister Theresa May told Parliament that the attacks constitute a "perversion of a great faith"[2], while Manchester Mayor Andy Burnham described the man who murdered 22 in his city as "a terrorist, not a Muslim"[3].

Mohammed (taking into account its spelling varieties) is now the most common baby name in England and Wales[4]. Despite 47% of the British public stating they want an end to immigration from Muslim countries[5], the Muslim population of Britain surpassed 4.1 million (6.3% of the entire population) in 2017[6]. According to some analyses, the Muslim population doubles every decade.

---

2 Jon Stone, Political Correspondent, "Theresa May Says It Is Wrong to Describe London Attack as 'Islamic Terrorism'," The Independent, March 23, 2017, accessed April 25, 2018, http://www.independent.co.uk/news/uk/politics/theresa-may-london-attack-islamic-terrorism-wrong-westminster-bridge-prime-minister-commons-a7645626.html.
3 Adrian Sherling, "Manchester Mayor: Bomber Was A Terrorist, Not A Muslim," LBC, May 24, 2017, accessed April 25, 2018, http://www.lbc.co.uk/radio/presenters/nick-ferrari/manchester-mayor-bomber-was-a-terrorist-not-muslim/.
4 Jacob Dirnhuber, "Parents Name Kids Neymar, Messi, and Ronaldo - but Muhammed Is Overall No 1 for Boys If Different Spellings Are Taken into Account," The Sun, September 20, 2017, accessed April 25, 2018, https://www.thesun.co.uk/news/4505719/muhammad-replaces-william-in-the-top-10-most-popular-boys-names-in-the-uk/.
5 Samuel Osborne, "Most Europeans Want Immigration Ban from Muslim-majority Countries, Poll Reveals," The Independent, February 07, 2017, accessed April 25, 2018, http://www.independent.co.uk/news/world/europe/most-europeans-want-muslim-ban-immigration-control-middle-east-countries-syria-iran-iraq-poll-a7567301.html.
6 Soeren Kern, "The Islamization of Britain in 2017," Gatestone Institute, accessed April 25, 2018, https://www.gatestoneinstitute.org/11648/britain-islamization-2017.

THE UNITED STATES
OF AMERICA

FREE SPEECH IN THE USA

"Islam isn't in America to be equal to any other faith, but to become dominant. The Koran should be the highest authority in America."

Omar Ahmad,
FOUNDING CHAIR OF THE COUNCIL ON
AMERICAN-IslamicRELATIONS

THE SHARIA-BASED ISLAMIC political movement is expanding throughout the world, and sadly the United States is no exception. A matter of supreme importance in the USA debate involves restrictions on free expression, a demand consistently made by Islamist groups there, often with the implication that speech critical of Islam amounts to racism or Islamophobia (as in the UK).

To put this into context, I must include the full wording of the First Amendment to the US Constitution – the supreme law of the United States.

Congress shall make no law respecting an establishment of religion, or prohibiting the free exercise thereof; or abridging the freedom of speech, or of the press; or the right of the people peaceably to assemble, and to petition the government for a redress of grievances.

Hassan al-Qazwini is the leader of North America's largest mosque (i.e., not a fringe extremist), based in Dearborn, Michigan. Following the 2012 online publication of the movie *Innocence of Muslims*, which portrayed Mohammed in a negative light, Al-Qaswini urged the US Government to respond in a way that was "stronger than verbal condemnation"[1]. The US suffered from the reaction to this film when one of its ambassadors was murdered in Libya, and US Consuls were attacked the world over.

This wasn't enough for the Muslim Brotherhood[2]. It called on the Obama administration to prosecute the 'madman' behind the video[3]. At least partly, President Obama appeared to defend freedom of speech, but he also condemned the film-makers and others critical of Islam, and transmitted a confused and muddled response with regard to free expression.

> *"Americans have fought and died around the globe to protect the right of all people to express their views, even views that we profoundly disagree with. We do not do so because we support hateful speech, but because our founders understood that without such protections, the capacity of each individual to express their own views and practice their own faith may be threatened. We do so because in a diverse society, efforts to restrict speech can quickly become a tool to silence critics and oppress minorities."*

Obama also said, "The future must not belong to those who slander the prophet of Islam[4]."

---

1 David Wood, "Dearborn Imam Hassan Al-Qazwini Calls on U.S. Government to Enforce Sharia Blasphemy Laws," Answering Muslims, January 01, 1970, accessed April 25, 2018, http://www.answeringmuslims.com/2012/09/dearborn-imam-hassan-al-qazwini-calls.html.
2 The Muslim Brotherhood's Official English Website, accessed April 26, 2018, http://www.ikhwanweb.com/.
3 David D Kirkpatrick, "Anger Over Film Fuels Anti-American Attacks in Libya and Egypt," The New York Times, September 11, 2012, accessed April 26, 2018, http://www.nytimes.com/2012/09/12/world/middleeast/anger-over-film-fuels-anti-american-attacks-in-libya-and-egypt.html?_r=0&adxnnl=1&pagewanted=all&adxnnlx=1350907754-iNQBh9wd19NDth yknLJfQ.
4 "Obama's Speech to the United Nations General Assembly – Text," The New York Times, September 26, 2012, accessed April 25, 2018, http://www.nytimes.com/2012/09/26/world/obamas-speech-to-the-united-nations-general-assembly-text.html?pagewanted=all.

Nakoula Basseley Nakoula was the man behind the *Inno-cence of Muslims* film, and he lived in California. Born in Egypt, Nakoula was sentenced to jail time in the USA for bank fraud, having pleaded guilty in 2010. In what must have been a gift to the authorities there, in producing *Innocence of Muslims*, Nakoula had allegedly broken the terms of his parole and was re-arrested in September 2012. Nakoula's lawyer went into hiding as a result of the film, and security was bolstered at his trial. (Nakoula was released on probation in August 2013.)

In Manchester, Tennessee, in 2013, a group called the American Freedom Defense Initiative (AFDI) gathered to protest against a talk which addressed "how civil rights can be violated by those who post inflammatory documents targeted at Muslims on social media"[5]. The group alleged that the purpose of the event was to warn people against criticising Islam, and to educate people as to how they could use the law of the land to stamp out such criticism. The meeting was addressed by Bill Killian, US Attorney of the Eastern District of Tennessee, FBI Special Agent Kenneth Moore, and Zak Mohyuddin of the American Muslim Advisory Council. According to the American Freedom Defense Initiative, the intent of the evening was to aid "the imposition in the US of Islam's blasphemy laws forbidding criticism of Islam"[6].

An interesting case on free speech, which may support the AFDI's claims, came before the courts in 2012. Talaag Elbayomy was filmed appearing to launch a physical attack on a man, dressed as a Zombie Mohammed, in a Hallowe'en parade in Pennsylvania. Ernest Perce V filed a complaint against Elbayomy, alleging "He grabbed me, choked [me] from the back, spun me around to try to get [my Muhammad of Islam sign] off that was wrapped around my neck"[7].

Elbayomy claimed that Perce had instigated the attack and that he did not, in fact, physically touch him.

The case against the alleged attacker was dismissed, but it

5 "Group Sets Meeting to Increase Tolerance of Muslims, Culture," Tullahoma News, accessed April 26, 2018, http://www.tullahomanews.com/?p=15360.
6 Robert Spencer and Pamela Geller, "Manchester Protesters Stood for Free Speech," Manchester Times, June 19, 2013, accessed April 25, 2018, http://www.manchestertimes.com/?p=11879.
7 "Judge Rules In 'Zombie Muhammad' Case," The Huffington Post, February 28, 2012, accessed April 26, 2018, http://www.huffingtonpost.com/2012/02/27/pennsylvania-judge-musim-zombie-muhammad_n_1304764.html.

was the comments of the judge that understandably sparked controversy. Judge Mark Martin, a military veteran, made the following statement:

> *"If I were a Muslim, I'd find it offensive. But you have that right, but you're way outside your boundaries or First Amendment rights."*

He went on to tell Perce that he would be executed in some countries for portraying Mohammed in this way, and that "Islam is not just a religion, it's their culture. It's their very essence, their very being"[8].

The lawyer who represented Elbayomy then made these extraordinary comments:

> *"I think this was a good dressing down by the judge. The so-called victim was the antagonist and we introduced evidence that clearly showed his attitude toward Muslims. The judge didn't do anything I wouldn't have done if I was in that position."*

What conclusion can we draw from this? Evidence of a negative "attitude toward Muslims" makes you an antagonist, and if you are physically attacked, it is your own fault? In other words, punishment for insulting Islam has entered American law.

CAIR

I cannot talk about Islam and free speech in the US without giving some time to the Council on American-Islamic Relations (CAIR). CAIR was founded in 1994. Its website declares it has a presence in twenty US states, and it sells itself as an organisation that is "a natural ally of groups, religious or secular, that advocate justice and human rights in America and around the

---

8 Sarah AB, "Harry's Place," Politics, accessed April 26, 2018. http://hurryupharry. org/2012/02/24/zombie-mohammed/.

world"[9]. It should be called upon to prove this, given that its actions sometimes suggest a lack of commitment to the human rights of free speech, gender equality, and freedom of religion.

In August 2008, a trial began in the USA. The American Government sought convictions against the Holy Land Foundation, a registered charity, for funding the designated terrorist organisation Hamas. Following an initial mistrial in 2007, the 2008 jury returned a verdict of guilty on 108 charges including conspiracy to provide material support to a foreign terrorist organisation, providing material support to a foreign terrorist, and conspiracy to commit money laundering. Among the convicted individuals was Ghassan Elashi, a member of the founding Board of Directors of the Texas branch of the Council on American-Islamic Relations.

During the trial, FBI Special Agent Lara Burns was questioned about a wiretapped transcript made by the FBI during their investigations. A meeting of Islamists had been held in Philadelphia where it was suggested that a new organisation, one "whose Islamic hue is not very conspicuous"[10], be created to aid the spread of the Islamist message in the US. When questioned if any such group had been formed, Special Agent Burns answered, "CAIR".

Links with Hamas and other terrorist groups, as well as accusations of being a US front group for Islamism, have long plagued CAIR. In a book written by P. David Gaubatz[11], whose son worked undercover as an intern at CAIR, it is alleged that CAIR's membership is far smaller than it claims (many Muslims have been driven away by accusations of terrorist support), and that, if dependent upon donations from supporters, CAIR would fold. It is also alleged that women in the organisation have made discrimination claims, that CAIR has been sued by Muslims who sought what turned out to be ineffective legal advice, and that it discriminates against Shia Muslims. The book goes on to

---

9 "About Us," CAIR - Council on American-Islamic Relations – CAIR, accessed April 26, 2018, https://www.cair.com/about_us.
10 "FBI: CAIR Is a Front Group, and Holy Land Foundation Tapped Hamas Clerics for Fundraisers," Dallas News, October 07, 2008, accessed April 26, 2018, http://crimeblog.dallasnews.com/2008/10/fbi-cair-is-a-front-group-and.html/.
11 P. David Gaubatz and Paul Sperry, *Muslim Mafia*, (New York: WND Books, 2009).

claim that members of the Saudi royal family and government have directed funds amounting to millions of dollars into CAIR's accounts.

Despite its claims to share in the values of the United States and its Constitution, CAIR has a history of opposing free speech and advocating sharia in the US. In a booklet entitled *Understanding Sharia*[12], CAIR makes the claim that sharia is not incompatible with the US Constitution. The report does not criticise sharia's prohibition on blasphemy, its treatment of women, or its barbaric punishments – it merely denies that such punishments would ever occur in the US.

In another booklet, *Securing Religious Liberty*[13], CAIR attempts to silence criticism of sharia when it argues that such criticism is aimed at Islam generally, rather than sharia law, and 'bigots' who are actually 'anti-Muslim' merely disguise their irrational hatred by pretending they object to the cruelties of sharia.

This is standard. A very common method used by Islamists to silence criticism of sharia, which has been hugely effective in the West, is to turn this criticism into a form of oppression. CAIR's claim that those who oppose sharia are suggesting that Muslims are 'a foreign group' does not sit well with their own demands that Muslims be treated radically differently (see 'The US military and the FBI').

CAIR's record on matters of free speech becomes more dubious upon consideration of its relationship with the UN body, the Organisation of Islamic Cooperation (OIC). The OIC is a group of Islamic countries which has called several times for defamation of religion to be treated as an international criminal offence, and has described Islamophobia as the "worst form of terrorism"[14]. Since 1999, several non-binding resolutions have been passed at the United Nations condemning defamation of religion. Most attempts to push for what would in effect make insulting religion a criminal offence on a global scale have been

---

12 "Understanding Sharia: what it is, what it is not," CAIR Oklahoma, accessed April 26, 2018, http://virtuecenter.s3.amazonaws.com/files/2012-10-23-10/understandingsharia.pdf.
13 Cair, "Guides and Toolkits," CAIR - Council on American-Islamic Relations – CAIR, accessed April 26, 2018, https://www.cair.com/guides-and-toolkits.
14 Siraj Waheb, "Islamophobia Worse Form of Terrorism," Arab News, 17th May 2007, accessed 19th November 2012, http://www.arabnews.com/node/298472.

rejected by the US and other Western nations. However, one such resolution received US support.

UNHRC RESOLUTION 16/18

The United Nations Human Rights Council (UNHRC) Resolution 16/18 on "Combating Intolerance, Negative Stereotyping and Stigmatization of, and Discrimination, Incitement to Violence and Violence Against, Persons Based on Religion or Belief" initially appears laudable in seeking to protect people from discrimination and violence. The incitement to violence provision is problematic, however, as it leaves broad interpretive gaps in the definition of what does and does not amount to incitement.

It is of the utmost importance that 'incitement' is clearly defined. For example, can a cartoon be a recognised form of incitement to violence, and is the violence deemed an inevitable response? We are at risk of creating a situation where violent reaction implies incitement. Or to put it another way, Islamists could learn that if they react violently, the blame will be placed not on them, but on whatever it was they were reacting to.

At the invitation of then-US Secretary of State Hillary Clinton, representatives of 26 governments and four international organisations met in Washington, D.C., in December 2011 to discuss the implementation of Resolution 16/18. A report on this meeting, which you can read in full by following the link in the footnote[15], seems rather harmless and appears to change little, but the cooperation of the United States, on the global stage, in pursuing laws which *could* restrict free speech is worrying nonetheless.

The American author, and founder of Jihad Watch, Robert Spencer, worries about the direction the USA is travelling with regard to free speech, and has expressed unease about Resolution 16/18. His points are worth exploring.

---

15 Mission of the United States Geneva Switzerland, "US Report on the First Meeting of Experts to Promote Implementation of HCR Resolution 16/18," accessed April 27, 2018, http://geneva.usmission.gov/2012/04/19/implementation1618/.

On the actuality that the United States has supported a resolution which could, in effect, limit freedom of speech, Spencer
stated:

> "*The implications of that are staggering. For the first
> time, you have an American administration – the United
> States at the United Nations – actually supporting, co-spon-
> soring, a resolution that is in violation to the First Amend-
> ment to the Constitution*[16].
>
> "*There was lip service paid in this resolution, as it was
> passed, to the First Amendment to the Constitution, saying
> that the United States would be exempt from enacting any
> kind of statutes to criminalize Islamophobia, insofar as
> they were inconsistent with the Constitution.*"

This is worrying, because it could allow for reinterpretation
of the First Amendment, as Spencer goes on to point out.

> "*Once you have five Supreme Court Justices on your
> side, then it becomes not a difficult thing to narrow the
> interpretation of the First Amendment to such a degree
> that it becomes effectively meaningless. To introduce into
> its interpretation material having to do with hate crimes
> and hate speech, which of course are all interpreted in
> the eye of the beholder, are all interpreted in the way that
> the Obama administration in particular wants them to be
> interpreted at this time, the First Amendment could effec-
> tively be rendered null.*"

The importance of this point cannot be overstated. Anything
that allows *the possibility* of the reinterpretation of the First
Amendment is alarming, and should worry the free world. Many
people don't agree, but there is much validity to the claim that
the United States Constitution acts as the anchor of democracy in
the West. In Europe, we already have dangerous hate speech laws
that have stifled debate and regulated our opinions on matters

---

16 Robert Spencer, You Tube, http:// www.youtube.com/watch?v=5fUNo0ypdvs (page
discontinued).

that affect our democracy and culture in the most fundamental way. It would simply be a disaster if the US were to follow suit.

Spencer concluded that Obama was determined to allow hate speech laws in the US and, interestingly, described him as an "internationalist". I'll allow Spencer to describe what this means:

> *"The President does have an interest in submitting American law to the approval of international bodies, and the United States – up to this point – has been the only safeguard against the passage of this kind of law."*

The problem with the kind of internationalism that Spencer mentions is that there are countries on international bodies which are governed by people who simply don't recognise human rights, including the fundamental right to free speech. When they're negotiating international agreements that are aimed at accommodating all, one country is going to have to give way to another because there is no compromise – you either have free speech, or you don't. Countries that value free speech are either going to have to defend it, or give it up altogether in the name of accommodation.

Sadly, in the international arena, democracies often refuse to defend their values, and as a result, these values are being severely compromised.

The Istanbul Process was established in 2011 as a discussion platform for issues of concern to Afghanistan and the surrounding region, and is supported by the United States. The implementation of Resolution 16/18 is something of a priority for this grouping. In February 2013, Rizwan Saeed Sheikh, Director of Cultural Affairs at the OIC, General Secretariat, and Spokesman for the OIC Secretary General, said, "The Istanbul Process on Islamophobia will be held in the first half of this year, and the session will squarely focus on the issue of criminalizing denigration of religions."

In an interview with the *Saudi Gazette*, Sheikh made clear what the intended outcome of the process would be[17]: an end

---

17 "OIC Coming Back with Another Attempt to Stamp out Free Speech," National Secular Society, accessed April 27, 2018, http://www.secularism.org.uk/news/2013/02/oic-coming-back-with-another-attempt-to-stamp-out-free-speech.

to religious 'denigration'. He described Islamophobia as "a contemporary manifestation of racism mainly targeting Islam and Muslims".

Both of these points are important. Firstly, the definition of Islamophobia includes targeting Islam itself, not just Muslims. Secondly, we must consider what 'incitement' – such as cartoons – has previously led to violence to understand what it was that the OIC probably sought to criminalise. This is nothing short of blackmail – "You do something we don't like, we react violently, and that violence will be your fault because you did something we don't like."

Resolution 16/18 was adopted by the UN Human Rights Council in 2011, but with the reassurance that "international law requires states to prohibit discrimination against people on the basis of their religion or belief. It does not entitle individuals to have their religion, beliefs, opinions or ideas protected from scrutiny, debate, insult or even ridicule." It is worth noting, however, that states like Saudi Arabia have made their way on to the UN Human Rights Council. Saudi Arabia continues to execute its citizens for blasphemy regardless.

The UK too has committed itself to Resolution 16/18. Ambassador Mark Matthews gave a speech[18] confirming this at a conference in February 2017. He said that "all states should be required to monitor religious hate crime" and that "the teaching of religion in schools needs to be improved". Once again, the idea that the religion itself, rather than prejudice or discrimination, might actually be the problem is not entertained.

In 2013, a CAIR official took part in an OIC summit in Cairo where a meeting of heads of state discussed Islamophobia. According to a Facebook post[19], Nihad Awad – the national Executive Director of CAIR – would meet "with heads of state and other foreign dignitaries and...offer input on the growing phenomenon of Islamophobia in the United States and around

---

18 "UK Statement at the Implementation of Council Resolution 16/18 on Combating Religious Intolerance," GOV.UK, February 14, 2017, accessed April 27, 2018. https://www.gov.uk/government/news/uk-statement-at-the-implementation-of-council-resolution-1618-event-on-combating-religious-intolerance-hosted-by-universal-rights-group.
19 Facebook, "Dr. Ben Carson's Accomplishments, Awards, Honors, and Community Involvement," accessed April 27, 2018, https://www.facebook.com/notes/cair/cair-director-to-tweet-from-oic-summit-in-cairo/10151330302219442.

the world". Given the OIC's proposed solution to the problem of Islamophobia, one could be forgiven for believing that the CAIR agenda is quite clear: the prohibition of speech criticising Islam in the United States.

Back on the national stage, the Council on American Islamic Relations continues (successfully) in its domestic war against free expression. CAIR asked the Brandeis University President to rescind an honorary degree awarded to former Dutch MP Ayaan Hirsi Ali in 2014[20]. It said an honour bestowed on Hirsi Ali would be equivalent to "promoting the work of white supremacists and anti-Semites", and it has repeatedly celebrated the barring of other Islam-critics[21] from university platforms. Interestingly, CAIR didn't seem to have similar concerns about anti-Semitism when it argued (on free speech grounds) against an attempt by US Senators to "divest from entities that engage in commerce-related or investment-related boycott, divestment, or sanctions [BDS] activities targeting Israel"[22]. BDS events are notorious for promoting anti-Semitism, so much so that in 2017, Frankfurt became the first German city to refuse funds to BDS activities on the grounds of anti-Semitism[23].

ISNA

If you worry about CAIR and its war on free speech, worry more – because it has company. Another major group, which has been entertained at the White House, is the Islamic Society of North America (ISNA). This group is actively engaged in

---

20 CAIR, "CAIR Asks Brandeis University Not to Honor Islamophobe Ayaan Hirsi Ali," PR Newswire: News Distribution, Targeting and Monitoring, April 08, 2014, accessed April 28, 2018, https://www.prnewswire.com/news-releases/cair-asks-brandeis-university-not-to-honor-islamophobe-ayaan-hirsi-ali-254397281.html.
21 Brittney Baird, "Mae Beavers' Summit Nixed over Anti-Muslim Concerns," WKRN, January 11, 2018, accessed April 28, 2018, http://wkrn.com/2018/01/11/mae-beavers-summit-nixed-over-anti-muslim-concerns/.
22 Cair, "CAIR TESTIMONY IN OPPOSITION TO SB 739 AND HB 949," CAIR - Council on American-Islamic Relations – CAIR, accessed April 28, 2018, https://www.cair.com/cair_testimony_in_opposition_to_sb_739_and_hb_949.
23 "Frankfurt Becomes First German City to Ban 'antisemitic' BDS Movement," The Jerusalem Post | JPost.com, August 26, 2017, accessed April 28, 2018. http://www.jpost.com/Arab-Israeli-Conflict/Frankfurt-becomes-first-German-city-to-ban-antisemitic-BDS-movement-503399.

imposing its demands regarding what can and cannot be said about Islam, while its President has twice met with another President – one by the name of Obama. For its 50th annual convention, the US President sent a rather nauseating video message to ISNA[24]. Here is a snippet:

> *"Each and every one of you is committed to the vision that this country has always championed, that everyone deserves a chance to make their mark on our American story."*

Let's have a look at who is included in Obama's list of "each and every one of you"[25].

There's Jamal Badawi who defends a man's right to beat his wife[26], Muzammil Siddiqi (former president of ISNA) who apparently believes homosexuals have a "moral disorder" and "moral disease"[27], and several others who have endorsed sharia law and expressed hope that it will one day replace the Constitution of the United States. Given the line-up of speakers, it is difficult to argue that "each and every" person at the ISNA convention can be described as committed to the vision that everyone (women and homosexuals included) deserves to make their mark on the American story.

Obama similarly whitewashed Islam and endorsed Muslim victimhood in his first US mosque visit in early 2016 in Baltimore. Following a year of numerous terror attacks within the United States, the attempted murder of cartoonists, major jihad attacks on Western cities, and the growth of Islamic State on the world stage, Obama decided to focus his energies on how Muslims might be afraid of a potential backlash. Whether or not

---

24 "'My Administration Is Proud to Be Your Partner', Obama Tells Muslim Brotherhood Pro-Hamas Group," Frontpage Mag. June 23, 2015, accessed April 28, 2018, http://frontpagemag.com/2013/dgreenfield/my-administration-is-proud-to-be-your-partner-obama-tells-muslim-brotherhood-front-group-linked-to-terrorism/.

25 Islamic Society of North America, http://www.isna.net/annual-convention.html (page discontinued).

26 Ishaq Zahid, "Gender Equity in Islam," The Rightly-Guided Caliphs, accessed April 28, 2018, http://www.islam101.com/women/equity.html.

27 Muslim Information Service, "Islam and Homosexuality," The Rightly-Guided Caliphs, accessed April 28, 2018. http://www.missionislam.com/knowledge/homosexuality.htm.

Americans on the whole might feel afraid of terror attacks or repeated assaults on their free speech was not important.

PAMELA GELLER

There was little concern for a particular woman in Garland, Texas, in 2015, despite the fact that more than one attempt had been made on her life. She was deemed so unimportant that it was she, rather than the would-be murderers, who was roundly attacked by politicians and journalists.

I'm speaking, of course, of Pamela Geller.

Geller had organised an exhibition of cartoons of Mohammed in the city of Garland in response to another event that had been held there earlier the same year. In January, a 'Stand with the Prophet'[28] event was held in a publicly owned school building and featured New York City Imam Siraj Wahhaj. Wahhaj believes that American liberal democracy should be replaced by sharia, and endorses death by stoning.

In response, Geller and others organised a cartoon contest, featuring images of Mohammed, with keynote guest speaker Geert Wilders. On this occasion, free Americans exercising their fundamental rights were attacked by machine-gun wielding jihadists. Two jihadis opened fire outside the event and injured one guard. Police then killed both attackers. Thanks to the Americans' right to self-defence, only the jihadists were killed.

What is notable here is not just the fact that those calling for an end to American democracy can do so in safety, while those defending it cannot, but the reaction of the media to both stories. While there was scarcely a murmur about those seeking to crush democracy, those defending it were dealt a brutal blow.

The *Washington Post*[29] described Geller as "incendiary". Her

28 Breitbart News, "Outcry Over Coming 'Stand with the Prophet' Rally at Texas Public School Center," Breitbart, January 14, 2015, accessed April 28, 2018. http://www.breitbart.com/texas/2015/01/14/outcry-over-coming-stand-with-the-prophet-rally-at-texas-public-school-center/.
29 Https://www.facebook.com/lindseybever, "Pamela Geller, the Incendiary Organizer of Texas 'prophet Muhammad Cartoon Contest'," Washington Post, May 4, 2015, https://www.washingtonpost.com/news/morning-mix/wp/2015/05/04/why-a-woman-named-pamela-geller-organized-a-prophet-muhammad-cartoon-contest/.

words were described as "wild rhetoric", and her condemnation by the Southern Poverty Law Center, an organisation that claims to "fight hate", was treated as though it was all that was needed as proof of her 'guilt'. The Southern Poverty Law Center doesn't seem to have much of a problem with sharia, though[30]. On its website, it says the following about anti-sharia or anti-Islamisation groups:

> *"These groups also typically hold conspiratorial views regarding the inherent danger to America posed by its Muslim-American community. Muslims are depicted as a fifth column intent on undermining and eventually replacing American democracy and Western civilization with Islamic despotism. Anti-Muslim hate groups allege that Muslims are trying to subvert the rule of law by imposing on Americans their own Islamic legal system, Shariah law."*

But hang on, what about the fact that people were actually calling for an end to democracy, to be replaced by sharia, in Garland only months before Geller's cartoon exhibition? Where was the Southern Poverty Law Center then? Will it at least acknowledge that some Muslims are calling for sharia in America, and that it is those Muslims that Geller objects to? Don't bet on it.

The story doesn't end there. Not long after her cartoon exhibition, a further attempt was made on Pamela Geller's life. Yet again, she would receive no sympathy from the media. The unspoken argument was simply that she deserved it. For speaking her mind. In the land of the free.

CNN's Alisyn Camerota said, "What people are saying is that there's always this fine line, you know, between freedom of speech and being intentionally incendiary and provocative"[31].

This is how a person is treated when they utilise America's constitutionally guaranteed freedom of speech – particularly

---

30 "Anti-Muslim," Southern Poverty Law Center, accessed April 28, 2018, https://www.splcenter.org/fighting-hate/extremist-files/ideology/anti-muslim.

31 Https://www.facebook.com/erik.wemple, "Pamela Geller Beheading Plot: Who's Needlessly Provocative Now?," Washington Post, June 4, 2015, https://www.washingtonpost.com/blogs/erik-wemple/wp/2015/06/04/pamela-geller-beheading-plot-whos-needlessly-provocative-now/.

when that freedom is used to criticise aspects of Islam. But, where Geller is concerned, it was about to get even worse.

In March 2015, Usaamah Abdullah Rahim was killed by police in Boston, Massachusetts. According to MSNBC:

> "*Rahim, 26, was killed Tuesday morning after he was stopped for questioning. The FBI said Wednesday that Rahim was the subject of a terrorism investigation into an alleged plot to kill law enforcement officers sometime this week. The law enforcement sources said Rahim chose that course only after he worked on plans to travel to New York and behead Pamela Geller.*"

So a jihadist had made plans to murder Ms Geller. The media must have been on her side then, right?

No. A CNN host asked Geller if she relished being the butt of death threats [32].

There are a couple things implied here:

- Geller is just an attention seeker who doesn't care if that attention gets her killed
- There is no real problem with free speech and Islam in America, it's all just a crazy fantasy dreamt up by Pamela Geller
- The American media is in denial. It continues to insist that Geller is the problem, having apparently forgotten entirely about the most important document in this debate – the Constitution of the United States of America.

OBAMA'S MOSQUE VISIT

Back in Baltimore, the venue chosen by the US President for his first official mosque visit was controversial (but one wonders

---

32 "Pam Geller Asked by CNN if She Relishes Islamic Death Threats After Boston Beheading Plot Revealed," The Washington Times, June 4, 2015, http://www. washingtontimes.com/news/2015/jun/4/pam-geller-asked-cnn-if-she-relishes-death-threats/.

how easy it would have been to find one that wasn't). This was partly due to Mohamad Adam El-Sheikh, who had served as imam at the mosque over two separate periods from 1983–1989 and 1994–2003, and had been a member of the Muslim Brotherhood. According to Fox[33]:

> *"During his time in Baltimore, El-Sheikh was a regional director for the Islamic American Relief Agency, the international parent organization of which has been cited by the U.S. Treasury Department for connections to Al Qaeda and the Taliban. After 2003, he was the imam for the Dar Al-Hijrah Islamic Center in Falls Church, Va., near Washington. It was there that Awlaki, just months earlier, gave his fiery sermons, before going on to be a top Al Qaeda affiliate operative in Yemen. Awlaki, a U.S. citizen, was killed in a U.S. drone strike in 2011."*

The *Washington Post*[34] reports El-Sheikh as having said:

> *"If certain Muslims are to be cornered where they cannot defend themselves, except through these kinds of means, and their local religious leaders issued fatwas to permit that, then it becomes acceptable as an exceptional rule, but should not be taken as a principle."*

In Alabama in 1955, black people were expected to give up their seat on public transport if a white person wanted it. Buses were segregated between black and white, with black people at the back. One day in 1955, Rosa Parks refused to give her seat to a white man, and as a result, became an icon of the Civil Rights Movement in the US. I've no doubt whatsoever that had Barack

---

33 "Obama's Mosque Visit Demonstrates Tacit Acceptance of a Form of Gender Apartheid," Women in the World, February 3, 2016, http://nytlive.nytimes.com/womenintheworld/2016/02/03/obamas-mosque-visit-demonstrates-tacit-acceptance-of-a-form-of-gender-apartheid/.
34 "Facing New Realities As Islamic Americans (washingtonpost.com)," Washington Post: Breaking News, World, US, DC News & Analysis - The Washington Post, accessed April 28, 2018, http://www.washingtonpost.com/wp-dyn/articles/A14497-2004Sep11.html.

Obama been a political activist in 1955, he would have been right there fighting for black people to sit where they like.

In a certain Baltimore mosque, though, Obama didn't seem to mind the fact that women were 'sent to the back of the bus'. Muslim women protested because in the Baltimore mosque, women are relegated to partitioned prayer spaces, drab compared to the wide open space reserved for men[35]. Raheel Raza, an activist with the Muslim Reform Movement, was reported in the *New York Times*[36] as stating:

> "*While the free world awaits a Muslim reformation, the leader of the free world shows blatant disregard for gender equality by visiting a mosque that treats females like second-class citizens.*"

What is of equal importance is what Obama said when he was there. The visit took place shortly after surprise US Presidential contender, the billionaire Donald Trump, had made an extraordinary speech in December 2015, calling for a "*complete and total shutdown*" of the country's borders to Muslims[37].

Americans are of course entirely free to disagree with Donald Trump, and to utilise their First Amendment rights to oppose him robustly – with words. But the new developments in free speech in the US mean that opposition is being replaced by censorship. The then President of the United States appeared to concur. Not only did Obama use his Baltimore speech to tell Americans that the mosque he was speaking from was very similar to their church (are women made to sit in the cattle pen in US churches?), but he wasted no time in

35 "Muslim Women Protest Obama's Baltimore Mosque Visit," Algemeiner.com, February 4, 2016, accessed April 28, 2018, https://www.algemeiner.com/2016/02/04/muslim-women-protest-obamas-baltimore-mosque-visit/.
36 "Obama's Mosque Visit Demonstrates Tacit Acceptance of a Form of Gender Apartheid", Women in the World, February 3, 2016, accessed April 28, 2018, http://nytlive.nytimes.com/womenintheworld/2016/02/03/obamas-mosque-visit-demonstrates-tacit-acceptance-of-a-form-of-gender-apartheid/.
37 Diamond, Jeremy, "Donald Trump: Ban All Muslim Travel to U.S. – CNNPolitics," CNN, December 08, 2015, accessed April 28, 2018, http://edition.cnn.com/2015/12/07/politics/donald-trump-muslim-ban-immigration/.

letting the country know that what Trump had to say about Islam "has no place" in free America[38].

The free speech of a Presidential candidate, whether politically correct or not, whether offensive or not, has every place in America. Its place is guaranteed by the First Amendment to the US Constitution.

Obama went on to say:

> "No surprise, then, that threats and harassment of Muslim Americans have surged. Here at this mosque, twice last year, threats were made against your children. Around the country, women wearing the hijab...have been targeted. We've seen children bullied. We've seen mosques vandalized. Sikh Americans and others who are perceived to be Muslims have been targeted, as well."

Donald Trump later cancelled a rally in Chicago[39] when violent clashes broke out among protestors and supporters. In scenes not seen for decades in the United States, a Presidential political rally was deemed too unsafe to go ahead. This thinking is becoming more and more common in America, and will become more common still as the children in school get older.

38 "Remarks by the President at Islamic Society of Baltimore," The White House, February 03, 2016, accessed April 29, 2018, https://www.whitehouse.gov/the-press-office/2016/02/03/remarks-president-islamic-society-baltimore.

39 Buncombe, Andrew, New York, "Donald Trump Abandons Chicago Rally after Violent Clashes Erupt," The Independent, March 12, 2016, accessed April 29, 2018, http://www.independent.co.uk/news/world/americas/us-elections/donald-trump-calls-off-chicago-rally-due-to-security-concerns-a6927011.html.

INDOCTRINATION IN
THE UNITED STATES

ORGANIZED PRAYER IS banned in American state schools, having been ruled unconstitutional in 1963. It is a divisive and touchy area of debate in the US, and public opinion on the matter has fluctuated. It has also been an area of much legal to-ing and fro-ing (most of which is beyond the scope of this book), but in summary, case law over the years has determined that school-sponsored religious activity is prohibited, as is the promulgation of sponsored prayer. According to a 1971 ruling, any practices sponsored within state schools must neither advance nor inhibit religion, must be for a secular purpose, and must not entangle the church with the state. These are all very broad and I have no doubt will be debated in the courts for years to come.

You would be forgiven for assuming that as a result of this ruling, no religion can be advanced, no religious prose-lytising permitted, and no religion is given greater credence than another in US schools.

Let's see.

SCHOOLS

A very interesting story emerged from the state of Georgia in 2011. Following a discussion on school uniforms at a public middle school, a young girl brought home some material that the school had provided to facilitate discussion. Within the material was a letter from Saudi Arabia. This is what it said:

> "*My name is Ahlima and I live in Saudi Arabia...
> Perhaps two differences Westerners would notice are that
> women here do not drive cars and they wear abuyah. An
> abuyah is a loose-fitting black cloth that covers a woman
> from head to toe. I like wearing the abuyah since it is very
> comfortable, and I am protected from blowing sand...I
> have seen pictures of women in the West and find their
> dress to be horribly immodest...Women in the West do not
> have the protection of the Sharia as we do here. If our
> marriage has problems, my husband can take another wife
> rather than divorce me, and I would still be cared for...I
> feel very fortunate that we have the Sharia.*"

Interestingly, Ahlima omits to mention the campaigns by Saudi women seeking the right to drive cars, and the suppression of these campaigns . It is difficult to know quite what to say about the matter-of-fact way in which she refers to the dress of Western women: we dress "immodestly" and as such "do not have the protection of the Sharia". Protection from what? Is rape one of things sharia would protect us from? If so, then it's not surprising that so many men under sharia feel they can attack women outside its 'protection' with impunity.

Ahlima also omits to mention the sharia 'protection' of death by stoning, or the demeaning and degrading notion that a woman's word should be worth half of her husband's, or that she has no divorce rights of her own.

This is one of the most appalling pieces of propaganda it has been my misfortune to read. The father of one of the school pupils who was forced to read this argued that it amounts to a positive depiction of Islam (which, of course, it does), but the school authorities did not agree. Instead, they justified it as part of a 12-week study of life in the Middle East.

Similarly, the abysmal practice of female sartorial containment was promoted as 'just another culture' in the state of Texas in February 2013[1] when young women were asked to wear the burqa so that they could learn more about the lives of Muslim women. According to one pupil, the teacher told the class, "We are going to work to change your perception of Islam." The students were then urged to refer to Islamist terrorists as 'freedom fighters'.

A change of perception indeed.

Meanwhile in Florida, a school was forced to defend textbooks which matter-of-factly declared Mohammed the 'messenger of God'[2]. Several complaints followed, including from school board member Amy Kneessy who was particularly upset by seeing "such a blatant misportrayal of how women are treated in Muslim countries". According to one report, the book contained a 36-page chapter on Islam, and advised that "Jihad may be interpreted as a holy war to defend Islam and the Muslim community, much like the Crusades to defend Christianity". William Saxton, the chairman of Citizens For National Security, testified before the school board, stating that the books "promote Islam at the expense of Christianity and Judaism".

A field trip to a mosque from a Colorado[3] school in 2015 was preceded by dress code instructions. Despite it being against US law to treat boys and girls differently at school, only girls were instructed to dress in a sharia-compliant way and bring something to cover their heads.

Just like in Britain, American schools are showing intention to reschedule their timetables around Islamic holidays. The

---

1 Greenfield, Daniel, "Texas High School Tells Teenage Girls to Wear Burqas", Frontpage Mag. Feb 26, 2013, accessed April 29, 2018, https://www.frontpagemag.com/point/179005/texas-high-school-tells-teenage-girls-wear-burqas-daniel-greenfield.
2 "School Defends Textbook Calling Muhammad 'God's Messenger? | Education News," Education News, last modified August 13, 2014, http://www.educationviews.org/school-defends-textbook-calling-muhammad-gods-messenger/.
3 "Colorado School District Requires Girls to Cover Ankles, Wear Head Scarves on Trip to Mosque," EAGnews.org, last modified January 8, 2015, http://eagnews.org/colorado-school-district-requires-girls-to-cover-ankles-wear-head-scarves-for-trip-to-mosque/.

Waterbury Board[4] of Education in Connecticut sent a note to schools, also in 2015, asking them to "be sensitive to the Muslim holidays in regards to scheduling assessments and major events that happen through the district".

Americans had better get used to it. In Pine Bush, New York, a celebration of Foreign Languages meant that the morning's school announcements, including the Pledge of Allegiance (where US school-children plead loyalty to the United States), were made in Arabic. It seems odd that Arabic was the language chosen for Foreign Language Week – not French, or Spanish, or German, or Japanese. The decision divided the school, and apparently the Arabic Pledge of Allegiance caused significant outrage among students – and from some parents.

According to one report[5], this is the not the first time the school in question had caused some controversy. "In 2013, Jewish parents sued the district and administrators in federal court, accusing them of being indifferent to chronic anti-Semitic behavior."

Several further stories of Islam being propagated in American schools have come to light over the last couple of years. In New Jersey, for example, the Islamic shahada (declaration of faith –"There is no God but Allah and Mohammed is his messenger") was required to be stated by pupils in a homework assignment. After watching a cartoon to teach them of the five pillars of Islam, children were asked to fill in the blanks: "There is no God but [blank] and [blank] is his messenger". Two parents who complained said that the school district was "suppressing discussion about Christianity while prose-lytizing Islam"[6].

UNIVERSITY

While not endowed with the same non-religious obliga-tions as lower level schools, American universities – like their

---

4 Matt Buynak, "Waterbury Schools to Respect Muslim Holidays," WTNH, February 06, 2015, accessed April 29, 2018, http://wtnh.com/2015/02/05/waterbury-schools-to-respect-muslim-holidays/.

5 "Arabic Version of Pledge of Allegiance at Pine Bush High School Ignites Furor," Recordonline.com, March 19, 2015, accessed April 29, 2018, http://www.recordonline.com/article/20150318/NEWS/150319327.

6 Matt Katz, "Allegations of Islam Indoctrination Spread to New Jersey, WNYC, WNYC.org, April 10, 2017, accessed April 29, 2018, https://www.wnyc.org/story/allegations-islam-indoctrination-public-schools-spread-nj/.

British counterparts – are becoming increasingly embroiled in Islam-related disputes. One high-profile incident took place at an event at Portland State University, where some students had gathered to watch the award-winning film *Obsession*. The film documents what it calls "radical Islam's war on the west"[7]. During the broadcast, some students gathered to shout "Shame" at those in attendance. One protestor argued the following:

> "*This is not acceptable. I am a Muslim, and I am also an American. I'm extremely offended by what these people put forward. If PSU [Portland State University] wants to create a space where the Muslim students, and all the students of color, and of all races will be safe, if that is what they want to create, then they need to be held accountable. I understand, I am all about freedom of speech, I totally get that, but when you cross the line into preaching hate, then we are in this situation[8].*"

It appears that this man, by virtue of being a Muslim, believes that he should be the one to define when the line into preaching hate has been crossed. He also seems to believe that he should determine what the limits to free speech are. Finally, he has done the obligatory and implied that criticism of Islam amounts to racism.

Following this, a woman stood up and, referring to the Second World War, said:

> "*...and you guys cannot see the parallel? I am sorry. My first babysitter from my youngest daughter was a woman who fled [from Nazi Germany]...people died in that war to help free other people, I can't believe that you think this [the film] is hate.*"

7 "Obsession – Radical Islam's War Against the West", accessed April 29, 2018, Obsessionthemovie.com. http://www.obsessionthemovie.com/.

8 Theunitedwest, "Islam Supporters Bully College Republicans Out Of Their Own Event," YouTube, June 02, 2013, accessed April 29, 2018, http://www.youtube.com/watch?v=_jOzDykg_uo.

She was then subjected to a diatribe by a self-righteous (and I suspect self-appointed) spokesperson, wearing what appeared to be a keffiyeh – a scarf often worn by 'free Palestine' activists:

> "*The problem with this type of film is it basically paints a whole group of people in a certain type of way. It doesn't just deal with a certain kind of political ideology; what it does is it paints one group of people and one religion with a broad brush.*"

It is clear from her tirade that this sanctimonious spokesperson had not actually seen the film at all.

Here is part of the first few lines of the film:

> "*This is a film about radical Islamic terror. A dangerous ideology fuelled by religious hatred. It's important to remember, most Muslims are peaceful and do not support terror. This is not a film about them. This is a film about a radical worldview and the threat it poses to us all: Muslim and non-Muslim alike.*"

In a motion remarkably similar to the one passed at the London School of Economics, the Associated Students at the University of California (ASUC) at Berkeley voted unanimously to support a resolution "condemning Islamophobic hate speech at the University of California"[9]. Predictably, the resolution took it upon itself to define 'Islamophobia' as "the irrational fear of Islam, Muslims, or anything related to the Islamic or Arab cultures and traditions". Notably, the resolution doesn't limit itself, as it should, to harassment of or prejudice against Muslims as human beings. Yet again, it equates Muslims (human beings) with Islam (a religion). This immediately, and deliberately, confuses race and religion.

The resolution becomes even more troublesome by virtue of its "anything related to" clause. Presumably, sharia law is related to Islamic culture, and criticism of this is therefore out of bounds.

---

9 "ASUCD Senate Passes Resolution Condemning Islamophobia," The Aggie, last modified May 3, 2013, https://theaggie.org/2013/05/02/asucd-senate-passes-resolution-condemning-islamophobia/.

Like the LSE resolution, this one amounts to censorship of all things remotely connected to Islam, and given that few seem able to agree what is or isn't connected with Islam, students are likely to err on the side of caution and say nothing at all – which I suspect is the aim.

SHARIA IN THE US

Several US states, including Tennessee, Louisiana, and Arizona, have passed laws barring judges from consulting sharia, or more generally, foreign or religious laws. Oklahoma voters approved a ban on sharia law in 2010, but this was overturned on a religious freedom lawsuit. Accusations of hyperbole and prejudice have routinely been made against people arguing for a ban on sharia, many claiming that there is no need for a ban as there is no appetite for sharia. However, there is much evidence that a case in favour of sharia is being made in the US, and increasing numbers of Muslims are backing its introduction. Furthermore, there is also evidence of a growing appetite for hard-line Islamic punishments.

A survey of American Muslims was carried out by Wenzel Strategies, a public-opinion research and media consulting company, in 2012. The poll found[10]:

- 40% of American Muslims would prefer to live under sharia law
- 46% believe that those who insult Mohammed should face criminal prosecution
- 12% believe those insulting Mohammed should face the death penalty

The documentary 'The Third Jihad'[11] revealed that the attitudes being preached to American Muslims should cause serious alarm. The Islamic Thinkers Society at a rally in New York City

---

10 "WND Survey of Muslims in America", Wenzel Strategies, Wenzelstrategies. com, October 28, 2012, accessed April 29, 2018, http://www.wnd.com/files/2012/10/WenzelMuslimsQ14.pdf.
11 "The THIRD JIHAD | RADICAL ISLAM's Vision for America (Full Documentary HD)," YouTube, October 01, 2016, accessed April 29, 2018, https://www.youtube.com/watch?v=VwqdFMq7QYY.

castigated "dirty homosexuals", proclaiming: "We are Muslims; we will never stay silent against this act." Abu Mujahid, a spokesman, said he would give homosexuals "a choice of therapy, or abandoning their homosexual lifestyle" and if they didn't, they could "either leave or...face the punishment [as a criminal]". The punishment, he confirmed, was being thrown from a cliff.

Another spokesman for the Islamic Thinkers Society tells us that "Islam will dominate, that's how it will be."

HIZB UT-TAHRIR

Hizb ut-Tahrir (HT) is a notorious Islamist group active the world over. In 2013, the Anti-Defamation League[12] produced a document entitled 'Hizb ut-Tahrir Emerges in America'[13]. It claims that HT is "increasing efforts to spread a pro-sharia message in the US".

Hizb ut-Tahrir's message is quite unequivocal – it seeks a global caliphate under sharia law. The Anti-Defamation League report states that Hizb ut-Tahrir, formerly a clandestine organisation in America, has begun to emerge on to the public stage with conferences and street protests. It also claims that HT has increased its internet presence. At several conferences in the US over the last decade, HT has hosted speakers who have denounced democracy and called for the rule of Allah, and they have a very specific vision of what the rule of Allah will look like:

- Women must obey their husbands, cover themselves, not hold powerful positions, or be around men other than family members
- Muslims who "have by themselves renounced Islam... are guilty of apostasy (ridda) from Islam [and] are to be executed"
- Societies must support an economic model which

12 Chomsky, Noam, "Necessary Illusions", ©1989, accessed April 29, 2018, http://home.nvg.org/~skars/ni/ni-c10-s20.html
13 "Hizb ut-Tahrir Emerges in America", Anti-Defamation League, updated July 25, 2013, accessed April 29, 2018, http://www.adl.org/assets/pdf/combating-hate/Hizb-ut-Tahrir-Emerges-in-America-2013-07-25-v1.pdf.

reserves public ownership of utilities, public transport, health care, energy resources such as oil, and unused farm land

(You can see where they find common ground with the political Left.)

There is no doubt that HT seeks a global state under sharia law where there will be no free speech, women will be servants, and who knows what fate will await the Jews. The anti-Semitism of HT is not hard to uncover. Fadi Abdelatif, Hizb ut-Tahrir's spokesman in Denmark, was found guilty of distributing racist propaganda by passing out leaflets containing a quote from the Koran which read, "And kill them wherever you find them, and turn them out from where they have turned you out", followed by a passage stating, "The Jews are a people of slander...a treacherous people"[14].

It is also of little doubt that HT is increasing its visibility and presence in the US. According to the website Hizb ut-Tahrir Watch[15]:

> "[Hizb ut-Tahrir America's] *membership has swelled, putting on track its objective of persuading the global ummah that the establishment of a caliphate—ostensibly through non-violent means—is essential to reverse the decline of Islamic society. Globally, HT presents itself as confident and optimistic, and it is progressing according to the strategy its founding members outlined in 1953. Hizb-ut-Tahrir America (HTA) is enjoying a similar pattern of progress.*"

This group is, of course, entitled to free speech, but my question is this: where is the mainstream opposition to what Hizb ut-Tahrir is saying?

---

14 "Programmes | Newsnight | Hizb Ut Tahrir," BBC News, August 27, 2003, accessed April 29, 2018, http://news.bbc.co.uk/1/hi/programmes/newsnight/3182271.stm.
15 "Hizb-ut-Tahrir Activities in America", Terrorism Monitor 5, no. 16 (August 22, 2007), Posted March 11, 2013, accessed April 29, 2018, http://thehizbuttahrirwatch. wordpress.com/category/news-about-hizb-ut-tahrir/hut-america/activities-in-us/.

MUSLIM MAFIA

In the controversial book *Muslim Mafia,* the authors allege that a concerted effort is being made to Islamise America and subject it to sharia law. One of them spent time working with the Council on American Islamic Relations and removed some documents, which he published to provide evidence of this effort.

The foreword to the book was written by Republican Member of Congress Sue Myrick, who included the statement:

> *"Most Americans do not know about recently declassified documents detailing their secret plot to take over the United States from within – a plot launched by Islamist groups tied to the dangerous Muslim Brotherhood, which is based in Egypt and which is funded primarily by wealthy Saudis and Emirates. And these groups are already in this country, building an impressive infrastructure of support for the jihadist enemy."*

The book caught the attention of other Congress members who insisted the claims that key national-security committees which had had 'spies' planted in them by CAIR be investigated[16]. The comments of these Congress members were denounced as racist by CAIR, and many Democrats were equally displeased, Loretta Sanchez of California describing it as a "witch-hunt".

Given its propensity to do so, CAIR began a lawsuit against the author and attempted to have him barred from publicising documents he had taken during his time there. The suit alleged conversion, breach of fiduciary duty, breach of contract, trespass, and violation of the Electronic Communications Privacy Act – but interestingly, not libel. The full Memorandum of Opinion can be found here: https://ecf.dcd.uscourts.gov/cgi-bin/show_public_doc?2009cv2030-10

---

16 Jordy Yager, "House Republicans Accuse Muslim Group of Trying to Plant Spies," TheHill, February 04, 2016, accessed April 29, 2018, http://thehill.com/homenews/house/63023-republicans-accuse-muslim-advocacy-group-of-trying-to-plant-spies.

Here are some highlights:

- CAIR alleges that Defendants conceived and implemented a deliberate and concerted scheme to place Defendant Chris Gaubatz in an internship with CAIR under an assumed name and based upon other false representations and material omissions. CAIR further alleges that, as a consequence of these false representations and material omissions, Defendant Chris Gaubatz obtained access to CAIR's facilities and documents and proceeded to remove more than 12,000 of CAIR's internal documents and to make video and audio recordings of private meetings and conversations involving CAIR's officials and employees without consent or authorization.
- CAIR requested a Temporary Restraining Order and a Preliminary Injunction.
- CAIR alleged that Chris Gaubatz, under the pseudonym David Marshall, dishonestly secured a position as an intern, and had they known his real name or intentions – which they described as "spying on CAIR and other Muslim organizations" – they would not have allowed him access to their property or documentation.
- CAIR argued that Gaubatz had signed a Confidentiality and Non-Disclosure Agreement, of which he was now in breach.
- It was also alleged that Gaubatz had accessed information beyond the scope of what was permitted to him.
- CAIR claimed that Gaubatz had stolen documents that were confidential and not for distribution and had caused such to be published.
- CAIR have, since publication, received 'threats'.
- CAIR sought an order to: (1) enjoin Defendants from making any use, disclosure or publication of any (a) documents (including emails and other electronic documents) or copies thereof obtained from any office or facility of CAIR, or (b) recording (whether audio or video) of meetings of or conversations involving CAIR

officials or employees, or copies thereof; (2) require Defendants to promptly remove such documents and/or recordings from any blog or other Internet site under their control; and (3) require Defendants to promptly return such documents and recordings to CAIR.

- The Court made an order that Gaubatz return any documentation featuring attorney-client privileged information, proprietary donor information, and personnel information. It also ordered that such information be removed from P. David Gaubatz's blog [Chris's father and primary author of the book].

Below is a list of claims made in *Muslim Mafia*:

- CAIR planted spies inside key law enforcement agencies; while a few have been busted for tipping off terrorist suspects, many others still operate undetected
- CAIR has previously unreported ties to al-Qaida – in addition to Hamas – and has worked closely with al-Qaida field commanders inside America
- The group is running an influence operation against members of key homeland security committees on Capitol Hill and planting Islamist spies in congressional offices
- CAIR and its sister organization the Islamic Society of North America have struck a secret pact to attack Wall Street firms who do not comply with Islamic financing principles
- Executives from CAIR travel regularly to the Middle East to raise cash, and wire transfers show Saudi princes have donated hundreds of thousands of dollars to CAIR – even though the group claims to have received no foreign support
- A CAIR official working out of the group's Washington headquarters was the ringleader of a terrorist cell that chauffeured the 9/11 imam to secret meetings during which they plotted to kill Americans
- During the 2004 presidential campaign, CAIR organised

a 'task force' of Muslim Brotherhood fronts to hammer out an agenda which included supporting Osama bin Laden

- CAIR sent $40,000 to a Hamas front group just months before that same group wired $40,000 overseas to Hamas
- The organization's founder hosted the notorious Blind Sheik at his home during the period when the cleric was plotting to blow up the World Trade Center
- CAIR board members and advisers have privately advocated "Uzi jihads" against American cities and attacks on military planes transporting American soldiers from Fort Bragg
- CAIR defrauded poor Muslim immigrants out of thousands of dollars in a legal scam, and then covered up the scandal when the victims threated to go to American media sources
- The group launched campaigns to blacklist media personalities Bill O'Reilly, Dr. Laura Schlessinger, Glenn Beck, and Michael Savage, while successfully pressing 24 and National Review to acquiesce to their demands

I am, for obvious reasons, not going to display all of the details or evidence provided by the writers to back up these claims, but it is fair to say that they demonstrate a damning indictment of the Council on American Islamic Relations.

CAIR is also, according to P David Gaubatz, the primary author of *Muslim Mafia*, "putting books into neighborhood libraries across the country advising men to beat their wives – but only lightly – when they disobey them" and "lobbying the Justice Department and local law enforcement to exempt Muslim wife-beaters from laws against domestic violence, or at least look the other way and let Muslim clerics intervene when Muslims are involved in spousal battery cases". This mirrors campaigns in the UK by Muslim groups which seek to self-police Islamic communities in matters of domestic violence. Of course, domestic violence is permitted under sharia law, and as such it is the right of Muslim husbands to beat their wives.

THE AMERICA CIVIL LIBERTIES UNION

The America Civil Liberties Union (ACLU) describes itself as the nation's guardian of liberty[17]. It also claims to fight for equal protection under the law and to stand up for women's rights. One might expect the ACLU, therefore, to work in opposition to CAIR, or any Islamist group, to make absolutely sure that sharia law can never be applicable, or have any effect on the lives of women in America. But no, it does not.

In August 2013, a Federal Court overturned a ban that had been voted for by the people of Oklahoma on the use of sharia law in any courts there. The campaign to have the ban over-turned was led by the Council on American Islamic Relations and the American Civil Liberties Union.

The ACLU's line on this was that "Laws that single out Sharia violate the First Amendment by treating one belief system as suspect"[18], and as such it amounted to an infringement of the right to equality (and no doubt religious freedom). It didn't occur to the ACLU that sharia might deserve to be singled out because of the very real threat it poses to women. Nor did it occur to it to examine the reality of sharia in other countries, or the intent of those who seek it in the US. Instead, the ACLU presumably swallowed the argument that the harsh elements of sharia would not be employed in America because a new 'American sharia' would emerge.

This is, on the face of it, a considerable argument. But it supposes that sharia is fluid and is distinct from nation to nation. However, when it comes to the treatment of women, rules are rigid and apply irrespective of where one happens to be. ACLU might want to look to the UK and examine 'British sharia' and see exactly how women suffer under its dictates here. Sharia in the UK, in terms of domestic violence and family law, is identical to that of any Islamic state.

If the ACLU is unconvinced that CAIR has a sharia law agenda at all, it might be interested to learn of a meeting which

---

17 "About the ACLU," American Civil Liberties Union, accessed April 29, 2018, https://www.aclu.org/about-aclu-0.
18 "Bans on Sharia and International Law," American Civil Liberties Union, accessed April 29, 2018, https://www.aclu.org/religion-belief/bans-sharia-and-international-law.

took place in Detroit in 2013. According to *The Arab Amer-ican*[19], an article that one of its writers produced on the difficul-ties Muslim women experience in obtaining an Islamic divorce prompted the meeting.

On 25 September 2013, a number of imams got together to discuss the idea of setting up a tribunal network to handle Islamic divorce cases. The meeting was attended by the execu-tive director of CAIR who is quoted to have said that the imams agreed that Muslim women were subject to injustices in relation to marriage. To fix this, they suggested a network of sharia tribu-nals, not unlike those in the UK. I have described these in detail in the 'United Kingdom' section, but in summary, these tribunals are known to deny women divorce, even in cases of domestic violence. They make decisions on child custody, as well as on criminal matters such as violence and marital rape. Women are treated appallingly in British sharia tribunals, and the Executive Director of CAIR would like to see the same in America – and all with the tacit support of the ACLU.

The ACLU's defence of sharia law really matters. It allows Islamists to disguise its true dangers, and portrays those of us who understand these dangers as haters or bigots. The ACLU position causes much confusion. If a group which describes itself as a defender of women also defends sharia, its followers will likely erroneously believe that sharia presents no threat to women.

THE US MILITARY AND THE FBI

The sanitisation and misrepresentation of sharia, as well as the use of 'rights' language, is key to its advancement. Within the US military and security services, this is particularly dangerous. In order to shape our understanding of sharia or Islamist aims, Islamists must have control of our perception of the threat they pose, which in turn enables them to control our responses. It is

19 Natasha Dado, "For women, getting an Islamic divorce can be difficult", The Arab American News, September 20, 2013, accessed April 29, 2018, http://www.arabamericannews.com/2013/09/20/For-women-getting-an-Islamic-divorce-can-be-difficult/.

no secret what the intentions of the Muslim Brotherhood are – "eliminating and destroying the Western civilisation from within and sabotaging its miserable house by their hands"[20]. It is also no secret that it has front groups all over the Western world. It is no secret what CAIR leaders have said, what key figures in the Muslim Council of Britain have said, or what these organisations think of women, free speech, and democracy. Why people in the West do not vehemently oppose them stems from a combination of fear, guilt, and sheer bloody-minded denial. We refuse to see what is staring us in the face, and the US military is every bit as guilty as the rest of us.

According to a report by the American think-tank, the Center for Security Policy[21], a member of the Muslim Brotherhood, Lousay Safi (also an activist with the Islamic Society of North America), taught the principles of Islamic doctrine to American troops as they prepared for deployment to Iraq and Afghanistan. The report also describes the 2010 versions of the Pentagon's Quadrennial Defense Review, the Homeland Security Department's Quadrennial Review, and the National Security Strategy of the White House. All reports adhere to the demand that the words 'shariah', 'Islam' or 'jihad' not be used when discussing the terrorist threat facing the United States.

These terminological constraints resulted from demands made by the Muslim Brotherhood.

The FBI also panders to Islamists, and in doing so, undermines American security. The Council on American Islamic Relations, for example, has trained FBI officers on Islam, and on how to treat Muslims. CAIR argues that Muslims should not be treated like other Americans, but be given special considerations. This separate and distinct treatment of Muslims is deliberately sought because it lays the foundations for the application of sharia within America. The message is this: "Muslims cannot live

---

20 Mohamed Akram, "An Exploratory Memorandum on the General Strategic Goal for the Brotherhood in America", The Investigative Project on Terrorism, May 19, 1991, accessed April 29, 2018, https://www.investigativeproject.org/document/20-an-explanatory-memorandum-on-the-general.

21 Adm. James "Ace" Lyons, "Forcing our all-volunteer force to fail", The Center for Security Policy, August 10, 2012, accessed April 29, 2018, https://www.centerforsecuritypolicy.org/2012/08/10/forcing-our-all-volunteer-force-to-fail/.

with the same laws as everyone else. We are different, we must have our own laws. If you don't allow this, you are oppressing us. You are racist."

According to the author of *Muslim Mafia*, CAIR has trained the NYPD, several FBI offices, Detroit Police, Sacramento Police, Elk Grove (California) Police, California Highway Patrol, Cleveland Police, Chicago Ridge Police, Texas Police Association, and many other law enforcement agencies. Interestingly, it has also trained the US Citizenship and Immigration Services, US Immigration and Customs Enforcement, and US Customs and Border Protection. The type of training that law enforcement and officials received from CAIR is displayed in its 'Law Enforcement Official's Guide to the Muslim Community'[22]. This demands that officers create a culturally-sensitive environment between American Muslims and law enforcement. It makes clear that Islam requires believers to work together to promote good and forbid evil, but does not offer a definition of either word. It also highlights the accommodation that should be made with regard to dogs and the separation of the sexes. Law enforcers are further required to respect the privacy of the suspect if frisking or conducting a strip-search.

The guide goes on to condemn anti-Muslim remarks as engendering distrust of authority among Muslims in America. What is meant by 'anti-Muslim remarks' is not clear.

Separate and distinct rules for Muslims lay the foundations of division, and by extension, the policing of Muslims in America by other Muslims. It is exactly as we have seen, and continue to see, in the United Kingdom – a country increasingly divided by a multicultural ethos that affords minority communities a separate status.

---

22 "A Law Enforcement Official's Guide to the Muslim Community," Council on Islamic Relations, April 30, 2003, article about it accessed April 29, 2018, https://www.cair.com/law_enforcement_community_offered_guide_to_muslims (linked page for the document discontinued).

DONALD TRUMP

US PRESIDENTIAL ELECTIONS are anxious affairs at the best of times. The rest of us, especially in the West, peer out from behind our cushions, waiting to see who or what the people of the world's superpower are going to inflict upon us next.

But the 2016 election was an anxiety-fest greater than any I've known before, and the media (or 'enemedia' as Pamela Geller calls it) could as usual be relied on to make the whole thing that much worse. It would pitch the first potential female American President, Hillary Clinton, against the flamboyant billionaire, Donald Trump.

Clinton was seen as the obvious favourite from the start, and the mainstream media made little secret of their preference for her. In the run-up to the election, Trump was painted as the devil incarnate. The media and the global elite went after him all guns blazing. This wasn't because of his business past, nor was it because he appears to be something of a womaniser. None of this really mattered (though the media pretended it did). Trump was the enemy because he said he would put the needs of Americans first, he would control his country's borders, and he would keep America safe from Islamic terrorists. The world's globalist elites simply would not permit such a show of nationalism and nation-state identity.

As night follows day, Donald Trump soon found himself labelled a 'racist'. It's right there in the *Washington Post* headline: "Donald Trump is the Most Unpopular Presidential Candidate Since the Former Head of the Ku Klux Klan"[1]. The *Huffington Post* doesn't leave you wondering what it means: "Trump's History of Misogyny is Worse Than You Thought"[2].

The media criticism wasn't limited to the US. Just days after Trump won the election, Conservative MP David Davies lashed out at the BBC for its blatant anti-Trump bias during the election campaign:

> *"All I know about Donald Trump is what I've seen through the British media, which is heavily biased against him. On the BBC it was clear that the TV presenters were appalled by his election. Yet many millions – half the American voters – must have believed they had good reasons for voting for him[3]."*

Here's a BBC headline from December 2015: "'Racist', 'Fascist', 'Utterly Repellent': What the World Said About Donald Trump[4]". Another one from August 2016: "Is the 2016 US Election Campaign Racist?[5]" This article contained the following paragraph:

> *"Who could imagine in 2016 that a vice-presidential candidate from one side would accuse the man running for*

1 "Donald Trump is the most unpopular presidential candidate since the former head of the Ku Klux Klan," The Washington Post, Last modified March 21, 2016, accessed April 29, 2018, https://www.washingtonpost.com/news/the-fix/wp/2016/03/21/the-last-presidential-candidate-who-was-as-unpopular-as-donald-trump-david-duke/.
2 JM Rieger, "Trump's History Of Misogyny Is Worse Than You Thought," The Huffington Post, September 30, 2016, accessed April 29, 2018, http://www.huffingtonpost.com/entry/donald-trump-misogyny-worse-thought_us_57edaa7be4b0c2407cdd1ca6.
3 Matt Dathan, Political Correspondent For Mailonline, "Tory MP Leads Furious Backlash against the BBC over Its 'biased' Coverage of Donald Trump's Election," Daily Mail Online, November 09, 2016, accessed April 29, 2018, http://www.dailymail.co.uk/news/article-3921030/Tory-MP-leads-furious-backlash-against-BBC-biased-coverage-Donald-Trump-s-election.html.
4 "'Racist', 'fascist', 'utterly Repellent': What the World Said about Donald Trump - BBC News", BBC, December 09, 2015, accessed April 29, 2018, http://www.bbc.co.uk/news/world-us-canada-35050186.
5 Gavin Hewitt, "Is the 2016 US Election Campaign Racist? - BBC News," BBC, August 30, 2016, accessed April 29, 2018, http://www.bbc.co.uk/news/election-us-2016-37219433.

president from the other side of pushing the 'values of the
Ku Klux Klan'? But that is what Tim Kaine said of Donald
Trump, denouncing him, in effect, for wanting to restore
white supremacy."

WHITELASH

The obvious contempt for Trump didn't stop after the election. BBC's *Question Time* (a panel discussion show immediately following the election) was extraordinary – extraordinary for someone who is not used to the BBC and its blatantly unapologetic left-wing bias, that is. Sarah Churchwell, Professor of American Literature, was the first to speak when she was asked why America had chosen Trump. After saying how complicated it all was, she mistakenly said, "Trump's re-election". She quickly followed this up with "heaven forbid" (cue sycophantic laughter and applause from the left-wing audience). More applause followed when she said Trump's victory had partly been the result of a "disinformation and character assassination campaign against Hillary Clinton". Yes, she actually said that.

When Jan Halper-Hayes of Republicans Overseas said that Clinton "represented the worst about capital cronyism and the problems of our government", she was booed. Halper-Hayes could scarcely get a word in edgeways. The chair David Dimbleby repeatedly had to silence the audience and panel.

My favourite, however, was Tasmina Ahmed-Sheikh – a Scottish MP who used sharia law in family disputes when she was a practising solicitor[6]. Ahmed-Sheikh found Trump's misogyny terribly problematic and complained about gender inequality generally.

Britain's politicians debated in Parliament whether or not to ban Donald Trump from the UK[7]. This is the same UK that has jihadi clerics inciting violence against women and Jews with absolute impunity.

I discuss anti-white hatred elsewhere in this book, and the

6 "MP and Former Lawyer Defends Use of Sharia 'courts'," Christian Concern, February 25, 2016, accessed April 30, 2018, http://www.christianconcern.com/our-concerns/islam/mp-and-former-lawyer-defends-use-of-sharia-courts.
7 "MPs to Debate Call to Ban Donald Trump from UK - BBC News," BBC, January 18, 2016, accessed April 30, 2018, http://www.bbc.co.uk/news/uk-politics-35321834.

US Presidential election result really brought it out into the open. Donald Trump's victory was declared a "whitelash" with widespread complaints that whites had inflicted this terror on America. Most strikingly, though, Trump's victory revealed not only a hatred of whites across America and the West, but an intense fear. Some might say that this is understandable given white people's previous dominance and cruelty to non-whites. But if generations of whites are presumed to be dangerous because of the actions of their ancestors, then the implication is that whiteness itself is the problem. Furthermore, it is only whites who should carry the perpetual burden of their forefathers' sins. People are bad because they are white.

That is the very essence of racism.

Take this example from the UK's *Guardian* the day after Trump's win[8]:

> *"But what this election also shows, what it will painfully bring out over the next four years, is that the ideology of whiteness in America is not going to bed without a fight."*

Got that? Being white is an ideology, apparently, and not a very nice one, either. Call Islam (which is an ideology) an ideology and you'll find yourself labelled a racist.

The UK's Left is no better, of course. Laurie Penny (the 'feminist') declared[9]:

> *"Today, all over America, black, brown and Muslim children are too frightened to go to school. Facts and figures may not win votes the way feelings do, but today's polling tells us that this election was not just about class, or gender, or partisan positioning. This election was, more than anything, about race. It was about white resentment, which is now among the greatest threats to global security.*

8 Moustafa Bayoumi, "Muslims Are Terrified, but We Won't Be Intimidated by Trump | Moustafa Bayoumi," The Guardian, November 10, 2016, accessed April 30, 2018, https://www.theguardian.com/commentisfree/2016/nov/10/muslims-trump-islamophobia?CMP=soc_3156.
9 "On the Election of Donald J Trump," New Statesman | Britain's Current Affairs & Politics Magazine, accessed April 30, 2018, https://www.newstatesman.com/world/north-america/2016/11/election-donald-j-trump-4.

It was about white rage, and there are a lot of us who need to own that inconvenient truth today lest it own us all tomorrow."

This is truly extraordinary. The white vote won an election so all non-whites are now in danger. It's as if the last few decades of race equality in the West have not taken place with the agreement of white people. This kind of rhetoric condemns white people as a threat to all non-whites; it's as insulting to one group as it is to the other. It is race hate in its purest form, but because white people are on the receiving end, it is never acknowledged as such, especially on the international stage.

THE UNITED NATIONS

The United Nations (UN) is not known for its consistency. It has a habit, for example, of singling out Israel for criticism while allowing vicious Islamic states to sit on human rights boards. Since the election of Donald Trump, however, the UN has had a new pariah to attack. It has denounced Trump's plans to build a wall on the border with Mexico and his notorious 'travel ban', while ignoring (even elevating) real human rights abusers around the world.

When Trump announced his plans to keep America safe from Islamic terrorism by preventing migration from specific Muslim nations, the UN was quick to respond and condemn. In February 2017, it stated that Trump was in breach of his human rights commitments as a result of the ban. A statement on the UN website[10] reads:

"Expressing concern that a new Executive Order by the United States President Donald Trump is in breach of the country's human rights commitments, a group of United Nations rights experts have called on the US to live up to its human rights obligations and provide protection for those fleeing persecution and conflicts.

10 "US Travel Ban a 'significant Setback' for Those Needing International Protection – UN Rights Experts | UN News," UN News Center, accessed April 30, 2018, http://www.un.org/apps/news/story.asp?NewsID=56082#.Wm66rJOFjow.

"Such an order is clearly discriminatory based on one's nationality and leads to increased stigmatization of Muslim communities."

One might conclude that if the UN is serious about nations living up to their human rights obligations, Saudi Arabia, a country that enslaves women and executes its citizens for blasphemy, would be top of its list for condemnation. But Saudi Arabia instead sits on its human rights council.

When the US President recognised Jerusalem as the capital city of Israel, the United Nations jumped. An emergency session of the General Assembly was convened in December 2017. No such emergency sessions take place when Islamic countries brutalise their own people for exercising their core rights, but this is par for the course with the UN.

The General Assembly, including the UK, voted overwhelmingly to condemn Trump. Trump's representatives were quick to reply.

"The United States will remember this day when it was singled out in the United Nations for the act of exercising our sovereignty. We will remember it when we are called upon to once again make the world's largest contribution to the United Nations. And we will remember it when so many countries come calling on us, as they so often do, to pay even more, and to use our influence for their benefit[11]."
Nikki Haley, Trump's Ambassador to the UN

This show of strength by the United States is precisely the right approach to take when dealing with an obviously biased UN. Sadly, the United Kingdom won't exercise its power in the world in a similar way, something it so desperately needs to do. Instead, the UK has joined in the demonisation of Trump, and the country will continue to suffer as a result.

---

11 Tim Hains, "Nikki Haley Threatens U.N. With Defunding Over Resolution Condemning U.S. Jerusalem Decision," Video | RealClearPolitics, accessed April 30, 2018, https://www.realclearpolitics.com/video/2017/12/21/nikki_haley_threatens_un_with_defunding_over_resolution_condemning_us_jerusalem_decision.html.

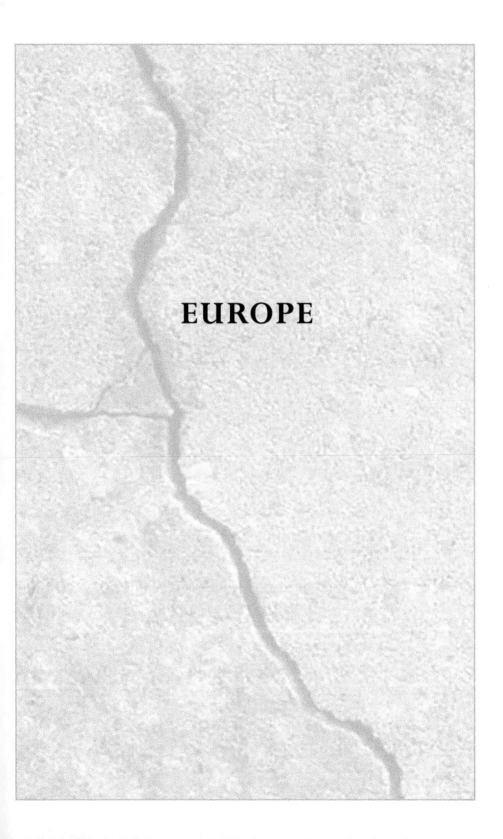

EUROPE

AUSTRIA, BELGIUM
AND DENMARK

AUSTRIA

ONE OF THE most controversial stories to emerge from Austria is that of Elisabeth Sabaditsch-Wolff. Sabaditsch-Wolff was convicted of denigrating religious beliefs under Section 188 of the Austrian Criminal Code when she was alleged to have made disparaging remarks to the Freedom Education Institute about the Islamic Prophet Mohammed at a conference in Vienna in 2009. She was secretly recorded doing so by a journalist.

Referring to Mohammed's marriage to nine-year-old Aisha, Sabaditsch-Wolff was reported to have said that Mohammed "had a thing for little girls" and compared his conduct to paedophilia. She was ordered to pay a fine of €480 when she was found guilty of the Section 188 charge (but not of original charges of hate speech). The judge in the case claimed that Mohammed's sexual contact with nine-year-old Aisha could not be considered paedophilia because the Prophet continued his marriage to her until his death. An interesting, and rather unfamiliar, analysis of paedophilia.

After the trial[1], Sabaditsch-Wolff said her conviction repre-sented "a black day for Austria". The Vienna Federation of Academics (*Wiener Akademikerbund*) said the ruling represented "politically and sentimentally motivated justice" and marked "the end of freedom of expression in Austria".

Also in 2009, a similar case was pursued against a member of Austria's Parliament, Susanne Winter, who was fined €24,000 for saying that "in today's system Mohammed would be considered a child molester". Winter also received a three month suspended jail sentence for the offence. She had been convicted of "incite-ment and degradation of religious symbols".

These cases received little to no coverage in the Western media. Austria's rape epidemic, however, could not be so easily ignored.

When Germany announced to the world that it was open to all comers in 2015, Austria and other European countries found themselves on the front line. Waves of migrants from the Middle East and Africa flooded into Austria, and the rape of Austrian women (and children) began immediately. Between January and April 2016, 28 rapes and sexual assaults were reported in the media[2]. This included a Cologne-like mob assault (see 'Germany') on New Year's Eve 2015 in the cities of Vienna, Salzburg, and Innsbruck.

One particular story which would make international head-lines was the rape of a young boy in Austria's increasingly perilous swimming pools. An Iraqi refugee known as Amir A raped a 10-year-old boy in a swimming pool toilet cubicle in Vienna in late 2015. The child was reported to have suffered "horrific inju-ries"[3]. After the rape, Amir calmly returned to the pool while a devastated and seriously injured child sought help.

Memorably, Amir told the world he had raped the child because he had suffered a "sexual emergency". Austria threw its

---

1 Soeren Kern, ""A Black Day for Austria"," Gatestone Institute, December 26, 2011, accessed April 30, 2018, http://www.gatestoneinstitute.org/2702/sabaditsch-wolff-appeal.

2 Soeren Kern, "Migrant Rape Epidemic Reaches Austria," Gatestone Institute, May 5, 2016, accessed April 30, 2018, https://www.gatestoneinstitute.org/7995/migrants-rape-austria.

3 "Migrant Who Raped Boy, Ten, Austrian in Swimming Pool Has Sentence Cut," Mail Online, May 24, 2017, accessed April 30, 2018, http://www.dailymail.co.uk/news/article-4536856/Migrant-raped-10-year-old-boy-swimming-pool-sentence-cut.html.

laws and morals up in the air trying to play down the significance of the fact that many of Europe's new migrants simply didn't see anything wrong with rape – of women or children. Having initially been sentenced to a measly six years in prison, Amir A found his sentence later reduced to just four[4]. Austria's response to its imported rapists was as it is across Europe: the rights of the rapist are primary and their victims are mere collateral damage in the brave new world of multiculturalism and open borders.

Austria, unlike other parts of Europe, has shown some mettle: in 2017, it banned the burqa[5], sent troops to the Italian border to close that route of entry[6], and elected a coalition government that had placed opposition to mass immigration at the heart of its platform. This was denounced all over Western Europe's media as a revival of Nazism and the ever-dreaded far Right[7]. The same media were less concerned about the wave of rape and assault spreading through Austria at the hands of immigrants.

BELGIUM

Belgium's first sharia court opened in 2011. Located in Antwerp, the country's second city, the court was initiated by the campaign group Shariah4Belgium, and mediated on matters of family law, including marriage, divorce and child custody. Shariah4Belgium claimed that the purpose of the court was to create a parallel Islamic legal system in Belgium and to challenge the state's authority as enforcer of the civil law[8]. It also expressed

---

4 "Migrant Who Raped 10-Year-Old Boy To Have Sentence Drastically Reduced," Breitbart News, May 24, 2017, accessed April 30, 2018, http://www.breitbart.com/london/2017/05/24/migrant-raped-10-year-old-boy-sentence-drastically-reduced/.
5 "Veil-Wearing Muslims Leave Austria As the Niqab Ban Kicks In," Breitbart News, December 12, 2017, accessed April 30, 2018, http://www.breitbart.com/london/2017/12/12/veiled-muslims-leave-austria-niqab-ban/.
6 "Austria to Send Troops and Armoured Vehicles to Border with Italy to Block Migrants," The Telegraph, accessed May 1, 2018, http://www.telegraph.co.uk/news/2017/07/04/austria-send-troops-armoured-vehicles-border-italy-block-migrants/.
7 Philip Oltermann, "Muted Protests in Vienna As Far-right Ministers Enter Austria's Government," The Guardian, December 18, 2017, accessed May 1, 2018, https://www.theguardian.com/world/2017/dec/18/thousands-protest-as-far-right-ministers-enter-government-in-austria.
8 Soeren Kern, "Islamic Sharia Law Court Opens in Belgium," Gatestone Institute, September 15, 2011, accessed May 1, 2018, http://www.gatestoneinstitute.org/2425/belgium-islamic-sharia-law-court.

a desire to handle criminal cases under sharia, just as Islamists have done in the UK. It believed it would soon turn the country into an Islamic state under full sharia law, promising stoning and beheading, as well as the death penalty for homosexuality and adultery. A representative described Belgians as dirty and perverted[9].

Shariah4Belgium was dissolved in late 2012. The closure of the organisation followed the imprisonment of its spokesman Fouad Belkacem (aka Abu Imran). He had been convicted of posting videos online calling for Muslims to fight against non-believers, and received a two year sentence[10].

The videos were made following violent protests against police who had arrested a Muslim woman for violating Belgium's laws on wearing face coverings in public. Belkacem was released from prison in February 2013, but was rearrested soon afterwards during police raids in April, when six Islamists, including Belkacem, were detained on suspicion of recruiting fighters for the war in Syria.

Belgian prosecutor Eric Van der Sypt told a news conference that "the investigation shows that Sharia4Belgium is part of a broad international jihadist movement"[11].

For Belgians worried about the encroachment of sharia into their country, The Islam Party should perhaps be of even greater concern. The party won its first seats on Belgian town councils in 2012. At a ceremony for new councillors in Anderlecht, a citizen from the public gallery interrupted proceedings to inform delegates:

> *"It is illegal, it is illegal. This gentleman* [newly elected Islam Party councillor] *has said he wants to enforce sharia. Sharia is incompatible with Belgian laws, with democratic laws, with the European Convention on Human Rights. It is not democracy. Sharia is not democratic."*

---

9 "Belgistan? Sharia Showdown Looms in Brussels - CBN.com," YouTube, March 15, 2012, accessed May 1, 2018, http://www.youtube.com/watch?v=SbMnA3uO9As.

10 "Belgium Arrests Islamist for Hate Video After Riot over Face Veil Arrest," Reuters, June 7, 2012, accessed May 1, 2018, http://blogs.reuters.com/faithworld/2012/06/07/belgium-arrests-islamist-for-hate-video-after-riot-over-face-veil-arrest/.

11 Soeren Kern, "Belgium Vs. Islamic Jihadists," Gatestone Institute, April 19, 2013, accessed May 1, 2018, http://www.gatestoneinstitute.org/3679/belgium-vs-islamic-jihadists.

For his trouble, he was told to shut up and get out[12].

The elections prompted some Belgian politicians to propose national legislation to limit the power of elected Islamists if their beliefs clash with the provisions of the European Convention on Human Rights[13]. Alain Destexhe, a liberal member of the Federation Wallonia-Brussels, presented this proposal and told Parliament:

> *"The people of The Islamic party do not want to be mixed with others in public transport and other communal places...They advocate getting married and wearing a veil at 12 years old, based on Islamic law[14]."*

According to one report, The Islam Party has announced plans to put forward candidates for regional and parliamentary elections in Belgium, as well as the European Parliament.

In March 2016, 31 people died in coordinated bomb attacks at Brussels's main airport as well as a major underground rail station. The bombings occurred days after Salah Abdeslam had been arrested as a key suspect in the attacks on Paris months before (see 'France'). Abdeslam had been hiding out in the now notorious district of Molenbeek in Brussels, and had apparently been protected by local people for more than three months. Furthermore, riots in support of Abdeslam took place in Molenbeek following his arrest.

Following the killings, the media again agonised as to what could have been the cause of his 'radicalisation'. Everything from poverty to social exclusion to alienation was offered up as a reason – everything, that is, except a certain religion.

Over a 15-year period (2000–2015), one million people arrived in Belgium, a country with a current population of around 11 million. The Muslim population of the country is deemed to be somewhere between 4 and 6%, and growing. The

---

12 "A Brave Citizen Stands Up Against The Introduction Of Sharia In Belgium.
mp4," YouTube, December 4, 2012, accessed May 1, 2018, http://www.youtube.com/watch?v=n_wS9RVCc1c.
13 Soeren Kern, "Confronting Sharia Law in Belgium," Gatestone Institute, March 19, 2013, accessed May 1, 2018, http://www.gatestoneinstitute.org/3624/sharia-law-belgium.
14 "Belgian Islamophobia: MPs Vow to 'impeach' Muslim Extremists," RT International, accessed May 1, 2018, http://rt.com/news/proposal-belgium-limit-muslims-612/.

Muslim population of Brussels is around 17%, and growing. As the population grows, so do division and segregation.

DENMARK

Kaldet til Islam (Call to Islam) in 2011 declared the Tingbjerg suburb of Copenhagen a "sharia controlled zone". The group said it intended to disperse morality police throughout the area to enforce sharia law there. In a statement on its website, Call to Islam asks:

> "*How can we claim to be followers of the Sunnah and defend the best Deen* [Islam]*, when we prefer to live among the infidels, be subject to their laws, emulate them and fail to differentiate ourselves from the kufr? How can we claim to love Allah and His Messenger when we are embarrassed to call for Sharia? How can we be indifferent to the establishment of Allah's rule on Earth, which is a duty for every Muslim?*[15]"

A representative of Call to Islam told a Danish television reporter[16]:

> "*Initially we will not implement the penal system. Initially, we will patrol around grabbing people who drink and ban everything that is forbidden in Islam.... It is such that sharia must be spread. Because God says that His religion should be dominant. It must dominate over all other ruling systems. And that's why sharia should be spread.*"

He claimed that Call to Islam was already patrolling areas in Copenhagen and intended to expand such patrols across the country.

15 "The Cutting Edge News," The Cutting Edge News - Page One, accessed May 1, 2018, http://www.thecuttingedgenews.com/index.php?article=52983&pageid=&pagename.
16 "Liveleak.com - Muslims in Denmark Force Sharia Zones, Wtf," LiveLeak. com - Redefining the Media, accessed May 1, 2018, http://www.liveleak.com/view?i=673_1370269024&comments=1 (translation by LiveLeak).

Integration Minister Karen Haekkerup[17] told the *Jyllands-Posten* newspaper:

> *"I consider this to be very serious. Anything that attempts to undermine our democracy, we must crack down on it and consistently so."*

Little has happened to date to address this 'very serious' matter.

THE DANISH CARTOONS

On 30 September 2005, the Danish newspaper *Jyllands-Posten* published twelve cartoons depicting Mohammed. Perhaps the most notorious of the cartoons showed Mohammed with a bomb embedded in his turban. Visual depictions of the Prophet are considered blasphemous in most Islamic traditions. The newspaper said it was publishing the cartoons to provoke debate on the issue of self-censorship around Islam in the West.

Meetings of Islamic groups in Denmark, to discuss a response, soon followed. One outcome was a police complaint arguing that *Jyllands-Posten* had committed a criminal offence under sections 140 and 266b of the Danish Criminal Code, which outlaw "disturbing public order by publicly ridiculing or insulting the dogmas of worship" and "insult, threat or degradation of natural persons, by publicly and with malice attacking their race, colour of skin, national or ethnic roots, faith or sexual orientation" respectively. The public prosecutor dismissed the claims and said that there was no case to answer because the publications concerned a matter of public interest, and were thus protected from criminal charge.

The Organisation of Islamic Cooperation (OIC) and Arab League wrote a joint letter to the Danish Prime Minister expressing their concerns. Having received petitions from Danish imams, ambassadors from Turkey, Saudi Arabia, Iran, Pakistan,

---

17 The New Media Journal - The New Media Journal, accessed May 1, 2018, http://newmediajournal.us/indx.php/item/3385 (page discontinued).

Egypt, Indonesia, Algeria, Bosnia and Herzegovina, Libya, and Morocco, they asked for a meeting with the Danish Prime Minister in October 2005[18]. The letter stated, "Danish press and public representatives should not be allowed to abuse Islam in the name of democracy, freedom of expression and human rights, the values that we all share." It is interesting that Saudi Arabia, Iran and Pakistan claimed to share the values of freedom of expression when all three countries impose the death penalty for blasphemy.

Prime Minister Anders Fogh Rasmussen responded, saying that "freedom of expression is the very foundation of the Danish democracy" and as such "the Danish government has no means of influencing the press"[19].

Displeased by this lack of capitulation and apology from the Danes, a group of imams decided to take their case to the Middle East. They created a dossier of documents[20] as evidence of the appalling mistreatment to which Muslims were subjected in Denmark. It included a picture of a man in a French 'pig-squealing contest' that had nothing to do with the *Jyllands-Posten* publication. The dossier claimed that Islam and Mohammed were being mocked and ridiculed in Denmark in the guise of free speech, and it was soon distributed to countries across the Middle East.

Protests and riots followed[21] and hundreds of people were killed. Churches were targeted, embassies burned to the ground, and several death threats were issued to the cartoonists. Kurt Westergaard, the creator of the infamous turban cartoon, was attacked in his home in Aarhus by Somali Muslim Mohamed Geele[22]. Geele had entered Westergaard's home with an axe and a knife, and shouted, "You must die" and "You are going to hell". He was convicted in 2011 and sentenced to 12 years imprisonment, followed by deportation.

Let me summarise these events and their significance. A

18 Hjem, accessed May 1, 2018, http://www.rogerbuch.dk/jpabrev.pdf.
19 Wayback Machine, accessed May 1, 2018, http://web.archive.org/web/20060219083657/gfx-master.tv2.dk/images/Nyhederne/Pdf/side3.pdf.
20 «Akkari-Laban Dossier,» Wikipedia, the Free Encyclopedia, January 20, 2018, accessed May 1, 2018, http://en.wikipedia.org/wiki/Akkari-Laban_dossier.
21 "BBC NEWS | South Asia | Muslim Cartoon Fury Claims Lives," Home - BBC News, February 6, 2006, accessed May 1, 2018, http://news.bbc.co.uk/1/hi/4684652.stm.
22 "Danish Cartoonist Attacker Guilty," BBC News, February 3, 2011, accessed May 1, 2018, http://www.bbc.co.uk/news/world-europe-12353863.

newspaper in a country in northern Europe had utilised its demo-cratic right to free expression, and in doing so had apparently insulted Islamic sensibilities. Riots followed and people were killed. Free speech came under attack in the West, and complaints were made by countries that execute their own citizens for blas-phemy that the Danish government was failing in its human rights obligations by allowing free expression that insulted them. Not a single paper in the UK would publish the cartoons, and in the USA, two editors of an Illinois paper which did print them were suspended "pending an investigation into how the cartoons had ended up in the paper"[23]. In short, another nail had been driven hard and fast into the coffin of Western democracy.

LARS HEDEGAARD

Islam in Denmark cannot be discussed without mention of Lars Hedegaard, who founded the Free Press Society there in 2004. A journalist, historian, and editor, Hedegaard had been an active socialist and previously described himself as a Marxist. But it is his criticisms of Islam for which he is best known.

Hedegaard was convicted under Denmark's section 266b in 2011 following comments he made about rape within Muslim families. He is reported to have said that "girls in Muslim fami-lies are raped by their uncles, their cousins or their dad"[24].

In the film *Silent Conquest*, Hedegaard clarified his view:

> *"It is a troubling aspect of Muslim culture... it tends to be a problem in Muslim families and I think that is well documented. You can also read about it in, for example, Ayaan Hirsi Ali's books, Taslima Nasrin's books... If you force your daughter, who is perhaps 12 or 13 years old, to marry someone she doesn't want – it could be a man of my age, for example – then... that is like forcing rape upon her."*

23 Monica Davey, "Illinois Student Paper Prints Muslim Cartoons, and Reaction Is Swift", The New York Times, February 17, 2006, accessed May 1, 2018, http://www.nytimes.com/2006/02/17/national/17cartoons.html?_r=0
24 "President of Danish Free Press Society Convicted for 'Racism'," EuropeNews, accessed May 1, 2018, http://europenews.dk/en/node/42859.

I disagree: it isn't *like* forcing rape upon her; it *is* forcing rape upon her. I document elsewhere in this book the prevalence of child marriage in many Islamic states, so Hedegaard is not being untruthful. Even if one does not approve of Hedegaard's language, the fact remains that he was prosecuted in a court of law merely for speaking the truth.

Having initially been convicted, Hedegaard appealed to the Supreme Court and his conviction was overturned in 2012. In a speech to the Supreme Court at the time, he made the following remarks[25]:

> "I am... baffled at one of the claims about my person that has been circulated in connection with this case, namely that I am a racist. I have never been, I am not now, and I shall never be a racist. On the contrary, all my life I have opposed racist attitudes, by which I mean hatred towards and denigrating speech about people due their descent, skin colour or other so-called racial characteristics – in other words, antipathy against or ill treatment of people due to circumstances over which they have no control. Islam is not a race and therefore criticism of Islam cannot be racism."

Hedegaard is entirely right. Islam is not a race; it is a system of belief which must be held up to as much scrutiny as any other. Sharia law, however, does not allow criticism of Islam, so one could argue that the charges Hedegaard faced were sharia-based charges, delivered via the Danish judicial system.

We have seen many accusations of racism quickly follow criticism of Islam from white Europeans like Hedegaard. But what happens when someone who is not white makes similar criticisms? The Danish judicial system delivered an answer to that in 2012 when an Iranian woman was charged with racism for making comments very similar to those of Lars Hedegaard.

Firoozeh Bazrafkan, an Iranian-born artist living in Denmark,

---

25 "Lars Hedegaard's 'Racism' Case Goes Before Supreme Court," Frontpage Mag, April 15, 2012, accessed May 1, 2018, http://www.frontpagemag.com/2012/frontpagemag-com/lars-hedegaards-racism-case-goes-before-supreme-court/.

is reported to have said "I am also deeply convinced that Muslim men to a great extent, and everywhere in the world, rape, mistreat and kill their daughters[26]." She was found not guilty, but the seeds had been sown, and another powerful message sent: no matter who you are, don't criticise Islam.

What is remarkable about this story is the fact that the Danish prosecutor did not accept Bazrafkan's justification that her comments could not be racist because she was criticising her own people. In other words, the prosecutor proved that these charges had nothing to do with racism and everything to do with Islam. One can be charged with racism offences for criticising a religion, and those charges can, and will, be brought irrespective of the race of the parties involved.

Not long after his trial, Lars Hedegaard would discover that his troubles were not behind him. A would-be assassin, posing as a postman, shot at Hedegaard outside his home and he narrowly escaped with his life. Though the attack was widely condemned, there were some who argued that he had brought it on himself, thus further empowering the Islamist cause to destroy free speech in the West.

For example, the *New York Times* reported in February 2013[27] that Mikael Rothstein, a religious history scholar at the University of Copenhagen, said, "I think that Hedegaard wanted this conflict...brutal words can be as strong as the brutal physical act of violence." What this comment signifies is just how deeply in trouble freedom of speech is in Denmark. It equates insult with deadly violence and panders to the Islamist as it does so. It is difficult to quantify the damage this can cause.

Hedegaard's troubles had still not come to an end. Later in 2013, when he was moving house, his removal van was followed by two journalists seeking out the location of his new abode.

26 "Denmark Charges Iranian Woman with Racism for Criticising Islam," Frontpage Mag, June 22, 2015, accessed May 1, 2018, http://www.frontpagemag.com/2012/dgreenfield/denmark-charges-iranian-woman-with-racism-for-criticising-islam/.

27 Andrew Higgins, "Lars Hedegaard, Anti-Islamic Provocateur, Receives Support From Danish Muslims," The New York Times - Breaking News, World News & Multimedia, February 27, 2013, accessed May 1, 2018, http://www.nytimes.com/2013/02/28/world/europe/lars-hedegaard-anti-islamic-provocateur-receives-support-from-danish-muslims.html.

According to Bruce Bawer[28], another prominent critic of Islam, Danish newspaper *Ekstra Bladet* ran with the headline *"Lars Hedegaard Moves"* in a story penned by Bo Paulsen. Bawer wrote that the newspaper had published a picture of the removal van at Hedegaard's home. The reporters then followed the van and published a description of the route it had taken. Paulsen and a photographer, whose plan was clearly to identify Hedegaard's new address for public consumption, were pulled over by police who prevented their despicable plan coming to fruition.

According to Bawer:

> *"The tone of his* [Paulsen's] *article is that of a citizen – and member of the fourth estate* [the press] *– who has been deeply wronged by the law-enforcement establishment, in league with, and doing the bidding of, a racist, Islamophobic Enemy of the People."*

What is most remarkable about this is the skewed morality. A journalist intends to reveal the location of a fellow writer – who has done nothing but speak his mind and face an assassination attempt for doing so – to be put to good use by further potential assassins. The same journalist apparently believes that Hedegaard is the source of the problem, and is a man of dubious ethics.

I asked Lars Hedegaard about the events that he had had to endure, particularly the attempt on his life. He gave me this rather hard-hitting response – one which shed an even more disturbing light on the identity of those who wanted him dead:

> *"As the Daily B.T. reported in January* [2014], *the police is convinced that the attempt on my life was a meticulously planned political assassination – a very rare occurrence in Denmark. In a way, I'm flattered. At least it goes to show that I'm far from the bumbling, know-nothing conspiracy peddler most of the media have portrayed me*

---

28 "Media Try to Report Lars Hedegaard's New Address," Frontpage Mag, June 22, 2015, accessed May 1, 2018, http://www.frontpagemag.com/2013/bruce-bawer/ekstra-bladet-vs-lars-hedegaard/.

*as. Whoever ordered the hit would hardly have bothered
if I was as inconsequential as the media claim. Why call
attention to an idiot?*

"However, my glee at this unexpected recognition
turns to despair when I consider the broader implications.
We have now passed the point where an unofficial jurisprudence based on sharia law has taken hold. If the public
authorities will not or cannot silence critics of Islam by
legal means, some Muslims will take it upon themselves to
do so by paralegal means.

*"We are yet to hear what the Danish state intends to do
about this intolerable situation. Meanwhile, Muslims from
all corners of the world are allowed to settle in Denmark.
They are permitted to go to holy war in Syria and return to
Denmark to collect their social security benefits.*

*"Our government has entered into a suicide pact with
barbarians based on its belief that it is only expendable
people like me that have to pay the price."*

People like Mr Hedegaard did indeed pay a price when free
speech campaigners were attacked with machine guns at an event
in Copenhagen in 2015. On Valentine's Day in the Krudttønden
Cultural Centre, a man opened fire on attendees at a debate to
discuss free speech, particularly in the context of Islam. Swedish
cartoonist Lars Vilks was in attendance (as were friends of mine)
and is believed to have been the prime target. Vilks has drawn
and published cartoons of the Muslim Prophet Mohammed.

One person was killed in this attack, but more was to come as a
further shooting took place early the following morning at a Synagogue in the city where a Jewish man was murdered[29]. An attack on
free speech followed by an attack on Jews, reminiscent of the major
jihadi attack in Paris a short time previously (see 'France').

As with other countries, the above are merely snippets of the
problems being faced by Denmark, but before I move on, I want
to mention the following:

---

29 "Media Try to Report Lars Hedegaard's New Address," Frontpage Mag, June 22,
2015, accessed May 1, 2018, http://www.frontpagemag.com/2013/bruce-bawer/ekstra-
bladet-vs-lars-hedegaard/.

- In 2004, an imam in Copenhagen sparked an outcry when he quite bluntly told the Danes that women who did not wear headscarves were "asking for rape"[30]. Shahid Mehdi made the remarks in a televised interview and then reiterated them when questioned by the press.
- The *Copenhagen Post Online* commented, "As a mufti, a jurist who interprets Islamic law, Shahid Mehdi is in a special position of authority as a Muslim scholar". It claimed that Mehdi was affiliated with the Islamic Cultural Center in Copenhagen. Various public figures, from left and right, agreed that Mehdi's remarks could incite Muslim men to rape Danish women.
- Abu Bilal Ismail was secretly filmed at a mosque in Aarhus preaching that women should be stoned to death for adultery – this included divorced women who have sex, or "fornicate" as he put it. The footage was broadcast on national Danish television in early 2016. He added that those who abandon Islam also deserve to be killed.
- In March 2016 a group of undercover reporters found what they described as aims to build a parallel society for Muslims. A male and female reporter, posing as a couple, visited eight mosques in Aarhus, Odense, and Copenhagen to see what was being said behind closed doors.
- What they found was unsurprising: women should be stoned to death; people who leave Islam should be killed; a woman may not work without her husband's permission; polygamy is endorsed; women are not to deny men sex; men may beat their wives. There was also approval of the notion that Muslims should not mix with native Danes, and a rejection of engagement with the Danish state and criminal system. Some of the mosques involved were among the largest in the country, and many were believed to be 'moderate' in the public

---

30 JIM BALL (blog), accessed May 1, 2018, http://jimball.com.au/features/Political%20%20uproar%20over%20mufti%27s%20rmearks%20-The%20Copenhagen%20Post.htm (page discontinued).

face. Islamic misogyny is making itself increasingly felt in the once gender-equal nation of Denmark.

- In February 2017, the Danish People's Party called for a ban on Muslim refugees entering Denmark for a period of at least six years[31]. The Left described this as un-Danish, while the Danish Institute for Human Rights claimed every person had a right to "enjoy asylum from persecution". Everyone, one assumes, except Danish women facing a vastly increased possibility of rape.

Despite these denunciations, in early 2018, the Danish Prime Minister made similar pronouncements. In his New Year's address to the country, Lars Løkke Rasmussen said:

> *"We must break the chain in which generation after generation lives in a parallel society. A child has only one childhood. It must not be wasted. There are parallel societies throughout the country. I'm talking about neighbourhoods where teenagers are forced into marriages with someone they do not love; in which women are considered to be worth less than men[32]."*

---

31 "Leading Danish Politician Calls for Ban on Muslims Refugees," The Independent, last modified July 10, 2016, http://www.independent.co.uk/news/world/europe/denmark-muslim-refugees-ban-islam-apartheid-asylum-seekers-migrants-a7161786.html.
32 Voice of Europe, "Denmark's Prime Minister Extremely Worried About Parallel Societies and Islamisation," Voice of Europe, last modified January 3, 2018, https://voiceofeurope.com/2018/01/denmarks-prime-minister-extremely-worried-about-parallel-societies-and-islamisation/.

FRANCE

FRANCE'S RELATIONSHIP WITH Islam is one of the most fascinating of any country in Europe. It is characterised by several terror attacks, France's controversial ban on the burqa and niqab, which came into force in April 2011, and its notorious *banlieues* and ghettoisation. It has had its free expression and *laïcité* (secularism) viciously attacked in the form of the cold-blooded murder of cartoonists and writers at the *Charlie Hebdo* magazine offices in Paris.

Before I go into these in any detail, I will look at some of the lesser known developments in France involving Islam in recent years.

In November 2012, a protest took place in Paris – the first of its kind. The people involved complained that they were living under a politically correct establishment which refused to acknowledge the growth of Islam and sharia in France.

The march was not covered by the mainstream media, but CBN reported in the United States that protesters claimed to be increasingly angry at what they called "the Islamisation of France". CBN also reported that prayers were taking place on Paris streets, blocking traffic, but police were told not to intervene[1].

---

1 "Islamification of Paris-A Warning To The West," YouTube, last modified November 30, 2010, http://www.youtube.com/watch?v=wTXQ-vcsbK8.

CHARLIE HEBDO

Charlie Hebdo is a well-known satirical magazine based in the French capital. On 2 November 2011, its offices were fire-bombed and its website hacked[2]. Its crime had been to publish an issue 'guest-edited' by Mohammed. A cartoon of the Islamic Prophet appeared on the front cover with a speech bubble containing the quote, "100 lashes if you are not dying with laughter".

The attack was not the first *Charlie Hebdo* had endured. A less violent assault – though no less serious – afflicted the magazine in 2007 when its editor was taken to the courts by the Grand Mosque of Paris and the Union of French Islamic Organisations for depicting Mohammed on another front cover[3]. The Court ruled in favour of the magazine, but yet another silencing attempt had been made, and criticising or satirising Islam had become even more taboo.

In 2012, *Charlie Hebdo* hit the headlines when it yet again published depictions of Mohammed, this time during furore over the *Innocence of Muslims* film. In response to the publication, the French government increased security at its embassies across the world. Although politicians had broadly been supportive of the magazine on previous occasions, by this stage it seemed their patience had run out.

Foreign Minister Laurent Fabius criticised the publication, saying:

> *"In France, there is a principle of freedom of expression, which should not be undermined. In the present context, given this absurd video that has been aired, strong emotions have been awakened in many Muslim countries. Is it really sensible or intelligent to pour oil on the fire?[4]"*

---

2 "Attack on French Satirical Paper," BBC News, last modified November 2, 2011, http://www.bbc.co.uk/news/world-europe-15550350.
3 «BBC NEWS | Europe | French Cartoons Editor Acquitted,» Home - BBC News, last modified March 22, 2007, http://news.bbc.co.uk/1/hi/world/europe/6479673.stm.
4 Scott Sayare and Nicola Clark, «French Newspaper Publishes Cartoons Mocking Muhammad,» The New York Times - Breaking News, World News & Multimedia, last modified September 19, 2012, http://www.nytimes.com/2012/09/20/world/europe/french-magazine-publishes-cartoons-mocking-muhammad.html.

The *Charlie Hebdo* Editor in Chief Gérard Biard hit back with this wonderful comment:

> *"We're a newspaper that respects French law. Now, if there's a law that is different in Kabul or Riyadh, we're not going to bother ourselves with respecting it."*

It was the attack on *Charlie Hebdo* in January 2015 that would make the magazine a household name and reveal to France and Europe just how serious religious censorship had become. The *Charlie Hebdo* massacre is one of the most significant events to occur in Europe since the Second World War, and Europe's response to it starkly revealed our weakness; our complete lack of commitment to, and indeed understanding of, free speech, secularism, and the history of revolution and enlightened values that have made Europe one of the great civilisations of human history.

On 7 January 2015, brothers Saïd and Chérif Kouachi arrived at the offices of *Charlie Hebdo* in Paris. They proceeded to murder 12 people and injure others. Over the next couple of days, a further five people died when Amedy Coulibaly attacked a Jewish supermarket on 9 January and murdered four. He had already murdered a police officer the previous day.

Witnesses to the *Charlie Hebdo* shooting reported that the gunmen had shouted *"Allahu Akbar"* and "We have avenged the Prophet Mohammed" at the scene[5]. At the Jewish supermarket in Porte de Vincennes, Coulibaly reportedly said he would kill those inside (whom he had been holding hostage) if the Kouachi brothers were harmed[6]. Over the space of a few days, the usual targets of jihadis had come under attack in France: secularists and Jews. But still, no real lessons would be learned as to the catastrophe Europe had unleashed upon itself.

---

5 "Massacre at French Magazine Office," BBC News, last modified January 7, 2015, http://www.bbc.co.uk/news/world-europe-30710883.
6 "Paris Shooting: Armed Man Takes Hostages in Paris Kosher Store," The Sydney Morning Herald, last modified January 9, 2015, http://www.smh.com.au/world/paris-shooting-armed-man-takes-hostages-in-paris-kosher-store-20150109-12ldgt.html.

"JE NE SUIS PAS CHARLIE" – NO LESSONS LEARNED

A few days after the attacks, world leaders gathered in Paris for a rally to honour the victims. The free speech organisation Reporters Without Borders noted the fact that the march was attended by world leaders who themselves place restrictions on journalists and head countries where blasphemy is criminally prosecuted.

A statement from the group[7]:

> *"Reporters Without Borders welcomes the participation of many foreign leaders in today's march in Paris in homage to the victims of last week's terror attacks and in defence of the French republic's values, but is outraged by the presence of officials from countries that restrict freedom of information. On what grounds are representatives of regimes that are predators of press freedom coming to Paris to pay tribute to Charlie Hebdo, a publication that has always defended the most radical concept of freedom of expression?"*

Countries named by Reporters Without Borders included Russia, Egypt, United Arab Emirates, and Turkey. In Egypt, "ridiculing or insulting a heavenly religion or a sect following it" carries a sentence of up to five years in prison. According to the US State Department, in the United Arab Emirates:

> *"Proselytizing and distributing non-Islamic religious literature are prohibited under penalty of criminal prosecution, imprisonment, and deportation, on the grounds that such behavior transgresses core Islamic teachings[8]."*

In Turkey, as Islam increases its grip on that previously secular country, persecution or prosecution for blasphemy is increasing.

---

7 RWB Condemns Presence of ‹predators? in Paris March, Calls for Solidarity with ‹all Charlies? | Reporters Without Borders,» RSF, last modified January 25, 2016, https://rsf.org/en/news/rwb-condemns-presence-predators-paris-march-calls-solidarity-all-charlies.
8 "United Arab Emirates," U.S. Department of State, accessed May 1, 2018, http://www.state.gov/j/drl/rls/irf/2008/108495.htm.

While representatives of countries that imprison people for offending Islam 'honoured' those murdered for offending Islam, one of France's most popular leaders was excluded from events. Why? Because she offends Islam.

Marine Le Pen is the leader of the French National Front and is a hugely controversial but popular politician in France. In 2017, she lost the French Presidential election to a relatively unknown banker (and EU favourite) Emmanuel Macron. At the time of the *Charlie Hebdo* attacks, she described the jihadi murders accurately, saying, "This is a terrorist attack carried out in the name of radical Islam"[9].

Le Pen's exclusion from commemorative events was steeped in such extraordinary doublespeak that it provided the perfect demonstration of the hypocrisy that is allowing Europe to fall: the complete lack of commitment to our values. Le Pen had said that with the *Charlie Hebdo* attack, "Islamists have declared war on France"[10]. This was her crime.

Then-Prime Minister Manuel Valls said, "There should be no exclusion from national unity". But there's a catch: 'national unity' means "tolerance and refusal to link the religion of Islam with extremism". Read that again. According to the French Prime Minister, following an Islamist terror attack on his country's right to blaspheme, only those who refused to link the attacks with Islam could take part in 'national unity'. When honouring those who were killed for insulting Islam, we must exclude those who truthfully point out that they were killed for insulting Islam.

France had learned absolutely nothing.

France's Foreign Minister enlightened us, saying that "the terrorists' religion is not Islam, which they are betraying"[11]. Like many Western leaders, the French Foreign Minister presented

---

9 "Marine Le Pen Condemns 'murderous Ideology' in the Aftermath of Charlie Hebdo Shooting," Telegraph.co.uk, last modified January 7, 2015, http://www.telegraph.co.uk/news/11331595/Marine-Le-Pen-condemns-murderous-ideology-in-the-aftermath-of-Charlie-Hebdo-shooting.html.

10 Connexion France, "Le Pen Slams FN "exclusion"," The Connexion, accessed May 2, 2018, http://www.connexionfrance.com/france-front-national-charlie-hebdo-front-national-marine-le-pen-16528-view-article.html.

11 "Mosques Fire Bombed and Pelted with Pig Heads in Aftermath of Paris Terror Attacks," National Post, accessed May 2, 2018, http://news.nationalpost.com/news/mosques-fire-bombed-and-pelted-with-pig-heads-in-aftermath-of-paris-terror-attacks.

himself as an expert on all things Islamic, while ignoring Islam's scriptures and indeed the terrorists themselves.

Proving that it wasn't only the French who had learned nothing, Dutch Prime Minister Mark Rutte joined the Mayor of Amsterdam in that city's Dam Square to remember the cartoonists. Mayor Eberhard van der Laan told a large crowd, "Our message to the enemies of freedom is: we will not give way, not one millimetre"[12]. While this speech was being made, Geert Wilders was facing charges for criticising Muslim immigration to the Netherlands, proving that the Dutch have sacrificed far more than just a millimetre of their freedoms.

In the aftermath, several Western publications, including the *New York Times* and the UK's *Daily Telegraph*, along with cable news network CNN, refused to show the cartoons in question. They too demonstrated no understanding at all of the nature of the attacks or the need for defence of free speech in the face of them[13].

FRANCE'S BURQA BAN

It should come as no surprise that the robust stance by the French state to ban the burqa and niqab in 2011 in opposition to what is undoubtedly an important symbol of Islamic extremism and female subservience was widely denounced, primarily by Left-wing commentators across the globe. Often declaring a woman's right to wear what she likes, the debate omitted to acknowledge the fact that this garment is forced upon women in many societies. It is quite the sign of moral inversion when a garment used to oppress is deemed to be a human right.

Furthermore, while there is widespread concern for the women who want to wear this oppressive garment, there is little concern for those who don't.

12 "Dutch Take to the Streets in Support of Charlie Hebdo, Demonstrations Nationwide," DutchNews.nl, last modified January 9, 2015, http://www.dutchnews.nl/news/archives/2015/01/dutch-take-to-the-streets-in-support-of-charlie-hebdo-demonstrations-nationwide
13 "News Outlets Are Censoring Images of Cartoons That May Have Incited Charlie Hebdo Attack," Slate Magazine, last modified January 7, 2015, http://www.slate.com/blogs/the_slatest/2015/01/07/charlie_hebdo_cartoons_self_censorship_by_several_major_outlets.html.

One example of the Left's defence of female subservience came from the UK's *Guardian*, which described the burqa ban as having placed women "under house arrest"[14]. Angelique Chrisafis wrote that Muslim groups had reported "a worrying increase in discrimination and verbal and physical violence against women in veils". I would like greater detail on this before I pass judgement, but if women were being attacked in the streets of France, of course this must be condemned and the assailants brought to justice. What Chrisafis didn't address, however, was why women were wearing the veils in the first place, given that they had been banned by French law. The notion that these Muslim women were law-breakers did not seem to feature in her thinking.

Violence and riots have broken out across France in subsequent years as a result of the refusal of many French Muslims to obey the face-covering laws. One such incident took place in 2013[15]. A police spokesman, commenting on a riot in July of that year, stated:

> "*About 50 assailants were involved. They started to fight against the police, burned vehicles, rubbish, and public property.*"

His comments followed a second night of rioting in the Parisian suburb of Trappes which had flared when a man was arrested for allegedly assaulting a police officer carrying out an identity check on his veil-wearing wife. The court case that followed included a challenge to the constitutionality of the niqab ban.

Cassandra Belin was convicted of insulting and threatening police and given a two month suspended sentence, as well as a fine of €150 for wearing a niqab. Her lawyers had argued that the ban amounted to a violation of religious freedom, but this was thrown out by the court on the grounds that the legislation had already been examined by the French Constitutional Council[16].

14 Angelique Chrisafis, "France's Burqa Ban: Women Are 'effectively Under House Arrest'," The Guardian, last modified November 25, 2017, http://www.theguardian.com/world/2011/sep/19/battle-for-the-burqa.

15 "Clashes Erupt in France over Veil Ban," YouTube, last modified July 21, 2013, http://www.youtube.com/watch?v=Gsp3h0ErdDg.

16 "French Court Upholds Controversial Burqa Ban," last modified January 8, 2014, http://english.alarabiya.net/en/News/world/2014/01/08/French-court-upholds-controversial-burqa-ban-.html.

In one of its best ever decisions, the European Court of Human Rights ruled in the summer of 2014 that France's burqa and niqab ban was perfectly acceptable. It agreed with the French argument that fully covering one's face isn't conducive to community cohesion[17]. As a consequence, several other countries, including Denmark, Spain, and Austria, have discussed or introduced similar bans.

A different kind of Muslim women's attire hit the headlines in France in 2016 with the banning of the so-called 'burkini' (a play on burqa and bikini). Mayors of around 30 coastal towns banned people from wearing the burkini, which covers a woman from head to toe while she's swimming, on their beaches through the summer of 2016.

One Mayor told beach-goers, "If you don't want to live the way we do, don't come"[18]. It is quite obvious what he means. France is a secular country; its people do not appreciate overt religious symbolism in their public places. They tend not to cover up women's bodies in the name of 'modesty'. Despite this, the Mayors were over-ruled by France's administrative court. The Collective against Islamophobia was involved in pursuing this ruling[19].

Some towns, however, refused to heed the Administrative Court ruling and kept the ban in place[20].

I took part in several media discussions at the time regarding this ban and a couple of things were made clear to me: British 'feminists' are enraged by opposition to an item used to sustain the 'virgin-whore' view of women, and I ought to stay out of the argument in any case. On one radio show, the Muslim guest referred to me, on air, as a "white girl" who, she heavily implied,

---

17 Kim Willsher, "France's Burqa Ban Upheld by Human Rights Court," The Guardian, last modified July 1, 2014, http://www.theguardian.com/world /2014/jul/01/france-burqa-ban-upheld-human-rights-court.

18 Sheena McKenzie and Antonia Mortensen, CNN, "French Mayor on Burkini Ban: They Must Accept Our Way of Life," CNN, last modified August 30, 2016, http://edition.cnn.com/2016/08/30/europe/french-mayor-cogolin-burkini-ban/.

19 "French Resorts Lift Burkini Bans," BBC News, last modified September 1, 2016, http://www.bbc.co.uk/news/world-europe-37243442.

20 Angelique Chrisafis, «French Mayors Refuse to Lift Burkini Ban Despite Court Ruling,» The Guardian, last modified November 28, 2017, https://www.theguardian.com/world/2016/aug/28/french-mayors-burkini-ban-court-ruling.

had no right to express an opinion on the matter. This same attitude was expressed by some when inquiries into sharia courts in Britain took place.

I proceeded to inform the Muslim guest that 'white girls' do have a right to object to primitive misogynist ideas about women's bodies, previously defeated in Europe, which are making a spectacular comeback. I also pointed out that French people have a right to argue for the maintenance of their secular spaces, irrespective of what Muslims (or anyone else) might think about it, or what colour their skin happens to be.

I marvelled when she told me that 'feminists' in Britain were on their way to France to wear burkinis in solidarity. One can always rely on Western feminists to get on board with misogyny as long as it is Islamic.

France has, partly due to its burqa ban, been accused of being particularly Islamophobic, and in 2013, the Collective Against Islamophobia in France decided to do something about it. In a rather modern twist, the group encroached upon free speech and expression by launching a smartphone app which would allow users to report Islamophobic incidents as they happened[21]. The software allows people to film occurrences and instantly send them to the Collective so that they can be published or, if possible, the 'Islamophobes' stopped in their tracks.

"The primary goal is to allow people to send out instant reports," the group's spokesman Babacar Sene said. He also argued that Islamophobia had been trivialised in France.

Sami Debah, the group's president, added:

> *"We are seriously worried about the situation we have in France. When you see the results of surveys where 74% of people think that Islam is not compatible with French society, this view is reflected in acts of Islamophobia on the street, which rose by 38% between 2011 and 2012."*

---

21 «French Smartphone App Targets Islamophobia,» The Local - France›s News in English, last modified November 4, 2013, http://www.thelocal.fr/20131104/french-smartphone-app-targets-islamophobia.

Debah didn't specify what "acts of Islamophobia" were particularly worrying. What he did mention was where the blame should lie: "We blame political dialogue in the country"[22]. The Collective Against Islamophobia in France thus demonstrated its intent to monitor the public (through a smartphone app) and political dialogue to ensure that it does not offend Islamic sensibilities. French freedom of speech, and with it democracy, is being sacrificed in this endeavour as violent attacks on France escalate.

THE OPEN-BORDER THREAT

Meanwhile, the lives and freedoms of many women in France have been severely curtailed as a direct result of Muslim immigration. The mainstream media has stayed away from this, but in 2016, the Clarion Project[23] – a non-profit organisation that educates the public about the dangers of radical Islam – produced a report that revealed the terrifying scale of change in no-go zones in France, particularly Paris[24]. The report revealed areas of France where women are simply not visible in public, or are harassed in the streets to such an extent that many had changed their clothing, behaviour, or walking route to avoid it. This had coincided with the arrival to these areas of Muslim migrants from Somalia, Eritrea, Afghanistan, Sudan and other war-torn nations.

In short, men arrived in France, and other European countries, from places where women are often harassed, abused, and are unsafe alone in public. But despite the clear evidence of the threat faced by women as a result, Europe's borders remain open for more. Europe also remains open to jihadist terrorists, and the unelected President of the European Commission, Jean-Claude Juncker, has confirmed it is to stay that way[25].

---

22 Islamophobia Has Been Trivialized in France›,» The Local - France›s News in English, last modified February 15, 2013, http://www.thelocal.fr/20130215/islamophobia-has-become-trivialised-in-france.
23 "About Clarion Project," Clarion Project, accessed May 2, 2018, https://clarionproject.org/about-us/
24 "No-Go Zones For Women," Clarion Project, last modified May 22, 2017, https://clarionproject.org/paris-neighborhood-no-go-zone-women/.
25 Breitbart News, "Juncker: Borders Will Remain Open," Breitbart, last modified November 15, 2015, http://www.breitbart.com/london/2015/11/15/eu-commission-president-borders-will-remain-open/.

Here are some of the violent attacks that open borders have brought to France since the *Charlie Hebdo* massacre:

- November 2015 – the deadliest terror attack in the country's history took place in Paris. One hundred and thirty people were killed and hundreds injured when a nightclub, sports stadium, bars, and restaurants were riddled with bullets and grenades. ISIS claimed responsibility[26].
- January 2016 – a man drove his car at soldiers in Valence. Jihadi propaganda was found on his computer[27].
- June 2016 – a police officer and his wife were stabbed to death in Magnanville. ISIS claimed responsibility[28].
- July 2016 – 86 people were killed when the driver of a cargo truck drove his vehicle into crowds celebrating Bastille Day (the country's National Day) in Nice. ISIS claimed responsibility[29].
- July 2016 – a family were attacked with a knife in Garda-Colombe. The attacker was upset about the clothing being worn by the women of the family[30].
- July 2016 – an 86-year-old Catholic priest was beheaded in his church in Saint-Étienne-du-Rouvray. ISIS claimed responsibility[31].

---

26 Https://www.facebook.com/anthony.faiola, "Paris Attacks Were Carried out by Three Groups Tied to Islamic State, Official Says," Washington Post, last modified November 15, 2015, https://www.washingtonpost.com/world/string-of-paris-terrorist-attacks-leaves-over-120-dead/2015/11/14/066df55c-8a73-11e5-bd91-d385b244482f_story.html.

27 Man Who Drove Car at French Troops Had Jihadi Propaganda In..,» U.S, last modified January 2, 2016, http://www.reuters.com/article/us-france-attacks-mosque-idUSKBN0UG0ED20160102.

28 SITE Intelligence Group, "IS' 'Amaq Reports IS Fighter Behind Stabbing Death of Police Officer in Paris Suburb," June 13, 2016, accessed May 2, 2018, https://news.siteintelgroup.com/Jihadist-News/is-amaq-reports-is-fighter-behind-stabbing-death-of-police-officer-in-paris-suburb.html.

29 "Isis Claims Responsibility for Deadly Nice Lorry Terror Attack," The Independent, last modified July 16, 2016, http://www.independent.co.uk/news/world/europe/nice-terror-attack-isis-claims-responsibility-lorry-massacre-france-coastal-city-a7140381.html.

30 "Mother and Three Daughters Are STABBED in French Holiday Resort," Mail Online, last modified July 20, 2016, http://www.dailymail.co.uk/news/article-3697451/Mother-three-daughters-aged-8-14-STABBED-French-holiday-resort-scantily-dressed.html.

31 Julian Borger, «Isis Attackers Forced French Priest to Kneel Before He Was Murdered, Hostage Says,» The Guardian, last modified July 26, 2016, https://www.theguardian.com/world/2016/jul/26/men-hostages-french-church-police-normandy-saint-etienne-du-rouvray.

- February 2017 – a man shouting *"Allahu Akbar"* attacked a soldier standing guard at the Louvre museum in Paris with a machete. He was shot dead[32].
- April 2017 – ISIS claimed responsibility when jihadists opened fire on police officers on the Champs-Élysée in Paris[33].
- June 2017 – a man claiming to be a 'soldier of the caliphate' attacked a police officer with a hammer at the famous Notre Dame cathedral in Paris[34].
- October 2017 – two women are murdered by a man shouting *"Allahu Akbar"* at the Marseille-Saint-Charles train station[35].

This constitutes a mere sample of the Islam-related violence that occurs with regularity in France. There have been numerous attacks on police, soldiers and, of course, rabbis. Such is the fear of violence in France that a no-go zone app was created in 2017. The idea of it is to allow users to share information about instances of "aggression, theft, harassment or incivility" at locations in the city and mark them on a public map[36].

The new President of France isn't about to offer any comforting words, however. True to form for a mainstream European politician, Emmanuel Macron has blamed the French themselves for the troubles Muslim immigration has brought to their shores[37]. He said France needed to question itself as to why so many Muslims rejected mainstream French society. Islam, he made clear, was not the source of the problem.

---

32 "French Soldier Shoots Attacker at Louvre," BBC News, last modified February 3, 2017, http://www.bbc.co.uk/news/world-europe-38853841.

33 "'Guns and Gas' Found in Paris Attack Car," BBC News, last modified June 19, 2017, http://www.bbc.co.uk/news/world-europe-40332532.

34 "Footage Captures Paris Police Shooting Isis-supporting Hammer Attacker," The Independent, last modified June 7, 2017, http://www.independent.co.uk/News/world/europe/notre-dame-attack-video-footage-police-france-terror-paris-isis-farid-ikken-journalist-student-a7777871.html.

35 Angelique Chrisafis, "Man Shot Dead by French Army After Killing Two People at Marseille Train Station," The Guardian, last modified November 27, 2017, https://www.theguardian.com/world/2017/oct/01/french-police-operation-under-way-at-marseille-train-station.

36 Sofia Petkar, "'No-go Zone? New App Launched to Report Crimes in France As Terror Threat Remains Critical," Express.co.uk, last modified July 1, 2017, https://www.express.co.uk/news/world/823542/france-terror-threat-level-critical-paris-no-go-zone-app-report-crimes.

37 Breitbart News, "Macron Blames France for the Rise of Islamic Radicalisation," Breitbart, last modified November 15, 2017, http://www.breitbart.com/london/2017/11/15/emmanuel-macron-blames-france-rise-islamic-radicalisation/.

GERMANY

CHRISTA DATZ-WINTER, A Frankfurt judge, denied a divorce to a young Moroccan-German woman on the grounds that she and her husband came from a "Moroccan cultural environment in which it is not uncommon for a man to exert a right of corporal punishment over his wife"[1]. When the young woman protested, the judge quoted verse 34 of Sura 4 from the Koran, which reads: "...as to those [wives] on whose part you fear desertion, admonish them and leave them alone in the sleeping places and beat them".

Following a national outcry, Datz-Winter was removed from the case, but the message had been strongly delivered: Islam has entered the German courtroom and domestic violence has been condoned. A daily newspaper *Die Tageszeitung* ran a story on the case entitled: "In the Name of the People: Beating Allowed"[2].

German law requires one year of separation before a divorce can be granted, unless there are exceptional circumstances to

---

1 Kate Connolly, "German Judge Invokes Qur'an to Deny Abused Wife a Divorce," The Guardian, last modified November 26, 2017, http://www.guardian.co.uk/world/2007/mar/23/germany.islam.

2 SPIEGEL ONLINE, Hamburg, Germany, "German Justice Failures: Paving the Way for a Muslim Parallel Society - International," SPIEGEL ONLINE, last modified March 29, 2007, http://www.spiegel.de/international/germany/german-justice-failures-paving-the-way-for-a-muslim-parallel-society-a-474629.html.

expedite it. Despite the fact that there was little dispute over the extent of the violence this woman had suffered at the hands of her husband, Datz-Winter said that she could not find evidence of "an unreasonable hardship" that would justify an early dissolution of the marriage. According to *Der Spiegel*, an influential German publication:

> "*The judge argued the woman should have 'expected' that her husband, who had grown up in a country influenced by Islamic tradition, would exercise the 'right to use corporal punishment' his religion grants him.*"

On the upside, Germany had acknowledged the Islamic right of a husband to beat his wife. On the downside, it didn't object.

HATUN SÜRÜCÜ

Violence against Muslim women in Germany came to national prominence in 2005 following the killing of Hatun Sürücü, a young Kurdish woman, in Berlin. Hatun was murdered by her brother in an honour-killing at the age of 23. Her offence was to leave her husband (she had been forced to marry her cousin at the age of 16) and move in with a German boyfriend. She was killed by three shots while standing at a bus-stop. Her brother Ayhan confessed to the killing and was sentenced to nine years in prison. Two other brothers, Alparslan and Mutlu, one alleged to have obtained the murder weapon and one to have stood guard at the killing, were acquitted.

Ayhan insisted that he had carried out the killing of his own volition and his family members were not involved. However, the main prosecution witness known as Melek A – who was Ayhan's girlfriend at the time of the killing – disputed this version of events. Now living in hiding under a new identity, in December 2012, she was interviewed by a documentary team[3] and stated:

---

3 "Hatun Sürücü "honor" Killing in Germany," YouTube, last modified December 13, 2012, http://www.youtube.com/watch?v=2e4hdsaGIg4.

*"They were all in on it, I am 100% certain. Alparslan told me. He said that Mutlu got the gun and got the **confir-mation in a mosque** [my emphasis] that killing Hatun was permitted."*

The morning after the murder, Melek A, Alparslan and Ayhan took an underground train together. Melek claimed that Alparslan had told her, "Ayhan did it out of conviction. Do you see the people here? Killing them isn't a sin because they are infidels." She went to the police and the brothers were arrested. Following the acquittal of two of the brothers, the prosecution appealed and were granted a new trial, but by then they had fled to Istanbul from where extradition to Germany is not lawfully possible.

Mutlu was interviewed in Istanbul in 2012. He was asked about his sister, and his feelings towards her.

"I definitely felt hatred [for Hatun]. It started with the way she dressed and there were other things. Why did she change? Why did she want to dress up like that and go out that way? So that boys look and flirt with you. Everybody knows that."

Mutlu denied obtaining the murder weapon and, according to the reporter, said that Islam does not permit people to take justice into their own hands. He added, however, that if Hatun had lived in an Islamic country, she would have been punished.

"If four reliable witnesses were to see that, and she was sentenced in an Islamic state, she'd be sentenced to death... by stoning.... I accept the Islamic laws, I accept what Allah has prescribed."

When Ayhan himself was interviewed about killing his sister, he answered:

"She was very permissive, and very open in how she interacted with men. There were several relationships, and then there was the nightlife."

In March 2005, the BBC published a story on the killing which included a description of comments made by local schoolchildren in Berlin, some of whom had agreed with Hatun's killing because she had "lived like a German"[4].

A Berlin social worker, who wished to remain anonymous, explained that dozens of Muslim girls run away in Berlin every year because they fear being murdered by their families.

A Turkish women's magazine in 2006[5] revealed that six Muslim women had been murdered in Berlin, for the sake of 'honour', over a four month period. The report also claimed that judges often handed out lower sentences for such crimes – in two cases going so far as to reduce murder charges to manslaughter – out of deference to so-called 'cultural differences'. *Der Spiegel* agreed in an article in 2012 and stated that German courts had regularly seen the 'honour' argument in these murders as a mitigating circumstance[6].

In a separate report from *Der Spiegel* magazine, it was claimed that Islamic law – particularly in family matters – has been operating alongside the secular German system for several years. The report, published in 2012, states that Germany now has "two legal systems" and that women in Germany are suffering greatly as a result[7].

SHARIA AND WOMEN'S RIGHTS IN GERMANY

In the city of Recklinghausen, Haj Nur Demir – a 61-year-old Lebanese immigrant – runs a makeshift sharia court from the back room of his furniture store. He has no legal training whatsoever,

---

4 "BBC NEWS | Europe | 'Honour Killing' Shocks Germany," Home - BBC News, last modified March 14, 2005, http://news.bbc.co.uk/1/hi/world/europe/4345459.stm.
5 Stephan Theil, "The Barbarians Within," NEWSWEEK, March 28, 2005, in Papatya, accessed May 2, 2018, http://www.papatya.org/presse13.html.
6 SPIEGEL ONLINE, Hamburg, Germany, "The Role of the Father: Honor Killing Verdict Has Prosecutors Wanting More - International," SPIEGEL ONLINE, last modified May 24, 2012, http://www.spiegel.de/international/germany/prosecutors-focus-on-father-in-german-honor-killing-case-a-834752.html.
7 SPIEGEL ONLINE, Hamburg, Germany, "In the Name of Allah: Islamic Mediators and Germany's 'Two Legal Systems' - International," SPIEGEL ONLINE, last modified June 20, 2012, http://www.spiegel.de/international/germany/islamic-mediators-facilitate-two-legal-systems-in-germany-a-839580.html.

but exercises pseudo-legal authority over many Muslim families. His usual clients, according to reports, are men complaining about their wives and daughters. Marriages are performed, divorces granted, and child custody arrangements are 'advised'.

Terres des Femmes is an organisation devoted to protecting women's rights in Germany. It has reported that forced marriages take up a rather substantial chunk of the imams' time. Rosa Halide M., who runs a shelter for Muslim girls in Stuttgart, has "never witnessed an imam preventing a forced marriage"[8].

Meanwhile, in the state of Rhineland-Palatinate, Interior Minister Jochen Hartloff of the Social Democrats sold the joys of sharia to the German public.

"It [use of sharia] is certainly conceivable," he said, "when it comes to questions pertaining to civil law." What he means by civil law is marriage, divorce, child custody – those small matters that allow women to be beaten, lose their children, and be subjected to domestic slavery. Sharia would, he continued, "Serve the cause of integration"[9].

At the end of 2013, the Gatestone Institute in the United States documented matters of concern regarding Islam in Germany throughout that year[10]. Here are some of the relevant points:

- In January, the city of Bremen's governing council signed a treaty with local Muslim groups guaranteeing:

  "The protection of Muslim community properties, the approval of the construction of mosques with minarets and domes, the allotment of land for Muslim cemeteries, the supplying of halal food in prisons and hospitals, the recognition of three Muslim holidays, Muslim representation in state institutions and several other rights and privileges."

---

8 Ibid.
9 "Politician Blasted for Support of Islamic Law," SPIEGEL ONLINE, February 3, 2012, accessed May 2, 2018, http://www.spiegel.de/international/germany/sharia-in-germany-politician-blasted-for-support-of-islamic-law-a-813148.html.
10 Soeren Kern, "The Islamization of Germany in 2013," Gatestone Institute, last modified January 15, 2014, http://www.gatestoneinstitute.org/4130/islamization-germany.

- It was, according to Gatestone, the second such agreement to be signed in Germany, the first being in Hamburg in November 2012.
- Peer Steinbrück, the Chancellor candidate for the Social Democratic Party, said in Berlin that he supported the idea of physical education classes in German schools being divided by gender as a courtesy to Muslims.
- Bavaria became the first German state to classify 'Islamophobia' as extremism. The German intelligence agency reportedly began to monitor activists who had opposed the building of a so-called 'mega-mosque' in the city of Munich. The result of this is quite clear – the state wants to regulate what German citizens are allowed to campaign against.
- In 2014, 'sharia police' were patrolling the streets of a German city. A propaganda video, entitled 'Sharia Police: Coming Soon to Your City', showed a group of men roaming the streets of Wuppertal at night and urging people to embrace Islam.

But it was the year 2015 that would change Germany forever.

THE COLOGNE RAPES

Chancellor Angela Merkel opened the borders of Europe's biggest power and invited the world to come and join it, triggering a mass exodus from the Middle East and Africa towards her quiet and civilised country, almost all of the migrants young men. What happened next?

Rape happened. Lots of it.

The rape crisis in Germany came to the public consciousness like a shovel to the head in early 2016 in the city of Cologne. The city's police chief reported on New Year's Day that the previous night's festivities had been "largely peaceful"[11]. It might

11 ABC News, "International News: Latest Headlines, Video and Photographs from Around the World -- People, Places, Crisis, Conflict, Culture, Change, Analysis and Trends," ABC News, accessed May 2, 2018, http://abcnews.go.com/International/ wireStory/18-asylum-seekers-linked-crimes-cologne-year-36159623.

have been that Germany had already taken to using the word 'peaceful' in the Islamic sense, or it could have been that a political police force was unwilling to be seen to be critical (by telling the truth) of the Chancellor's insane open border.

What had actually happened the night before in 'largely peaceful' Cologne was that hundreds of women had been sexually assaulted in the street by a 1,000-or-so-strong group of men in full view of an apparently helpless police force. People were assaulted, mugged, and beaten on a public square that fronts the city's main railway station. Several women had been raped, some by gangs.

Over days the news filtered out, each report worse than the last. *France 24* reported in mid-January that over 500 people had been assaulted. Worse still, this had happened all over Germany. Organised gangs had sexually assaulted German women in Berlin, Hamburg, Stuttgart, Dusseldorf...and these are just the cities we know of. All of it was kept undercover at first, because the German establishment did not want Germans to know that it had unleashed Islamic misogyny, as well as savage and violent behaviour, on to the country's streets. Almost all of the men involved were from the Middle East and Africa.

Henriette Reker, the Mayor of Cologne, responded to this crisis by placing restrictions on the movement of women. The Mayor was simply emulating the approach of other authorities throughout Germany when women or girls had been attacked.

In the town of Mering in Bavaria, where a 16-year-old girl had been raped, police warned parents not to allow their children to go out alone. In Pocking, parents were asked to ensure their daughters weren't dressed a certain way, in case this led to 'misunderstandings' (i.e. rape), and grown women were to avoid going to the train station alone because it was close to a refugee centre[12].

And so it began – the Islamisation of women's lives in Germany. Women need to be accompanied; they need to cover up, or failing that, they should stay inside altogether. This is the

---

12 ABC News, "International News: Latest Headlines, Video and Photographs from Around the World -- People, Places, Crisis, Conflict, Culture, Change, Analysis and Trends," ABC News, accessed May 2, 2018, http://abcnews.go.com/International/ wireStory/18-asylum-seekers-linked-crimes-cologne-year-36159623.

future for Germany unless the German people change direction very quickly.

DOUBLE STANDARDS AND DENIAL

Following the mass sexual assault in Cologne, Pegida attempted to hold a rally in that city, but police used water cannon to disperse these 'terrible criminals' for utilising their democratic rights[13]. These are the same police who had stood by and allowed the gropers, robbers, and rapists of New Year's Eve free rein.

Having initially tried to keep the assaults quiet, then issuing guidance on how women ought to be behave, then using water cannon on protestors, the EU (the real government of Germany) pretended the assaults had had nothing to do with the masses of men pouring into Europe every day. For a further stroke of duplicitous genius, it referred to itself as 'the voice of reason' while doing so.

The *Telegraph* reported this as follows[14]:

> *"The sex attacks that took place in Cologne on New Year's Eve were simply a 'matter of public order' and had nothing to do with the refugee crisis, Jean-Claude Juncker's inner circle believe.*
>
> *"The European Commission will be the 'voice of reason' and tell the public that there is no link between the migration crisis affecting the continent and attacks on women in Germany... "amid growing fears of a 'xenophobic' backlash. The minutes of the European Commission's weekly cabinet meeting from January 13 hint at officials' fears that the events in Cologne could turn public opinion sharply against the million migrants who have entered Europe.*

---

13 "German Police Fire Water Cannons at PEGIDA Protesters in Cologne," RT International, accessed May 31, 2018, https://www.rt.com/news/328379-police-pegida-cologne-rally/.

14 "EU Leaders: 'No Link' Between Cologne Sex Attacks and Migrant Crisis," Telegraph.co.uk, last modified January 29, 2016, http://www.telegraph.co.uk/news/worldnews/europe/germany/12130843/EU-leaders-No-link-between-Cologne-sex-attacks-and-migrant-crisis.html.

"The Interior Minister, days after the attacks, said that 'people with a migration background were almost exclusively responsible for the criminal acts'.

"One perpetrator is alleged to have told police he was Syrian, adding: 'You have to treat me kindly. Mrs Merkel invited me.'

"'As far as the crimes in Cologne were concerned, he said that these were a matter of public order and were not related to the refugee crisis,' the minutes say. He went on to set out how a growing proportion of the arrivals are economic migrants, rather than refugees.

"He also observed that the flow of migrants at EU borders was not slowing down and estimates suggested that only about 40% of them, mostly Syrians, were fleeing war and therefore in need of international protection; meanwhile more and more third country nationals were slipping in who were driven by mainly economic reasons and did not qualify for such protection.

"During the discussion that followed, Mr Juncker's team stressed 'the importance of the Commission's continuing to play its coordinating role and sounding the voice of reason to defuse tensions and counter populist rhetoric.'

"They called for 'the unconditional rejection of false associations between certain criminal acts, such as the attacks on women in Cologne on New Year's Eve, and the mass influx of refugees.

"At the same time, they agreed that they must 'respond to the concerns of European citizens, particularly by stressing that Europe was also a union of security and values'."

There is so much wrong with this, it is difficult to know where to start. First, a spectacular lie – the mass attacks by migrants had nothing whatsoever to do with migrants. The Commission fears that public opinion might turn against these migrants. They do not fear for ordinary German people who are attacked in the streets. They acknowledge that the bulk of people coming are not actually refugees, and they acknowledge the crimes being committed by these people, and then their only concern is to control public opinion.

Other arguments from the Left post-Cologne included the notion that the migrant rapists should simply be punished like everyone else. There should be no talk of preventing them entering the country in the first place. This does two things: it makes the victim of rape a mere statistic (the individual is unimportant), and it wrongly supposes that the criminal standard of evidence can be met in cases where women are surrounded by crowds of men in public squares and assaulted. The women are very unlikely to be able to identify these men afterwards. It matters not that rape is such a difficult crime to prosecute; the powers that be decided that open borders are more important, and they are willing to allow people to be raped for that cause. The effect is that every single person on the planet is owed a duty by Germany; all they have to do is go there. Being a German citizen is meaningless, the notion of the national citizen breaks down, and the leftist dream of borderlessness continues unabated.

Another leftist-approved idea is to provide 'guidance' to Muslim immigrants, the guidance being "please don't rape women". In doing this, the Left yet again finds itself in something of a quandary: why on earth would we need to provide guidance if there is no threat? The message is effectively this: "these men are just the same as us, but we'll give them classes and ask them not to rape anyone – in honour of our shared values". Keep in mind that in most cases, these guidance classes were voluntary. Common sense should tell us that the men who would volunteer for a class on how to treat women with a bit of respect are in fact the men who least need it – but common sense has no place in this debate.

When the truth becomes so widely known that lies no longer work, the politically correct contort themselves in and out of the most absurd positions. As countries began to announce plans for classes for migrants on how to be civilised towards women, an extraordinary article[15] in Britain's *Independent* revealed just how casually our media establishment treats rape when non-Westerners are involved.

---

15 "Refugees Are Being Given Classes on 'Western Sexual Norms' in Norway," The Independent, last modified January 9, 2016, http://www.independent.co.uk/news/world/europe/norway-refugees-given-classes-on-sexual-norms-a6803666.html.

The article's author, Jake Alden-Falconer, wrote of European politicians:

> *"Many were previously reluctant to suggest that men from more conservative societies would misinterpret women's behaviour, for fear of stigmatising migrants as potential rapists and playing into the hands of anti-immigrant politicians."*

Conservative societies? So rape is a conservative value?

That aside, this creates the impression that we are importing only conservatism – nothing to worry about. The migrants don't *really* come from a brutal misogynist society. Alden-Falconer goes on to suggest that these conservatives may "misinterpret women's behaviour". So by implication, it is women's behaviour that is the problem. If only women would behave differently – maybe more like women in 'conservative' Muslim societies – we wouldn't have this problem.

It gets worse. The classes on how not to rape would not take the form of a lecture. Instead, they were to have a 'group discussion' feel about them.

Linda Hagen, a spokeswoman for a Norwegian company that runs 40% of Norway's asylum centres, said, "Our aim is to help asylum seekers avoid mistakes as they discover Norwegian culture."

Mistakes? Does she mean sexual assault?

She continued:

> *"There's no single cultural code to say what is good or bad behaviour because we want a free society. There has to be tolerance for attitudes that may be seen as immoral by some traditional or religious norms."*

Boom! There it is.

There is no single cultural code to say what is good or bad behaviour. This is the scourge of the moral relativism destroying Western society. Essentially, raping a woman is no better or worse than not raping her. Who are we to judge other people's 'conservative' cultural practices?

PSEUDO-FEMINISM

The 'feminist' response to Cologne was even worse.

Gaby Hinsliff is a feminist and a *Guardian* writer (something that increasingly sounds like a contradiction in terms). After Cologne, she implied that those of us who were opposed to mass immigration were delighted by these horrific events[16]. This moral judgement comes from a woman who still supports mass migration while knowing for certain it will cause women to be raped. She throws in the obligatory nonsense about how millions of uneducated men (often illiterate in their own language) are going to provide a much-needed boost to our economy.

She also employed more leftist slipperiness when she said that stopping immigration isn't possible. This is propaganda regularly used by the Left – to pretend the idea of stopping immigration is ridiculous and border control unrealistic even though most countries in the world have perfectly functional border controls.

Laurie Penney, a well-known 'radical feminist', provided her thoughts on Cologne in the *New Statesman*[17]. According to her, the oppression of women is a global phenomenon because patriarchy is a global phenomenon. It's embedded in the economic and social structures of almost every nation and community on earth.

Here are excerpts from a response I wrote to Laurie Penney at the time:

> This is important. It is a direct message to all feminists who support the massive and unprecedented immigration that Europe is experiencing now, and has experienced for the last couple of decades. It is not enough to dismiss us all as racists and bigots; this may make you feel more comfortable, but it simply isn't true. It isn't bigotry or racism to observe and acknowledge reality, and there are some harsh realities that I wish you would take on board.

16 Gaby Hinsliff, "Let's Not Shy Away from Asking Hard Questions About the Cologne Attacks | Gaby Hinsliff," The Guardian, last modified November 28, 2017, http://www.theguardian.com/commentisfree/2016/jan/08/cologne-attacks-hard-questions-new-years-eve.
17 "After Cologne, We Can't Let the Bigots Steal Feminism," New Statesman | Britain's Current Affairs & Politics Magazine, accessed May 31, 2018, http://www.newstatesman.com/politics/feminism/2016/01/after-cologne-we-cant-let-bigots-steal-feminism.

Human beings are not all equal.

Like it or not, there are a lot of people out there who want violence and misogyny, who want the right to marry off their daughters, or to mutilate girls' genitals. Some people are rapists, some are jihadists, and some take great pleasure from tearing the clothes from a woman in a public square on New Year's Eve. The executioner is a human being; the sharia oppressor is a human being; the mutilator is a human being. Not all human beings have good intentions.

Not all cultures are equal, either, and nowhere is this more evident than in the treatment of women. You rightly point out that sexual assault is a serious matter regardless of where it takes place, but the fact is that these attacks did not take place in Germany prior to now, and German men were not responsible for them. These were attacks carried out by immigrants in Germany, and most have come from Muslim-majority countries.

Everywhere that Islam has influence, women suffer because of it. The severity varies, but I would argue that it varies depending upon how much influence Islam actually has.

Sharia law, a law based on Islam, is uniquely terrible to women. You need to confront this reality, and realise that it is right here in Britain, and thriving. Even if you argue that sharia councils are a matter of choice, which they're not, are you happy with the availability of that choice? Do you think treating women like that is something we should be able to choose to do? Or should it be disallowed on principle? Why aren't you, as a feminist, speaking out about that?

Not all religions are the same. To argue that they are is to argue that the religion itself, its scripture and its practices aren't actually relevant. Today, the Western world is not influenced in any significant way by Biblical literalism. The Islamic world, on the other hand, is enormously influenced by Quranic literalism, so much so that you can be executed (by law of the land) for questioning or criticising it. These are two different worlds, and like it or not, they are not compatible.

Immigration is bringing Islamic norms and attitudes towards women to the West, and it is making free women less free, and safe women less safe. We are turning back the clock on all of the achievements that have been made in the Western world. This is bad news for all women, regardless of where they live.

GERMANY'S ROLL OF SHAME

The Muslim population of Germany skyrocketed in 2015 and 2016. Despite gains for the only party with the courage to oppose migration in Germany, the AfD (*Alternative für Deutschland*), Chancellor Merkel stated clearly that she will not change course. In 2016, a further 300,000 Muslim migrants entered Germany, putting the country in competition with France for the largest Muslim population in Europe. This will result in countless more rapes and several more deaths.

- July 2016 – An Afghan migrant shouting *"Allahu Akbar"* injured five people on a train in Wurzburg with an axe[18].
- July 2016 – Ali Sonboly, an 18-year-old Iranian, killed ten people (including himself) and wounded 35 others at a McDonald's in Munich[19].
- July 2016 – Mohammed Daleel, a Syrian migrant whose asylum application had been rejected, injured 15 people when he blew himself up at a concert in Ansbach[20].
- July 2016 – A 21-year-old Syrian murdered a Polish woman and her unborn baby with a machete in Reutlingen[21].

18 "German Police Kill Train Axe Attacker," BBC News, last modified July 19, 2016, http://www.bbc.co.uk/news/world-europe-36827725.
19 "Knifeman on Loose After People Attacked in Munich," The Independent, last modified October 21, 2017, http://www.independent.co.uk/news/world/europe/knife-attacker-munich-germany-police-twitter-several-injured-a8012411.html.
20 "Suicide Bomber in Ansbach, Germany, Pledged Loyalty to ISIS, Officials Say," The New York Times - Breaking News, World News & Multimedia, last modified January 20, 2018, https://www.nytimes.com/2016/07/26/world/europe/ansbach-germany-music-festival-explosion.html.
21 "Germany Machete Attack: Syrian Asylum Seeker Murders 'pregnant' Woman in Reutlingen," The Telegraph, accessed May 3, 2018, http://www.telegraph.co.uk/news/2016/07/24/syrian-refugee-kills-woman-with-machete-in-southern-germany/.

- August 2016 – Muslim 'sharia patrols' began operating around Hamburg[22].
- August 2016 – A man shouting *"Allahu Akbar"* stabbed a man and woman picnicking in Oberhausen[23].
- September 2016 – A report revealed that 1,475 married *children* are now resident in Germany[24].
- December 2016 – A 17-year-old Afghan was arrested for the rape and murder of 19-year-old medical student Maria Ladenburger in Freiburg[25].
- December 2016 – 12 people were murdered and dozens injured in Berlin when a Tunisian migrant drove a truck into shoppers at a Christmas market in the capital[26].
- February 2017 – a report revealed that 48,000 women and girls in Germany have been victims of female genital mutilation (FGM)[27].
- February 2017 – a woman was murdered by a Nigerian asylum seeker for rejecting his sexual advances[28].
- March 2017 – a woman was murdered for ending a relationship with a Moroccan asylum seeker[29].

---

22 Breitbart News, "New Sharia Police Patrol Forming In Hamburg," Breitbart, last modified August 12, 2016, http://www.breitbart.com/london/2016/08/12/new-sharia-police-patrol-forming-hamburg/.

23 James Cox, "Knifeman 'shouts Allahu Akbar' As He Attacks Couple at Music Festival Leaving Wife Fighting for Life," The Sun, last modified August 28, 2016, https://www.thesun.co.uk/news/1686934/knifeman-shouts-allahu-akbar-as-he-attacks-couple-at-music-festival-leaving-wife-fighting-for-life/.

24 Soeren Kern, "Germany Imports Child Marriage," Gatestone Institute, last modified October 6, 2016, https://www.gatestoneinstitute.org/9078/germany-child-marriage.

25 "Afghan Refugee 'raped and Killed EU Official's Daughter to Satisfy Sexual Urges'," Metro, last modified September 6, 2017, http://metro.co.uk/2017/09/06/afghan-national-raped-eu-officials-daughter-to-satisfy-sexual-urges-before-killing-her-6906912/.

26 "Berlin Attack: What We Know," BBC News, last modified December 24, 2016, http://www.bbc.co.uk/news/world-europe-38377428.

27 "50,000 Women in Germany Have Suffered Genital Mutilation: Report," The Local - Germany's News in English, last modified February 7, 2017, https://www.thelocal.de/20170207/50000-women-in-germany-have-been-genitally-mutilated-report.

28 "Nigerianer (27) in Der Schweiz Festgenommen - Festnahme Nach Mord an Flüchtlingshelferin," Bild.de, last modified February 14, 2017, http://www.bild.de/regional/ruhrgebiet/mord/fluechtlingshelferin-wohl-von-fluechtling-erstochen-50425302.bild.html.

29 Gabi Peters, "Mord in Rheydt: Polizei Identifiziert Mordopfer," Westdeutsche Zeitung, last modified March 5, 2017, http://www.wz.de/lokales/moenchengladbach/mord-in-rheydt-polizei-identifiziert-mordopfer-1.2391143.

- March 2017 – a migrant from Kosovo was arrested for injuring nine people with an axe at a train station in Dusseldorf[30].
- March 2017 – an 80-year-old man was attacked with a machete in Dusseldorf[31].
- May 2017 – a Somali asylum seeker murdered an 87-year-old woman at a retirement home in Neuenhaus[32].
- July 2017 – sharia patrols (enforcing sharia law in public) began in Berlin[33].
- July 2017 – an Iraqi-Kurdish asylum seeker opened fire with an M16 machine gun at a nightclub in Konstanz, killing one[34].
- August 2017 – a report revealed that murder rates in the city of Bremen had reached more than one per day[35].
- October 2017 – an assistant at a refugee centre in Ahaus was murdered by a migrant from Nigeria.[36]
- November 2017 – more than 200 churches were vandalised in Bavaria[37].

---

30 "Amoklauf Mit Neun Verletzten - Das Ist Der Axt-Mann Von Düsseldorf," Bild.de, last modified March 11, 2017, http://www.bild.de/regional/duesseldorf/amoklauf/der-amoklauefer-von-gleis-13-50796416.bild.html.

31 Erneute Attacke: Rentner in Düsseldorf Angegriffen Und Verletzt ? Täter Flüchtig - WELT," DIE WELT, last modified March 10, 2017, https://www.welt.de/vermischtes/article162735923/Rentner-in-Duesseldorf-angegriffen-und-verletzt-Taeter-fluechtig.html.

32 Mord in Neuenhaus: Angeklagter Verurteilt," GN-Online, October 5, 2017, accessed May 3, 2018, https://www.gn-online.de/neuenhaus/mord-in-neuenhaus-angeklagter-verurteilt-192676.html.

33 Soeren Kern, "Germany: Chechen Sharia Police Terrorize Berlin," Gatestone Institute, last modified July 8, 2017, https://www.gatestoneinstitute.org/10632/germany-chechens.

34 "Iraker (34) Schoss in Konstanzer Disko Um Sich - Holte Er Die Waffe, Weil Der Türsteher Ihn Rauswarf?," Bild.de, last modified July 30, 2017, http://www.bild.de/news/inland/news/konstanz-52704772.bild.html.

35 "13 Tote Im Großraum Bremen Seit 2014! - Immer Mehr Messer-Attacken," Bild.de, last modified August 23, 2017, http://www.bild.de/regional/bremen/stichwaffen/immer-mehr-messer-attacken-52951508.bild.html.

36 "13 Jahre Haft Für Anthony I," Hauptsache Heimat. WP.de, last modified October 12, 2017, https://www.wp.de/staedte/arnsberg/13-jahre-haft-fuer-anthony-i-id212210087.html.

37 "Anschläge Auf Gipfelkreuze Und Kirchen," TheEuropean, last modified November 9, 2017, http://www.theeuropean.de/valentin-weimer/11643-anschlaege-auf-gipfelkreuze-und-kirchen.

- December 2017 – 'Safe Zones' for women were established for the first time to prevent rape and sexual assault by migrants[38].

The above list does not include vast numbers of incidents of rape and sexual assault, attempted murder, inter-migrant violence, or foiled jihadi terror attacks. While these drastic changes to German society increased, German authorities continued the cover it up, attacking objectors while insisting immigration, and certainly Islam, bore no responsibility. The media was warned against reporting uncomfortable truths and police raids took place across the country to apprehend people who had made unpleasant comments on social media[39]. Anti-Semitism, like rape, has exploded across Germany and Jews are leaving the country en masse. Furthermore, age-old German festivals saw record low levels of attendance as the people of Germany became too afraid to venture outside.

But it appeared to make little difference to the German public. In September 2016, Angela Merkel was elected yet again, and hundreds of thousands of Muslim migrants continue to enter Germany[40].

38 "Berlin to Host New Year's Eve 'safe Zone' for Women As Authorities Crack Down on Harassment," The Telegraph, accessed May 3, 2018, http://www.telegraph.co.uk/news/2017/12/29/berlin-host-new-years-eve-safe-zones-women-authorities-crack/.
39 "Germany Raids Homes of 36 People Accused of Hateful Postings Over Social Media," The New York Times - Breaking News, World News & Multimedia, last modified December 22, 2017, https://www.nytimes.com/2017/06/20/world/europe/germany-36-accused-of-hateful-postings-over-social-media.html.
40 Kate Connolly, "German Election: Merkel Wins Fourth Term but Far-right AfD Surges to Third," The Guardian, last modified November 27, 2017, https://www.theguardian.com/world/2017/sep/24/angela-merkel-fourth-term-far-right-afd-third-german-election.

THE NETHERLANDS
AND NORWAY

THE NETHERLANDS

On 2 November 2004, the Netherlands awoke to news that would shake the nation and alter the discourse on the radical Islam growing in its midst. Film-maker Theo van Gogh had been murdered on the streets of Amsterdam for making a film critical of the treatment of women in Islam.

A collaboration with former Dutch MP and Somali dissident Ayaan Hirsi Ali, Van Gogh's film *Submission* portrayed a young Muslim woman forced into an abusive marriage and raped by family members. The film caused an outcry among some Dutch Muslims and forced Hirsi Ali into hiding; a note warning her that her life was also in danger was pinned to Van Gogh's chest. Following the killing, both churches and mosques were burned in tit-for-tat reprisals.

Dutch-born Mohammed Bouyeri would later be convicted of the murder.

Given that the killing of Van Gogh was an act of terror, and therefore not within the range of discussion of this book, I will not concentrate on it any further.

GEERT WILDERS

The fact is that democracy in the Netherlands faces numerous threats as a result of Islam – something evidenced in the persecution of an elected Parliamentarian by the name of Geert Wilders.

Wilders is a highly controversial and divisive figure. He has been described as everything from a hero to a racist to a Nazi. But the fact remains that Wilders is speaking his mind, and has an electoral mandate to do so. He has not called for violence nor threatened anyone's life, but he now lives under constant threat and resides in government safe houses. On top of this, he has been prosecuted by the courts of his own country. He is a prime example of the extent to which politicians and their words are under the control of, and subject to, Islamic sensitivity.

Wilders was eventually acquitted of the various charges brought against him, but it is the charges themselves that should worry us. They demonstrated a tendency towards group rather than individual rights, and thereby altered the relationship between citizen and state.

The legal journey of Wilders is long and complex so I will attempt to simplify it. He had been charged under section 137C and 137D of the Dutch Penal Code. Respectively, these read:

> "*A person who publicly, either orally, or in writing, or by image, intentionally makes a defamatory statement about a group of persons on the grounds of their race, religion or personal beliefs, or their hetero- or homosexual orientation, is liable to a term of imprisonment of a period of not more than one year or a fine of the third category.*"

> "*A person who publicly, either orally or in writing or by image, incites hatred of or discrimination against persons or violence against their person or property, on the grounds of their race, religion or personal beliefs, their sex or their hetero- or homosexual orientation, is liable to a term of imprisonment of not more than one year, or a fine of the third category.*"

The first word to spring to attention is 'defamatory'. To be defamatory, a claim must be false. If it is true, it cannot be defamatory. What also cannot be defamatory is the expression of an opinion that is based on truth.

Wilders was acquitted because the presiding judge ruled that his comments had been "acceptable within the context of public debate". In what he described as "a political trial", Wilders was denied the right to bring forward witnesses who he argued would confirm the truths contained within his criticisms of Islam[1]. Among the witnesses he sought to call was Mohammed Bouyeri, the murderer of Theo van Gogh.

Further ammunition that Wilders possessed to support his allegation that the trial was political included the fact that the prosecution had attempted to persuade the court there was no case to answer, and the charges against Wilders should be dropped[2]. This was ignored. Perhaps most strikingly, the initial trial (Wilders was tried twice) had collapsed because the panel of judges was deemed to be biased[3]. It emerged at the time that one of the judges, who had ordered Wilders to be tried, had had dinner with one of the potential witnesses and attempted to persuade him of the merits of prosecuting Wilders.

The trials of Geert Wilders were legally bewildering from start to finish. Even the prosecution argued there were no legal grounds, but the trial was ordered anyway – why? Was there a political message to be delivered by way of this trial? Wilders described the process as a farce and his eventual acquittal as a "victory for freedom of speech".

Much of the Western media at the time portrayed Wilders as a menace, and continue to do so – none more assiduously than the BBC.

---

1 "Http://webcache.googleusercontent.com/search'q=cache://www.dutchnews.nl/news/ archives/2010/02/court_limits_wilders_witness_l," DutchNews.nl Brings Daily News from The Netherlands in English, February 3, 2010, http://www.dutchnews.nl/news/ archives/2010/02/court_limits_wilders_witness_l.

2 "Pagina Niet Gevonden," Openbaar Ministerie, accessed May 31, 2018, http://www. om.nl/actueel-0/strafzaken/strafzaak_tegen/@154305/public_prosecution_0/ (page discontinued).

3 Ian Traynor, "Geert Wilders Hate Speech Trial Collapses in Netherlands," The Guardian, last modified November 26, 2017, http://www.theguardian.com/world/2010/ oct/22/geert-wilders-trial-collapses.

Before I describe the BBC's portrayal of Wilders, it is pertinent to address precisely what he has done to be denounced so widely. He is an outspoken critic of Islam and has described it not as a religion, but a totalitarian ideology comparable to communism and fascism. This is his opinion; he is surely entitled to it. He has called for the Koran to be banned under Dutch law because, he argued, it contains hate speech and as such should be held to the same standards as any other document.

His most notorious work, which gained global attention, was a short film called *Fitna*. This film superimposes verses from the Koran on to visual depictions of terrorist acts around the world, including the 9/11 atrocities, and implies that the Koran had inspired such acts.

As well as his judicial trial in Holland, Geert Wilders was also tried by the media, and he was guilty from the very beginning. The BBC screened a documentary that confirmed his guilt in the title: 'Europe's Most Dangerous man?'[4]

Among the Muslim representatives on the BBC documentary were members of the sharia-advocating Muslim Council of Britain. The most interesting Muslim voice was without doubt that of Khalid Yasin, who is matter-of-factly described as "having embarked on a mission to de-radicalise" young European Muslims.

Really?

As Melanie Phillips wrote at the time in an article entitled 'The World's Most Dangerous Broadcaster'[5], the documentary's creators appeared to have forgotten another occasion where we met Mr Yasin: Channel 4's 'Undercover Mosque'. In that film, Yasin was secretly filmed saying:

> "*We Muslims have been ordered to do 'brainwashing' because the kuffaar* [non-Muslims]...*they are doing 'brain defiling'...You are watching the kaffir TVs, and your wife is watching* [it] *right now, and your children are watch-*

---

4 "This World Geert Wilders Europes Most Dangerous Man Part 1," YouTube, last modified February 15, 2011, https://www.youtube.com/watch?v=0JJQffI4vbM.
5 "New English Review," New English Review, accessed May 4, 2018, http://www.newenglishreview.org/blog_email.cfm/blog_id/32762 (page discontinued).

ing it right now, and they are being polluted, and they are being penetrated, and they are being infected, so that your children and you go out as Muslims and come back to the house as kaffirs...The whole delusion of the equality of women is a bunch of foolishness. There's no such thing."

The BBC has a very strange idea of what constitutes de-radicalisation, it would seem.

Phillips also addressed the inclusion of the Muslim Council of Britain, which the BBC described as "an organisation seeking to promote a distinct Muslim identity in tune with British cultural norms and values". Again, it seems to have forgotten that the Muslim Council of Britain promotes sharia, something not in tune with British cultural norms and values at all.

Fast forward a couple of years, and Geert Wilders is again in the dock, this time for inciting discrimination[6]. He was found guilty, but the court refused to impose any sentence, saying the conviction alone was enough punishment for a politician. He was found not guilty of a separate charge of inciting hatred. These charges were brought following a fiery speech delivered by Wilders in which he asked his audience if they would like fewer Moroccans in the Netherlands[7]. His audience enthusiastically replied that indeed they would.

Moroccans are a significant minority in the Netherlands (it is difficult to find reliable figures, but some statistics state that Moroccans make up 9% of the population of Amsterdam, with males aged under 25 constituting 16% of that age/gender bracket)[8]. What makes the Moroccan population so controversial is its apparent overrepresentation in crime. The Gatestone Institute, reporting on findings of the Dutch Ministry of Interior, wrote in 2011 that 40% of Moroccan immigrants in the

---

6 "Geert Wilders Found Guilty of Inciting Discrimination," The Guardian, last modified November 28, 2017, https://www.theguardian.com/world/2016/dec/09/geert-wilders-found-guilty-in-hate-speech-trial-but-no-sentence-imposed.

7 Uri Friedman, "Should Calling for 'Fewer Moroccans? Be Considered Hate Speech?," The Atlantic, last modified November 2, 2016, https://www.theatlantic.com/international/archive/2016/11/geert-wilders-free-hate-speech/506018/.

8 "Moroccan-Dutch," Wikipedia, the Free Encyclopedia, last modified May 4, 2018, https://en.wikipedia.org/wiki/Moroccan-Dutch#cite_note-Buijsetal634-9.

Netherlands, aged between 12 and 24, had been arrested, fined, charged, or otherwise accused of a crime over a 5-year period[9]:

Showing he was not to be deterred, Wilders again denounced Moroccan crime in Holland when he referred to "Moroccan scum" while on the campaign trail for the 2017 Dutch general elections. Whatever one thinks of such language, it was resonating with the Dutch people, and Wilders was leading the polls[10].

Naturally enough, the Left-wing media focused solely on the language of Wilders, and ignored the levels of crime among Moroccan immigrants. The British Left-wing press was clear about who was in the wrong here. The *Independent*, for example, focused on how 'unsafe' Muslim migrants (primarily Turkish and Moroccan) were feeling in the Netherlands[11].

It clearly matters little to the Left-wing media if native Dutch are feeling unsafe as their country is transformed beyond recognition.

Despite Wilders riding high in the run-up to the elections of 2017, the Dutch people decided it was not the time, and Wilders's party came second at 13.1% of the vote. It was, however, the largest ever showing for Wilders in a national election, and a sign of the probable direction of feeling in Holland.

GAY RIGHTS IN THE NETHERLANDS

Pim Fortuyn had also been critical of Islam. Fortuyn was a politician and writer who denounced Islam as "a backward culture"[12]. He was openly gay and worried about the impact of

---

9 Soeren Kern, «Moroccan Crime in the Netherlands & the Myths of Multiculturalism,» Gatestone Institute, last modified November 28, 2011, https://www.gatestoneinstitute. org/2624/moroccan-crime-netherlands.

10 Robin McKie, "Far-right Leader Geert Wilders Calls Moroccan Migrants 'scum'," The Guardian, last modified December 1, 2017, https://www.theguardian.com/world/2017/ feb/18/geert-wilders-netherlands-describes-immigrants-scum-holland.

11 "Far-right Dutch Politician Geert Wilders Condemns 'Moroccan Scum' at Election Campaign Launch," The Independent, last modified February 18, 2017, http://www. independent.co.uk/news/world/europe/geert-wilders-moroccan-slum-election-campaign-launch-netherlands-holland-dutch-islamophobia-a7587711.html.

12 "BBC News | EUROPE | Obituary: Pim Fortuyn," Home - BBC News, last modified May 6, 2002, http://news.bbc.co.uk/1/hi/world/europe/1971462.stm.

Muslim immigration to the Netherlands with regard to the rights of homosexuals there (the BBC described him as having "used his sexuality as fuel for his fire against Islam, which – like many other religions – does not accept homosexuality").

Fortuyn was murdered by a Left-wing activist just days before Parliamentary elections in 2002. At his trial for the murder, Volkert van der Graaf (an animal rights campaigner whose compassion appears to have been for animals only), told the court that Fortuyn represented an "ever-growing danger" in Dutch society.

In a city once known to many as the gay capital of Europe, gay model Michael du Pree was dragged off stage at a fashion show and beaten, a group of lesbian women were injured with bottles during a protest against attacks on gays in the city, and the founder of Amsterdam Pride, Hugo Braakhuis, was also attacked, all in the space of a few short years. In an offender study by the University of Amsterdam in 2007, 201 hate crimes against homosexuals were recorded. Two thirds of the attackers in these cases were *"Muslim youths"*[13].

The people of the liberal, tolerant, and peaceful Netherlands have, in the 21st century, witnessed a political assassination, brought elected Parliamentarians to trial merely for speaking, and seen a film-maker butchered in the street. Some of their politicians are on the run for their lives. All of these cases have one thing in common: they all involved people who had criticised Islam.

NORWAY

Rape and anti-Semitism figures have exploded in Norway in recent years. Sexual assaults increased to such a degree in the Norwegian capital that extra police were drafted in from other parts of the country in 2011 to assist with the large number of investigations[14]. According to the Oslo police, *all* violent stranger

13 "(no Title)," Toronto Sun, last modified October 8, 2010, http://www.torontosun.com/comment/columnists/ezra_levant/2010/10/08/15630946.html.
14 Rolleiv Solholm, "More Police to Be Transferred to Oslo," The Norway Post, accessed May 31, 2018, http://www.norwaypost.no/index.php/news/latest-news/25917-more-police-to-be-transferred-to-oslo-25917.

rapes committed in that city over a three-year period were carried out by "non-western immigrants"[15].

Hanne Kristen Rohde is a senior police officer in Oslo. In April 2010, she said this on a major Norwegian TV channel about rapes of ethnic Norwegian women:

> "*The perpetrators are relatively young men...They are often asylum seekers who come from traumatised countries, or from countries where they have a completely different view on women than we have in Norway*[16]."

When asked if there were cases in Oslo of violent stranger rape committed by ethnic Norwegian men, she replied, "No, we have had no such cases in our department."

The response of the police to this rape epidemic at the time was to "educate" and "work with other agencies". The plan, it appeared, was to ask men nicely not to rape Norwegian women. If that didn't work, perhaps anthropologist Unni Wikan had a better plan.

> "*I will not blame the rapes on Norwegian women. But Norwegian women must understand that we live in a multicultural society and adapt themselves to it*[17]."

There you have it: to accommodate the violent misogyny arriving on the shores of Norway, Norwegian women must alter their own behaviour and limit their freedoms.

The American author Bruce Bawer, a resident of Norway for some years, highlighted what he called a "piece of propaganda"[18]

15 "41 Rapes in Norway by Non Indigenous Norwegians," YouTube, last modified June 12, 2011, https://www.youtube.com/watch?v=g7t5ZffkA0A.

16 "Oslo, Norway: 100% of Rapes Committed by 'non European Immigrants' (muslims)," YouTube, last modified October 10, 2013, https://www.youtube.com/watch?v=a56EqUPwyFQ.

17 "Letter to Professor Unni Wikan Celebrated Norwegian Anthropologist | Marculyseas," Marculyseas | Paradox in Paradise – Poems & Essays, accessed May 4, 2018, https://marculyseas.wordpress.com/category/letter-to-professor-unni-wikan-celebrated-norwegian-anthropologist/.

18 "Norway's Happy Lies on Muslim Immigration," Frontpage Mag, last modified June 22, 2015, http://www.frontpagemag.com/2013/bruce-bawer/norways-happy-lies-on-muslim-immigration/.

from the *Aftenposten* newspaper which ran the headline 'People with Immigrant Backgrounds Are Becoming More Like the Rest of Us' in 2013. Bawer claimed that the bureau which released that reassuring piece of information, Statistics Norway, "has a long record of massaging its numbers".

One parent, in a 2011 news report[19], said he planned to move his family out of Oslo as it was increasingly "difficult to be an ethnic Norwegian".

A kindergarten teacher, Patrick, claimed:

> "[There are] *almost no children or parents* [who] *speak Norwegian, and there are schools where children are threatened with beatings if they bring salami with them for their school lunch. Girls are bullied for being blonde, and they colour their hair dark to avoid it and fit in. It is especially not OK to be gay at the school, nor atheist, and especially not Jewish. Over the last three years it has been particularly frightening to watch and hear about every-thing that happens."*

NRK, Norway's national broadcaster, expanded on some of these issues in a special report in early 2012[20]. An eight-year-old boy, Elias, who lived in an area in Oslo with a 45% immigrant population, was interviewed about his life as young ethnic Norwegian there. Elias told reporters that he faced taunts of "Eww, you eat pigs" and "When you eat pigs, you go to the devil". Elias didn't like school much as he found it hard to make friends there, and no other children would play with him.

He also struggled to make friends at home, a fact confirmed by his mother, who said that Elias "stands out for being tall and blond".

Teachers at Elias's school admitted that pupils there are bullied for being non-Muslim.

---

19 Breitbart News, "Islam In Norway: Bullying Kids For Being Blond; Children Threatened If They Bring Salami To School," Breitbart, last modified March 25, 2011, http://www.breitbart.com/national-security/2011/03/25/islam-in-norway--bullying-kids-for-being-blond--children-threatened-if-they-bring-salami-to-school.
20 "Muslim Racism in Norway," YouTube, accessed May 5, 2018, http://www.youtube.com/watch?v=1250NUdBJ8c (video discontinued).

SHARIA IN NORWAY

As the Muslim population of Norway continues to grow, demands for sharia law inevitably follow. In a *Russia Today* report in 2012[21], a group called Ansar al-Sunna sent a letter to prominent Norwegian journalists and politicians threatening a "September 11 on Norwegian soil" if a section of the capital, Grønland, were not handed over to be governed by sharia law. The letter demanded:

> "*Our own ministers, border guards, police, and legal system, run according to sharia laws, and forbid all the evil you stand for and that violates Allah's laws*[22]...*We don't want to live together with filthy beasts like you.*"

If Norwegians were in any doubt as to what Grønland would look like under sharia, a rather ironically named 'peace conference' held in Oslo a year later would provide some helpful insight[23]. Fahad Qureshi, founder of the Norwegian Islam Net organisation, took to the stage to address a large audience. He complained that the media invariably identified the invited speakers to the conference – some of whom support "the death penalty for homosexuals" – as homophobic and therefore extreme. Qureshi explained that it wasn't just a speaker or two who held these extreme radical views, but that they were the "views that every Muslim actually has".

He went on to ask the audience members to raise their hands if they supported the notion that men and women should be segregated. Pretty much all of them (from what can be made out) complied. He made the same request with regard to stoning as a punishment for adultery; again, the vast majority of audience members raised their hands. Finally, he asked them to confirm that they were not extremists, or radicals. They did.

---

21 "Sharia Zones in Norway RT," MRCTV, accessed May 5, 2018, http://www.mrctv.org/videos/sharia-zones-norway-rt (video discontinued).

22 "Oslo Muslims Demand Sharia-Controlled Zone," Frontpage Mag, last modified June 22, 2015, https://www.frontpagemag.com/fpm/140897/oslo-muslims-demand-sharia-controlled-zone-bruce-bawer.

23 "Islamic Peace Conference Norway March 2013," MRCTV, accessed May 5, 2018, http://www.mrctv.org/videos/islamic-peace-conference-norway-march-2013.

The Muslim Brotherhood-linked Islamic Council of Norway stirred up controversy when it refused to condemn the death penalty for homosexuality[24].

ANDERS BEHRING BREIVIK

By far the most prominent and horrific story to emerge from Norway in several decades, and one linked inextricably to Islam, is that of mass murderer Anders Behring Breivik. In 2011, Breivik murdered 77 people – many of them children. On the morning of 22 July, he committed his first atrocity of the day when he blew up a government building in Oslo and killed eight people. Later that afternoon, he travelled to the island of Utøya and murdered 69 more. His target on the island was the Norwegian Labour Party youth camp.

He claimed that the purpose of the attack was to save Norway and Western Europe from a Muslim takeover, which he felt had been facilitated by the political Left, in particular the Labour Party.

Breivik is a vicious murderer and all decent people condemn his abhorrent acts. What is interesting about the fallout from these killings, however, is the response of the multicultural-ism-supporting Left-leaning press, and the immediacy with which they blamed all critics of Islam for his crimes.

Breivik had written a 'manifesto' prior to the killings, and in it had named several prominent people who had spoken out against Islamism and sharia. Among them were some British journalists, writers, and politicians, including George Orwell, Edmund Burke, and Winston Churchill. One of Britain's most prominent journalists to be named in the manifesto was Melanie Phillips. Phillips wrote an article[25] summarising the despicable attempts by many on the Left to associate legitimate criticism of

---

24 "Homosexuality - Punishable by Death?," Religion News Blog, last modified May 9, 2014, http://www.religionnewsblog.com/21959/islam-fatwa-homosexuality.

25 "MELANIE PHILLIPS: Hatred, Smears and the Liberals Hell-bent on Bullying Millions of Us into Silence," Mail Online, last modified August 1, 2011, http://www.dailymail.co.uk/news/article-2020924/Anders-Behring-Breivik-Liberals-hell-bent-bullying-silence.html.

Islam with Breivik's crimes.

"The atrocity has produced a reaction among people on the political Left in Britain, Europe and the US that is in itself shocking and terrifying."

Phillips pointed to the reaction of the former Norwegian Prime Minister, and chair of the Nobel Peace Prize Committee, who said that leaders who criticised multiculturalism were "playing with fire" in using rhetoric that could be exploited by the likes of Breivik.

As Phillips rightly stated, "It is perverse to suggest that no one should write about these things because some deranged person raving about such ideas has run amok." Far from criticism of Islamic extremism being exploited by Breivik, Phillips argues – again rightly, in my view – that it is in fact the Left-wing critics who are exploiting the murders to silence that criticism.

Anders Breivik alone is responsible for his terrible crimes, and criticisms of Islam in Europe, and elsewhere, are still entirely valid. Norwegian politicians, however, tend to 'to and fro' on the matter.

Erna Solberg has been Prime Minister of Norway since 2013. At the height of the migration crisis (when Germany invited the world to Europe, and it came), she made it clear that 'refugees' were increasingly unwelcome in Norway, and most of those en route to Europe were not refugees at all[26]. She also made it clear that there would be no free ride for migrants in Norway; that people would be required to work, and they would have to accept Norwegian cultural norms.

The country's Immigration Minister similarly said, "I think those who come to Norway need to adapt to our society" in 2016[27].

Inconsistency abounds, however, and Solberg has also been accused of pandering to Islam. According to one article,[28] Solberg

---

26 "Norwegian PM: Not Natural to Accept These Migrants into Europe," Speisa, accessed May 5, 2018, http://speisa.com/modules/articles/index.php/item.1186/norwegian-pm-not-natural-to-accept-these-migrants-into-europe.html.

27 "Minister Tells Muslim Refugees 'we Eat Pork and Drink Alcohol', is Told to Quit," The Independent, last modified October 21, 2016, http://www.independent.co.uk/news/world/europe/norway-integration-minister-muslim-eat-pork-drink-alcohol-show-face-sylvi-listhaug-a7372991.html.

28 https://www.gatestoneinstitute.org/10627/norway-political-elites-cheer-for-islam

has also claimed that Muslims in Europe "are now being harassed just as Jews were in the 1930s".

As so often with politicians in Europe, it appears Erna Solberg has a tendency to alter her arguments depending upon her audience.

SWEDEN

In MARCH 2012, a Swedish journalist wrote an anonymous account on a Danish website of how she perceived life in her country and the changes it had undergone. She called the article 'Sweden – A Raped Country'[1], and if you read it, you'll likely see why she kept her identity to herself.

Its content is shocking. She describes the widespread hatred of ethnic Swedes by vast numbers of immigrants; the crimes committed against Swedes solely because of their ethnicity; the rape epidemic sweeping this previously civilised and peaceful country; and the deafening silence on all of these matters from the Swedish press and government. It is worth noting that Sweden's press is subsidised with government money, so a cynic may suggest that Swedish leaders are reluctant to inform the public of what they have done to their beautiful nation.

RAPE CRISIS IN SWEDEN

Of the crimes being committed against Swedes because they are Swedes, by far the most disturbing is the epidemic of rape. Sweden now has the highest rates of rape in the western world[2].

---

1 "Sweden – A Raped Country," Cavatus's Blog, last modified March 24, 2012, http://cavatus.wordpress.com/2012/03/24/sweden-a-raped-country/.
2 "Sweden Tops European Rape League - but That Doesn't Tell the Whole Story," The Local - Sweden's News in English, last modified April 27, 2009, http://www.thelocal.se/19102/20090427/.

According to the anonymous journalist, Sweden's BRA – a government organisation charged with the prevention of crime – announced that a total of 1,091 rapes were reported in just one month in the summer of 2012. This was an increase of 18% on the previous year. The number of children under 15 years old reporting rape had shot up by 53% over the same period. Sven Granath, a BRA investigator, put the increase down to good weather. But, of course!

As the journalist wrote, "If the BRA were in a dictatorship, it would be known as The Board for Making Non-Desirable Facts Invisible".

The figures for rape in Sweden saw a further 10% increase in 2017[3]. Mainstream media, however, consistently denies any problem. The BBC posted a report (labelled a "reality check") in February 2017 that matter-of-factly stated that increasing numbers of rapes in Sweden were solely attributable to "the strictness of Swedish laws and how rape is recorded in the country"[4]. Once again, the BBC presented a view as a fact. However, its 'fact' does not explain the following:

- Reza Mohammed Ahmadi and Maysam Afshar were jailed in 2017 for raping a woman and broadcasting this live on Facebook. They received miniscule jail sentences of respectively two years and four months, and one year. Emil Khodagholi, a 'Swede', was jailed for six months for filming and broadcasting the rape[5].
- A wheelchair-bound woman in her 30s was raped by six migrants at an asylum centre when she asked if she could use their toilets. The perpetrators were arrested and almost immediately released[6].

---

3 "Reported Rapes in Sweden Up by 10 Percent," The Local - Sweden's News in English, last modified January 18, 2018, https://www.thelocal.se/20180118/reported-rapes-in-sweden-up-by-10-percent.

4 "Is Malmo the 'rape Capital' of Europe?," BBC News, last modified February 24, 2017, http://www.bbc.co.uk/news/uk-politics-39056786.

5 "Three Men Jailed for Gang Raping Woman on Facebook Live," Metro, last modified April 26, 2017, http://metro.co.uk/2017/04/26/three-men-jailed-for-gang-raping-woman-on-facebook-live-6597934/.

6 "Wheelchair-bound Woman 'gang-raped at Swedish Asylum Centre'," Mail Online, last modified October 11, 2016, http://www.dailymail.co.uk/news/article-3831991/Wheelchair-bound-woman-gang-raped-six-migrants-Swedish-asylum-centre-asking-use-toilet.html.

- A 23-year-old woman was kidnapped in Malmö and taken to a 'hookah shop' where she was raped by several men. Seven suspects were charged; only two were convicted (from Kuwait and Syria). They would not be deported[7].
- A 13-year-old girl was raped (vaginally and anally) in a school toilet by a 19-year-old Syrian. He was sentenced to two months in prison[8].
- A mother of two children was gang-raped at a refugee camp in Mariannelund, Småland by nine 'refugees'. Forensic examination revealed 48 different kinds of semen at the scene[9].

In an article for *Front Page* magazine in February 2017, Dawn Perlmutter wrote[10]:

"If the Swedish Government would acknowledge that the increase in sexual assaults and other crime is a direct result of refugees' cultural and religious beliefs, it would prevent the rise of nationalist movements in their country. What the Swedish Government does not understand is that women in Islam are viewed as explicitly sexual beings in which every part of their body is thought to be erotic. The reason for being covered from head to toe is that a woman's entire body is viewed as private parts. So, if you shake hands with her it is the same as touching her crotch. If she displays her hair, it is the equivalent of exposing her pubic hair. Every square inch of her is sexual.

7 Breitbart News, "Migrants Jailed After Woman Abducted At Gunpoint, Gang-Raped In Hookah Bar," Breitbart, last modified January 14, 2017, http://www.breitbart.com/london/2017/01/14/migrants-jailed-woman-abducted-gunpoint-gang-raped-hookah-bar/.
8 "Muslim Rapes Child in Sweden, Gets Two Months, Not Deported," Www.independentsentinel.com, last modified February 7, 2017, http://www.independentsentinel.com/muslim-rapes-child-in-sweden-gets-two-months-not-deported/.
9 "48 Stains of Semen Found After Refugee Gang Rape Mother of Two," 10News.dk, last modified May 10, 2018, http://10news.dk/48-stains-of-semen-found-after-refugee-gang-rape-mother-of-two/.
10 "The Refugee Rape Gangs of Sweden," Frontpage Mag, last modified February 23, 2017, https://www.frontpagemag.com/fpm/265873/refugee-rape-gangs-sweden-dawn-perlmutter.

"For this reason, Sharia Islamic Law not only justi-
fies rape and sexual assault of infidel women and children,
it incites extreme acts of brutality. Western noncompliant
non-Muslim women are viewed as the epitome of impurity
and disrespect. They are perceived as a personal affront, a
cultural dishonor and a threat. How dare Swedish women
think they have the same freedoms as Muslim men? Hence,
rape is a method of shaming women into submission and
restoring male honor."

THE SWEDISH AUTHORITIES'
RESPONSE TO THE RAPE CRISIS

Despite the obvious pattern of particularly violent rapes committed by Muslim migrants, despite the cultural and religious aspect of this, Sweden continues to insist its high rape rates have nothing to do with Muslim migration, and those who say otherwise are to be punished.

Mauricio Rojas was once the Immigration Spokesman for the Liberal Party. In 1974, Mr Rojas fled to Sweden as a political refugee from Chile. In 2004, he fled his adopted country – where he had required 24 hour protection. His crime? Publishing an article that described possible cultural reasons for some crimes committed by immigrants.

According to various reports in Sweden, immigrant men – particularly from Islamic and Muslim societies – are over-represented in rape statistics by a staggering 450%. Is it difficult to work out why this might be? According to the anonymous journalist, a young man named Hamid helped to explain the reasons. Following the gang rape of a young Swedish girl in 2000, Hamid is reported to have said:

"It's not as wrong to rape a Swedish girl as it is to rape
an Arab girl.... The Swedish girl gets a lot of help after-
wards, and she had probably been fucked already. But the
Arab girl will get problems with her family. For her it is a
great shame to be raped. It is important that she retains

her virginity when she marries. I do not have much respect for Swedish girls. You could say that they get fucked until they are broken."

In Stockholm in the summer of 2012, there was an average of five rapes per day[11].

I asked BRA representatives to provide me with information about the high incidence of rape in Swedish society. I made it clear that I was seeking only the truth, and that if they wished to quash the myth of migrant rape, I would print the truth. I specifically asked them about rape and the ethnicity or religious identity of those accused, but in their response, these issues were avoided.

Here is some of the information that was provided and the reasons behind it, according to BRA:

1. The quantity of sexual offences in Sweden has increased five-fold over the last thirty years.

Reasons: increased contact with strangers via the internet; increased alcohol consumption; rise in the number of victims reporting offences.

2. Sweden is perceived to have high levels of rape in comparison to most other countries.

Reasons: Sweden has a broader definition of rape than many other countries and registration of assault crimes is more extensive than most countries.

3. It is two and a half times as likely for persons born abroad to be registered as crime suspects as it is for Swedish-born persons with two Swedish parents. For those born in Sweden to two foreign-born parents, it is twice as common for them to be crime suspects as those born in Sweden to Swedish-born parents. The proportion of persons suspected of offences is greater in groups from certain geographical areas, in particular North Africa and Western Asia.

---

11 Swedish Rape-jihad: "police Reported an Average of Five Rapes a Day in Stockholm",» Jihad Watch – Exposing the Role That Islamic Jihad Theology and Ideology Play in the Modern Global Conflicts, accessed May 5, 2018, http://www. jihadwatch.org/2012/08/swedish-rape-jihad-police-reported-an-average-of-five-rapes-a-day-in-stockholm.

Reasons: it is difficult to make the break from one's homeland and settle in a country with vastly different living conditions; social factors such as poverty increase the risk of involvement in crime among some immigrants; the reception given to immigrants in Sweden is flawed.

It will come as no surprise that the BRA believes it is the fault of Swedes themselves that crime is so high among immigrant groups, particularly from North Africa and Asia. The report BRA provided goes to great pains to highlight prejudices faced by immigrants arriving in Sweden and the discrimination that they face. I have no doubt that there is discrimination and racism in Sweden, just as there is everywhere, but surely this cannot explain rape. Attitudes to women may do so, but this is not something that many in Sweden are prepared to talk about.

It is not in dispute that rape statistics in Sweden vastly increased just as immigration did. While correlation does not equal causation, if it is true that immigration has had no impact on rape figures, why does the Swedish Government refuse to provide statistics on just this issue[12]? Surely it would put the matter to rest if it did. However, the Swedish establishment is determined to keep this information from the people, and to do so, it needs the complicity of journalists.

In 1987, an extraordinary agreement was reached at a meeting of the Swedish Journalists' Organisation. The agreement was known as the Little Saltlake Bath Agreement[13] and it provided guidance that Swedish journalists should follow when reporting on crime figures and statistics. In summary, the guidelines demanded that the ethnicity or religion of perpetrators of crimes never be made public.

I asked Ingrid Carlqvist, a prominent Swedish journalist, for her view. Here is her answer in full:

---

12 Scandinavian Rape, Scandinavian Blinders,» Frontpage Mag, last modified June 22, 2015, http://www.frontpagemag.com/2013/bruce-bawer/scandinavian-rape-scandinavian-blinders/.

13 "The Crisis in Swedish Media," Cavatus's Blog, last modified April 8, 2010, http://cavatus.wordpress.com/2010/02/11/crisis-swedish-media/.

"Sweden has forbidden statistics about ethnicity and religion – it is absolutely insane. The reason that you keep statistics on crime and criminals is to see what is happening in a society and try to do something about it. Now we can see that crime is growing (especially rapes), but we have no idea what to do about it as we don't know what is the reason or who is behind it.

"Yesterday, BRA came [out] with a new report saying that young women are increasingly worried about going outside – in fear of being raped or abused. This was presented in TV4 as a problem. But the problem as they saw it was not that women have a real fear, but that they fear something that is not there. A woman who teaches self-defence said that it is much more likely that a woman will be abused in her home by someone she lives with than be raped by an unknown, so the best thing would be for young women to practise going [out] by themselves in the dark!

"The Swedes are kept in the dark. They can read about all the crimes in the media, but then BRA tells them everything is alright – don't worry. And no one is doing anything about the fact that crime has exploded in Sweden since we started mass immigration. They pretend it is not true.

"A few years ago I talked to a person who had worked with statistics his whole life. He said that the government had made it impossible for him to do his job. As he saw it, the whole thing is meaningless now. And you have to wonder why the government made it illegal to show who is behind certain crimes. The answer is obvious: they don't want people to know the truth, because then Swedes would protest against mass immigration."

The political response in Sweden to this national rape crisis has mirrored that of Germany – the focus has been on restricting the freedoms of Swedish women, while allowing the immigration to continue. When the tiny town of Östersund, population 45,000, endured eight sexual assaults over a period of just three weeks, police reported that they had never seen such violent incidents against women, all of them committed by 'foreign men'[14]. However, their response was to hold a press conference warning women to stay indoors. This produces the desired effect of keeping women under control and subdued, just as they are in Islamic societies.

Östersund cancelled its 'Earth Hour' event in March 2016 because of even more sexual assaults. Earth Hour involves the switching off of lights in towns around the world to highlight climate change issues.

Chief Constable Stephen Jerand said, "Keeping the lights on creates security and is in line with our common efforts to increase security under current conditions[15]." What he meant by 'current conditions' was the widespread sexual assault of women on the streets of a small town in rural Sweden by immigrants.

The police in Sweden have admitted they can't cope; there is simply too much rape[16]. The admission arose following the case of a 12-year-old rape victim whose alleged rapist still had not been questioned a month after the event, despite the police admitting they knew his name.

ANTI-SEMITISM

It isn't only women who are increasingly suffering violent attacks in Sweden. In the third largest city of Malmö, Jews are fleeing in vast numbers because they no longer feel safe.

Judith Popinksi was a victim of the Nazi holocaust and had spent time in a concentration camp. She later fled to Sweden where she lived and raised her family for over sixty years.

---

14 "EXCLUSIVE: The Small Swedish Town Terrorized by String of Sex Attacks," Mail Online, last modified March 16, 2016, http://www.dailymail.co.uk/news/article-3485473/ The-small-Swedish-town-terrorized-string-sex-attacks-eight-assaults-past-three-weeks-leaves-women-terrified-walk-dark.html.

15 "Swedish Town Refuses to Turn Lights off to Protect Women from Attacks," Mail Online, last modified March 18, 2016, http://www.dailymail.co.uk/news/article-3499108/ Earth-hour-cancelled-migrant-rape-Swedish-town-refuses-turn-lights-protect-women-attacks.html.

16 "So Many Rapes, So Few Police: Swedish Authorities 'can't Cope' with Growth in Rape Cases," YouTube, last modified September 15, 2017, https://www.youtube.com/ watch?v=V8EwVnQZTlE.

She left in 2009, saying, "I never thought I would see this hatred again in my lifetime. Not in Sweden anyway[17]."

The hatred she was referring to probably included the repeated violent attacks against synagogues and Jewish community centres across Malmö. In 2012, a Jewish centre was attacked with *"explosives and bricks"*[18], and Jews in the city subsequently described a surge in anti-Semitic hate crimes. Rabbi Shneur Kesselman stated that he had personally experienced around 90 such incidents in the seven years he had lived there, including having "Palestine" scratched into the paintwork of his car.

Following an attack on attendees at a pro-Israel rally in 2009, the then-Mayor of Malmö, Ilmar Reepalu, created a storm of controversy by suggesting that Sweden's Jews should "distance themselves from Israel"[19] if they were to avoid such attacks. He justified anti-Semitic violence by adding that Malmö's Jews "chose to hold a pro-Israel demonstration" which could "convey the wrong message to others".

The wrong message? I assume he means having an opinion on the Middle East which does not adhere to the 'correct' view.

In the Swedish capital of Stockholm, young Jews are also heading for the exit. Rabbi Yitzhak Nahman, who presides over a Stockholm synagogue which had been moved to Sweden from Hamburg due to Nazi persecution, has reported numerous threats on the streets of the city. According to the Rabbi, *"It has become more dangerous"*, and he has been advised not to visibly identify himself as a Jew in public. He has reluctantly stopped wearing his Kippah on Stockholm's streets[20].

Lena Posner-Korosi, President of the Council of Jewish Communities in Sweden, stated in 2011 that the attacks were

17 Nick Meo in Malmo, Sweden, "Jews Leave Swedish City After Sharp Rise in Anti-Semitic Hate Crimes," Telegraph.co.uk, last modified February 21, 2010, http://www.telegraph.co.uk/news/worldnews/europe/sweden/7278532/Jews-leave-Swedish-city-after-sharp-rise-in-anti-Semitic-hate-crimes.html.

18 "Attack on Jewish Community in Sweden Follows Surge of Hate Crimes," Haaretz.com, last modified September 28, 2012, http://www.haaretz.com/jewish-world/jewish-world-news/attack-on-jewish-community-in-sweden-follows-surge-of-hate-crimes-1.467351.

19 "Swedish Mayor Blasts Zionism," Ynetnews, last modified January 2258, http://www.ynetnews.com/articles/0,7340,L-3841278,00.html.

20 Dennis Zinn, "The Jewish Community of Sweden," Vimeo, accessed May 5, 2018, http://vimeo.com/14907669.

not coming from ethnic Swedes, but from Muslim fundamental-
ists. She said that most Jews in Sweden do not feel comfortable
walking in areas with a large Muslim population, and "if you are
a visible Jew, you are bound to be cursed or abused in one way
or another"[21].

Daniel Radomski wrote in *Haaretz*, a prominent Israeli newspaper, in late 2013 of the rise of anti-Semitism in Sweden[22]:

> "*It is no coincidence that Malmö, with its large
> Muslim population, has seen a vast increase in anti-Semitic
> attacks... the recent rise in anti-Semitic activity in Sweden
> originates largely from the Arab and Muslim communities.
> Here, many immigrants have backgrounds that are directly
> linked to the Israeli-Arab conflict and hail from countries
> where classic anti-Semitism is commonly accepted, encour-
> aged by politicians and even taught in schools.*"

The extent of growing anti-Semitism in Sweden reached a trag-
ically ironic crescendo in 2015 when Jews were not invited to a
town's commemoration of *kristallnacht* – a night in which hundreds
of Jews were murdered in Germany and tens of thousands more
were sent to concentration camps[23]. Given the rise in attacks on
Jews across the country, it was not deemed safe for Jews to gather in
large numbers, even to commemorate anti-Semitic attacks.

THE SILENCE OF THE PRESS

I said in my introduction how difficult it was to find information on the Islamisation of the West, particularly in the mainstream press. Sweden, however, was by far the most difficult. It
is a country in total lockdown. So silent is the Swedish press on
matters concerning Islam that a Somali journalist has described

---

21 Ibid.
22 "The Clear and Present Danger Facing Sweden's Jews," Haaretz.com, last modified
December 12, 2013, http://www.haaretz.com/opinion/.premium-1.563147.
23 Nima Gholam Ali Pour, "A Smorgasbord of Swedish Anti-Semitism," Gatestone
Institute, last modified January 2, 2016, http://www.gatestoneinstitute.org/7163/swedish-
antisemitism.

the country as being worse than Mogadishu.

Amun Abdullahi arrived in Sweden in 1991 as a refugee from Somalia. She became a reporter for a Stockholm radio station, and carried out an investigative report into a youth centre in that city that was allegedly recruiting young men into the radical Islamist group Al-Shabab. Following her report, her car was torched and she received several death threats.

Abdullahi had, she said, been prepared for a backlash from the Somali community, but she had not been prepared for the response from the mainstream Swedish media, which dismissed the results of her investigation as "hearsay" and "rumour". She lost her family and moved away from Stockholm.

Abdullahi has since returned to Somalia.

FREE SPEECH IN SWEDEN

The Swedish courts have naturally played a part in the destruction of democracy in Sweden. Take Michael Hess, for example, a Sweden Democrats politician who said rather frankly:

> *"It is deeply rooted in Islam's culture to rape and brutalise women who refuse to comply with Islamic teachings. There is a strong connection between rapes in Sweden and the number of immigrants from MENA [Middle East and North Africa]"*[24] *countries.*

His day in court was fantastically revealing. The court cared not a jot whether what Mr Hess said was true – what mattered was that it was Islamophobic. Mr Hess's problem was that he is Swedish, and being Swedish in Sweden is a distinct disadvantage.

Sweden took in a total of 163,000 people in 2015 – its total population is around 10 million. Following notorious crimes, such as the killing of two people in an Ikea store (an icon of Sweden)

---

24 Nima Gholam Ali Pour, "A Smorgasbord of Swedish Anti-Semitism," Gatestone Institute, last modified January 2, 2016, http://www.gatestoneinstitute.org/7163/swedish-antisemitism.

by migrants using knives lifted from the store's shelves[25], and the killing of Alexandra Mezher at a migrant centre[26], tensions began to rise and vigilante groups formed. In early 2016, frightening images emerged from Stockholm's main railway station revealing attacks on migrants by Swedish men, gathered in large numbers and dressed in black. A total of 14 people were arrested[27].

Sweden is a country with a previous reputation as clean, liberal, educated, gender-equal, peaceful, and having a very high standard of living. Mass migration, particularly from the Muslim world, has altered Sweden so that it is no longer safe for women or Jews, no longer free to speak its mind, and only a small step away from violent ethnic conflict. That reality becomes ever closer as Sweden's doors remain open – and open they certainly are.

Five people were killed and more than a dozen injured in a terror attack in the capital Stockholm in 2017 when a man drove a truck into crowds in a busy shopping street[28]. Rakhmat Akilov, who was arrested (he will be tried in 2018), had sworn his allegiance to the Islamic State in a self-recorded video the day before the attack.

Prime Minister Stefan Löfven assured the people of Sweden that mass immigration would now end. But in 2017, Sweden continued to grant asylum, and in that year alone, welcomed a further 27,205 'refugees'. These figures are from the Swedish Migration Agency only, and do not include asylum granted at The Migration Courts or the Migration Court of Appeal[29].

---

25 Https://www.facebook.com/michael.miller.1466, "In Sweden's Ikea Attack, Two Migrants, Two Slayings and Rampant Fear of Refugees," Washington Post, last modified September 29, 2015, https://www.washingtonpost.com/news/morning-mix/wp/2015/09/29/in-swedens-ikea-attack-two-migrants-two-murders-and-rampant-fear-of-refugees/.

26 "Mother of Swedish Girl 'killed by Refugee' Speaks out," Mail Online, last modified January 27, 2016, http://www.dailymail.co.uk/news/article-3418312/She-wanted-help-did-Mother-Swedish-refugee-worker-killed-Somali-migrant-says-country-fled-war-torn-Lebanon-no-longer-safe.html.

27 "Stockholm Special Squad to Stop Far-right Mobs," The Local - Sweden's News in English, last modified February 2, 2016, http://www.thelocal.se/20160202/stockholm-special-squad-to-stop-far-right-vigilantes.

28 "Stockholm Attack Driver 'deliberately Targeted Young Children' As He Drove Hijacked Lorry into Crowd," The Telegraph, accessed May 5, 2018, http://www.telegraph.co.uk/news/2017/04/07/truck-crashes-crowd-people-stockholm/.

29 "Asylum decisions, first time applications, Swedish Migration Agency, 2017," Migrationsverket, accessed May 6, 2018, https://www.migrationsverket.se/download/18.4100dc0b159d67dc6146d1/1514898751014/Avgjorda%20asyl%C3%A4renden%202017%20-%20Asylum%20decisions%202017.pdf.

AROUND THE WORLD

CANADA

Canada has shown itself to be particularly adept at bowing down to one demand of Islamism, and that is the humiliation and degradation of women. I'm not only referring to Muslim women, but to all women.

SEGREGATION OF WOMEN IN CANADA

Valley Park middle school in Toronto effectively created a mini-mosque in its cafeteria. In 2011, a photo of this mini-mosque was released, and caused something of an eruption in the Canadian media. There were three sections in the cafeteria-mosque: boys at the front, most girls behind, and then a little section behind them for a special kind of girl. The girls at the very back were there because they were menstruating.

Read that again.

A Canadian public school allowed young girls to be segregated because they had their period.

The columnist Tasha Kheiriddin asked:

*"Is this the Middle Ages? Have I stumbled into a time
warp, where 'unclean' women must be prevented from
'defiling' other persons?*[1]*"*

Kheiriddin also pointed out that these were not grown women
making a choice to exclude themselves (which would be bad
enough), but impressionable young girls being force-fed their own
'inferiority' and told that the natural functioning of their bodies
was a cause of contamination. The fact that menstruation is exclusively a female thing reinforces the 'awfulness' of being female.

In defence of this state of affairs, the Toronto District School
Board Education Director Chris Spence stated: "As a public
school board, we have a responsibility and an obligation to
accommodate faith needs".

A second example of the humiliation of women in the name
of Islamic appeasement came in the unlikely setting of a martial
arts class. In the city of Halifax, a young Muslim had joined an
Aikido class, only to insist that the class be segregated by gender
as he refused to touch or be in proximity to any person of the
female variety. His wish was granted.

Seventeen-year-old Sonja Power, a black belt in Aikido who
suddenly found herself in a women-only zone, said that the
accommodation of the segregation request had made her feel like
a "second class citizen; that I was so disgusting and unworthy
that this man doesn't even want to interact with me" and asked,
"Why would something you choose, your religion, trump something I'm born with, my gender?"

Good question.

A student at York University refused to do group work because
the presence of females interfered with his religious beliefs. J.
Paul Grayson, a sociology professor, received notice from the
student that he would not work with women, and passed this on
to the Dean of his faculty and the university's Centre for Human
Rights. Both responded that Grayson should accommodate the
student's wishes.

---

1 Tasha Kheiriddin: Religion Has No Place in Public School – and Neither Does Sexism,»
National Post, last modified July 11, 2011, http://nationalpost.com/opinion/tasha-
kheiriddin-religion-has-no-place-in-public-school-and-neither-does-sexism.

According to the *National Post*, the Vice Dean argued that the "academic integrity" of the course could be compromised if Mr Grayson did not respect the "sincerity of the student's beliefs"[2].

Some Canadian MPs objected to the accommodation. Justice Minister Peter MacKay said:

> *"This is what we've tried to combat in places like Afghanistan. Building schools there, and ensuring now that millions of girls are able to attend school alongside boys, I believe, is a very positive accomplishment of our country."*

Another MP said, "We live in a country seeking gender equality.... This is Canada, pure and simple."

Encouraging words indeed, but little appears to be changing.

BEING STONED TO DEATH IS GOOD FOR YOU?

Another day, another Islamist calling for somebody to be stoned to death – this time in Ontario. Sheikh Faisal Hamid Abdur-Razak enlightened us all when he recommended a good death by stoning for the cleansing of the soul. The Sheikh advised that homosexuals and adulterers would actually benefit from being stoned to death[3]:

If you're thinking that this man is a fringe lunatic in Canada, think again. Sheikh Faisal Hamid Abdur-Razak is both the President of the Islamic Forum of Canada and the Vice-president of the Islamic Council of Imams of Canada. There were no restrictions on the Sheikh's ability to make such speeches, but the same cannot be said for others who wish to exercise their right to speak their minds in Canada.

---

2 "York University Standing by Choice to Excuse Student from Group Work with Women over Religious Beliefs," National Post, accessed May 6, 2018, http://nationalpost.com/news/york-university-appears-to-be-standing-by-choice-to-excuse-student-from-group-work-with-women-over-religious-beliefs.

3 "President of the Islamic Forum of Canada Explains How Gays Benefit from Being Stoned to Death," Frontpage Mag, last modified June 22, 2015, https://www.frontpagemag.com/point/202318/president-islamic-forum-canada-explains-how-gays-daniel-greenfield.

FREE SPEECH IN CANADA

In 2007, a group of Islamists demanded that the widely read *Maclean's* magazine be censored for publishing part of a book by international journalist Mark Steyn that argued Islamic culture is not compatible with Western liberal democracy. The irony of arguing that Islam is compatible with liberal democracy while demanding free speech be curtailed appeared to have passed the Canadian Islamic Congress by.

This is how the *New York Post* reported it[4]:

> *"The plaintiffs allege that Maclean's advocated, among other things, the notion that Islamic culture is incompatible with Canada's liberalized Western civilization. They insist such a notion is untrue and, in effect, want opinions like that banned from publication."*

You really couldn't make this up.

The British Columbia Human Rights Tribunal and the Canadian Human Rights Commission agreed to hear the case – using powers to rule on cases of 'hate speech'. Fortunately, both bodies dismissed the case against *Maclean's,* but it served as a warning to passive and tolerant Canadians to be on their guard.

Maclean's had escaped punishment for its terrible crime, but the seeds were sown and Canadian journalists had been issued a caution. This was acknowledged by the Canadian Islamic Congress. Faisal Joseph, the group's lawyer, was "delighted" and took the opportunity to point out the "gaping hole" in human rights legislation in Ontario (the non-sharia-complaint gaping hole).

Attempting to shut down free speech is not the sole political activity of the Canadian Islamic Congress – pressing for the introduction of sharia law is also a popular pastime. It offered its full support to Marion Boyd (a prominent politician) who recommended that the Ontario government permit sharia tribunals in the province to hear cases of family law, and to issue binding sharia-compliant rulings. The proposal was opposed by

---

4 CANADA'S THOUGHT POLICE,» New York Post, last modified December 16, 2007, http://nypost.com/2007/12/16/canadas-thought-police.

the Canadian Council of Muslim Women and other non-Muslim women's groups, and happily was defeated.

Interestingly, the Canadian Islamic Congress has also called on the national government to remove Hamas and Hezbollah from its list of banned terrorist organisations[5].

The *Maclean's* affair is perhaps the most notorious example of Islamist attempts to stifle free speech in Canada, but it is certainly not the only one. The American author Pamela Geller was banned from speaking in a Toronto synagogue at the behest of the police[6]. Rabbi Mendel Kaplan – who is both Rabbi at the synagogue and local police chaplain – declared that Geller's attendance would "place [him] in conflict with the values of our organization, which support a safe, welcoming and inclusive community for all". A spokesman for the York Regional Police, in a highly sinister move, said that if Geller were allowed to attend, the police would "reassess our relationship" with the Rabbi.

Meanwhile in Alberta, Imam Jamal Hammoud told his audience in 2013, "Allah willing, Muslims will soon be the majority in Canada." He called it a "kind of Jihad"[7]. What I want to know is this: Why does he call for a Muslim majority? Isn't that intolerant, divisive, and racist?

The Muslim Council of Calgary, to which Mr Hammoud is affiliated, gave us a snapshot of what a Muslim-majority Canada would look like. For a start, it provided a platform to a certain Dr Bilal Philips[8]. Philips, an infamous Canadian-born Islamist who openly preaches death to homosexuals, was invited to speak at a "celebration of diversity" entitled the 'Power of Unity

5 Canadian Islamic Congress, last modified December 4, 2016, http://www. canadianislamiccongress.com/mc/media_communique.php?id=814.

6 Tzvi Ben-Gedalyahu, "Canada Forces Chabad to Ban Radical-Islam Critic Pamela Geller," The Jewish Press - Breaking News, Opinions, Analysis and More on Israel and the Jewish World I JewishPress.com, last modified May 7, 2013, http://www.jewishpress. com/news/canada-forces-chabad-to-ban-radical-muslim-critic-pamela-geller/2013/05/06/.

7 Imam Predicts Muslims Will Become the Majority in Canada,» Frontpage Mag, last modified June 22, 2015, http://frontpagemag.com/2013/dgreenfield/imam-predicts-muslims-will-become-the-majority-in-canada/.

8 "Bilal Philips Acknowledges That Sharia Commands the Killing of Homosexuals and Hopes for the Day That It Will Be Applied in Canada," Point De Bascule Canada, last modified September 25, 2012, http://pointdebasculecanada.ca/bilal-philips-acknowledges-that-sharia-commands-the-killing-of-homosexuals-and-hopes-for-the-day-that-it-will-be-applied-in-canada/.

Conference'. Calgary Alderman Diane Colley-Urquhart said she found this "rather ironic". Quite.

APOLOGISTS

Justin Trudeau – now Prime Minister of Canada – felt sorry for the two Chechen bombers who blew up a marathon in the United States city of Boston, and urged Canadians to ask why on earth they might have committed such an appalling act. But he has already decided. According to Trudeau, "There is no question that this happened because there is someone who feels completely excluded, completely at war with innocents, at war with a society"[9]. If the Boston bombers are at war with American society, it goes without saying, it is the USA's fault.

He went on to ask, "Where do those tensions come from?" Not a bad question, but will he like the answer? Director of the Monterey Terrorism Research and Education Program, Jeffrey M Bale, put forward the idea that "they had embraced a radical Islamist ideology that enjoined them to wage armed jihad against the 'infidel' enemies of Islam"[10]. The bombers had said that they were angered by American aggression. This excuse is nothing new, and it's regularly thrown around by Left-wing politicians as if it somehow makes violence OK. It does the trick, though, and takes the focus away from Islamist ideology, placing it back firmly at the feet of the West, the United States in particular.

But there's something missing from this rhetoric: Just what is it that makes two young Chechens so angry about Iraq and Afghanistan that they are willing to kill for it, and what do they think gives them that right?

---

9 Don›t ‹sit Around Trying to Rationalize It›: Harper Slams Trudeau for Response to Boston Bombing,» National Post, last modified April 17, 2013, http://nationalpost.com/2013/04/17/trudeaus-response-to-boston-marathon-bombing-was-unacceptable-made-excuses-for-terrorists-harper-says/.

10 IPT News, «Boston Bombers› Motivations No Mystery,» The Investigative Project on Terrorism, last modified April 30, 2013, http://www.investigativeproject.org/4005/boston-bombers-motivations-no-mystery.

Dzhokhar Tsarnaev, one of the bombers, explains: "When you attack one Muslim, you attack all Muslims"[11].

Ah, I see.

Back to Trudeau. When he's not busy feeling sorry for bombers, he has other important engagements, such as attending events hosted by the polygamy-endorsing, sharia-advocating Islamic Society of North America.

Like leaders all over the Western world, Trudeau ignores the truly moderate Muslim voices and bows down to the Islamists instead. In a discussion on Trudeau, and how he manages to reconcile being pro-gay rights and pro-woman with spending time in the company of some of the vilest homophobes and misogynists on the planet, Tarek Fatah – a Canadian commentator – made the following superb statement. It should be read by every Islamic apologist in the world:

> "This is orientalism. These are white folks who really don't think that Muslims are human beings. Maybe in 5,000 years, we will develop to be that state, but right now we are some underclass who need to be pandered to. We can make mistakes, and they will tolerate us and reach out to us under the diversity agenda. It is the racism of lower expectations. When a white man goes to a racial minority and says, 'I understand that you are bigoted against gays, you will in the next 1,000 years understand, but until then I will treat you like I treat my serfs'."

Thank you, Mr Fatah – Canada needs you.

OPPOSING SHARIA LAW

Canada also needs more people like Dalton McGuinty, who fiercely opposed the introduction of sharia in the province of

---

11 Boston Bombings Suspect Dzhokhar Tsarnaev Left Note in Boat He Hid In, Sources Say,» CBS News - Breaking News, Live News Stream 24x7, last modified May 16, 2013, http://www.cbsnews.com/news/boston-bombings-suspect-dzhokhar-tsarnaev-left-note-in-boat-he-hid-in-sources-say/.

Ontario in 2004. Faith based tribunals had been set up there by Catholic and Jewish communities following the passing of the Arbitration Act in 1991. In 2003, the Islamic Institute of Civil Justice said it intended to do the same. Sharia settlements were further recommended by Marion Boyd.

They probably didn't expect the backlash that this provoked. Women's rights groups and secular Muslims made it clear that they did not want sharia arbitration in Canada, and to his great credit, Premier McGuinty agreed.

> *"There will be no Sharia law in Ontario. There will be no religious arbitration in Ontario. There will be one law for all Ontarians*[12]*."*

Once again, the language of rights and freedoms was invoked by Islamists seeking to remove the rights and freedoms of Muslim women. Irfan Syed, chairman of the Toronto-based Muslim Lawyers Association, said sharia was a "legitimate way to give religious communities some autonomy[13]."

How about that for doublespeak! The autonomy of religious communities? But communities are not human beings and do not have autonomy. What this actually means is the imposition of sharia by 'community leaders' in an effort to remove autonomy, particularly the autonomy of Muslim women.

Homa Arjomand, a women's rights activist who organised a series of protests across Canada to convince the Ontario government not to allow sharia law, put it well:

> *"Everybody knows that in Sharia women are considered second class citizens, they have no rights at all.... The Islamic extremists were pushing for the legalisation of religious arbitration which would result in the absorption of religion into the Ontario justice system*[14]*."*

---

12 "BBC NEWS I Americas I Sharia Law Move Quashed in Canada," Home - BBC News, last modified September 12, 2005, http://news.bbc.co.uk/1/hi/world/americas/4236762.stm.
13 James Sturcke, "Sharia Law in Canada, Almost," The Guardian, last modified August 26, 2008, https://www.theguardian.com/news/blog/2008/feb/08/sharialawincanadaalmost.
14 "Canada: Statement by Homa Arjomand Against Religious Schools in the Public System I Women Reclaiming and Redefining Cultures," Women Living Under Muslim Laws, accessed May 5, 2018, http://www.wluml.org/node/3898.

Canada most definitely needs Ms Arjomand as well. It is almost as if she knows something that the likes of Marion Boyd do not.

JIHADIST ATTACKS AND BARBARIC CULTURAL PRACTICES IN CANADA

Quiet and civilised Canada, which isn't really used to being in the world's headlines, now finds itself there with increasing regularity since Islam started pushing its weight around. In 2014, two terror attacks occurred in Canada – one of them inside its Parliament in Ottawa. Michael Zehaf-Bibeau shot and killed Corporal Nathan Cirillo, who was on ceremonial duty at the time. He then managed to enter Canada's Parliament building and engage in a shoot-out with security forces. He was shot dead. This alarming incident took place a mere two days after Martin Couture-Rouleau drove his car at two other Canadian soldiers, killing one, in Quebec. Both were designated terrorist attacks by the Canadian government, and both were committed by Muslim converts.

At the time, Justin Trudeau was the future Prime Minister of Canada, and he wasted no time at all in telling Canadians that the attacks had nothing to do with Islam[15]."

Further jihadist attacks included an assault in early 2016 when Ayanle Hassan Ali stabbed two Canadian soldiers. Allah had told him to carry out the attack, he informed us[16]. Despite the fact that ISIS had urged so-called 'lone wolf' attacks on Canada[17], and all three attacks on Canadian soil had been carried out by Muslims stating clearly they were acting in the name of Islam, the priority of police following the 2016 attack was to ensure that nobody blamed this on Islam.

---

15 "'Canada Will Not Be Intimidated': Top Political Leaders Address Ottawa Shooting News," CBC, last modified October 24, 2014, http://www.cbc.ca/news/politics/ottawa-shooting-harper-mulcair-trudeau-speak-about-attack-1.2809530.
16 "'Allah Told Me to Do This,' Military Centre Stabbing Suspect Said During Attack News," CBC, last modified March 15, 2016, http://www.cbc.ca/news/canada/toronto/toronto-stabbing-military-recruitment-centre-1.3491719.
17 "Canadian Who Joined ISIS Calls On Canadian Muslims To Conduct Lone-Wolf Attacks," International Business Times, accessed May 5, 2018, http://www.ibtimes.com/canadian-who-joined-isis-calls-canadian-muslims-conduct-lone-wolf-attacks-1740896.

"I don't want this categorizing a large group of people; that will be very unfair and very inaccurate," police chief Mark Saunders said, adding he doesn't want to see any of this "Islamophobia nonsense"[18].

Priorities indeed.

A new tried and tested method of jihadist murder, ramming into crowds of people with a car or truck, was used in Edmonton in 2017. Luckily nobody was killed when a Somali asylum seeker with an Islamic state flag in his vehicle deliberately drove into pedestrians during a high-speed chase after he had stabbed a police officer[19]. This attack occurred in the same year that the Canadian Parliament voted to condemn criticism of Islam.

The M-103 motion was passed by 201 votes to 91 and called upon politicians to "condemn Islamophobia and all forms of systemic racism and religious discrimination"[20]. Islamophobia was not defined, and once again, Islam had been singled out for special protection and compared with race. The Islamophile and now Prime Minister of Canada, Justin Trudeau, was fully behind the motion, as were his MPs.

Meanwhile, 'asylum seekers' (mostly Muslim) continued to flow into Canada[21]. These 'asylum seekers', as well as other Muslim immigrants, would not necessarily be expected to obey Canadian law. During the premiership of Stephen Harper, Canada had passed the so-called 'Zero Tolerance for Barbaric Cultural Practices Act' into law. It was not to last, however. When Trudeau became PM, the words 'barbaric cultural practices' suddenly became offensive.

Liberal Senator Mobina Jaffer argued:

18 "'Allah Told Me to Do This,' Military Centre Stabbing Suspect Said During Attack News," CBC, last modified March 15, 2016, http://www.cbc.ca/news/canada/toronto/toronto-stabbing-military-recruitment-centre-1.3491719.

19 "Edmonton Terror Attacks: Suspect Was Known to Canadian Security Services," The Guardian, last modified November 27, 2017, https://www.theguardian.com/world/2017/oct/01/canadian-police-edmonton-van-knife-attack-terrorism.

20 "Canadian Parliament Passes Anti-Islamophobia Motion," The Independent, last modified March 24, 2017, http://www.independent.co.uk/news/world/americas/canada-parliament-anti-islamophobia-motion-pass-muslim-irqa-khalid-david-anderson-racism-faith-a7647851.html.

21 "Fearing U.S. Rejection, Asylum Seekers Flee to Canada," PBS NewsHour, last modified January 27, 2018, https://www.pbs.org/newshour/show/fearing-u-s-rejection-asylum-seekers-flee-to-canada.

> *"The issue here, frankly, is the pairing of the words 'barbaric' and 'cultural.' By pairing these two words, we are removing the agency from the individual committing an action that is clearly wrong and associating it instead with a cultural group at large. We are implying that these practices are part of cultures and that these cultures are barbaric[22]."*

The fact that these practices *are* associated with cultures and that they *are* barbaric is neither here nor there, as far as this Senator was concerned. What mattered was not the victims of these cultural crimes, but whether or not calling them barbaric may cause offence.

A citizenship guide aimed at immigrants to Canada had once warned them against the abhorrent practice of female genital mutilation (FGM), but according to Conservative Michelle Rempel in 2017, "Canada's Prime Minister has decided to delete this information"[23].

Trudeau's response to this:

> *"We will continue to lead the way, pushing for an end to these barbaric practices of female genital mutilation everywhere around the world...and here in Canada...this is something we take very seriously."*

Trudeau would continue to lead the way against FGM around the world, as he said, but would do little to defeat it in Canada. This is a standard response from Western politicians regarding FGM. They insist they're against it and want it eradicated all over the world. Simultaneously, they do nothing at all to prevent it in the only place they have power – their own country.

---

22 "Senate Passes Bill to Remove Mention of 'barbaric Cultural Practices' from Harper-era Law," National Post, last modified December 12, 2017, http://nationalpost.com/news/politics/senate-passes-bill-to-remove-mention-of-barbaric-cultural-practices-from-law-passed-by-harper-conservatives.
23 "Tories Push Trudeau To Keep FGM Warning In Citizenship Guide," HuffPost Canada, last modified November 29, 2017, http://www.huffingtonpost.ca/2017/11/29/tories-push-trudeau-to-keep-fgm-warning-in-citizenship-guide_a_23292216/.

In extraordinary scenes[24] in the Canadian Parliament in late 2017, the country's immigration minister Ahmed Hussen refused to answer questions about whether FGM would be condemned in guidance issued to immigrants by the Canadian government. One would think this would have been easy to answer: will Canada tell immigrants that they cannot and should not remove the clitoris of young girls in order to prevent them experiencing any kind of sexual agency, pleasure, or autonomy? Yes or no?

Ahmed Hussen is a Somali immigrant, where FGM is practised by above 90% of people. Whether this is relevant is up to each of us to decide.

Canada, like all Western countries, is busily transforming itself from a free society to one where Islam increasingly calls the shots. Causing offence to Muslims is deemed far more important than the crimes carried out in its name.

Robert Spencer described it like this[25]:

"Canada is slipping down a dangerous slope. The government and Islamic supremacists have now partnered to attempt to silence anyone who criticizes Islam."

---

24 "RAW: Canada's Immigration Minister Hussen Avoids Questions About FGM for Nearly 10 Minutes," YouTube, last modified December 11, 2017, https://www.youtube.com/watch?v=WdRr2cRf9fg.
25 "Canadian Parliament Passes Anti-Islamophobia Motion," Jihad Watch – Exposing the Role That Islamic Jihad Theology and Ideology Play in the Modern Global Conflicts, last modified January 26, 2017, https://www.jihadwatch.org/2016/11/canadian-parliament-passes-anti-islamophobia-motion.

AUSTRALIA

RACIALLY MOTIVATED RAPE

IN 2000, SEVERAL young girls were raped by a group of at least nine men in Sydney. All of the men were Lebanese Muslims, and victims were told that they deserved to be raped for being Australian, or "Aussie pigs". When New South Wales Premier Robert Carr revealed the ethnic element of the crimes, he was accused by Keysar Trad of the Lebanese Muslim Association of being "unfair because it reflected badly on the community"[1].

There are a couple of points to make here. First of all, it was the rapists and *their* racial hatred that reflected badly on the Islamic community; Mr Carr was merely stating the facts. Secondly, as race was a motive for the rapes, it was relevant, regardless of how unrepresentative it was, or how badly it reflected on Australia's Muslims. One might argue that it would certainly have been relevant if the roles had been reversed, and white Australian men had been accused of gang-raping non-white women because of their ethnicity.

---

1 "Wayback Machine," Wayback Machine, accessed May 5, 2018, http://web.archive.org/web/20060524105853/www.cnsnews.com/ViewForeignBureaus.asp?Page=\ForeignBureaus\archive\200207\FOR20020716b.html.

Also in Sydney, two years later, four Pakistani brothers were jailed for raping an Australian girl, and police suspected it was not their only crime. According to news reports, one of the brothers told the judge that his Islamic beliefs convinced him he had a right to rape Australian girls because they "are promiscuous, don't wear headscarves, drink, and go about unaccompanied"[2]. Why is this relevant to Islam? Islamists routinely teach the supremacy of the Muslim over the non-Muslim, and of men over women. Are we to believe that these teachings have no effect or impact whatsoever on the views of some of the young men exposed to them?

The leader of Sydney's largest mosque (again, not a fringe lunatic) Sheikh Taj Din al-Hilali, in response to the rapes, said this:

> "*If you take out uncovered meat and place it outside... without cover, and the cats come to eat it...whose fault is it, the cats' or the uncovered meat's? The uncovered meat is the problem. If she was in her room, in her home, in her hijab* [the headdress worn by some Muslim women], *no problem would have occurred*[3]."

This is male supremacism defined. If a woman doesn't play by certain social rules, she will be raped as punishment. Sheikh Taj Din al-Hilali is a prominent speaker in Sydney and his words will inevitably be heeded by many.

Australian-born Sheikh Feiz Muhammad was filmed in the Channel 4 documentary 'Undercover Mosque' as stating "The pinnacle, the crest, the summit of Islam is Jihad". He told an audience of over 1,000 in Sydney that a woman has only herself to blame if she is raped. According to the *Sydney Morning Herald* in 2005[4], he said:

---

2 "Gang Rapist Claims Right to Assault - National - Smh.com.au," Australian Breaking News Headlines & World News Online I SMH.com.au, last modified December 9, 2005, https://www.smh.com.au/news/national/gang-rapist-claims-right-to-assault/2005/12/09/1134086806845.html.

3 Mark Tran, "Australian Muslim Leader Compares Uncovered Women to Exposed Meat," The Guardian, last modified October 26, 2016, http://www.theguardian.com/world/2006/oct/26/australia.marktran.

4 "Muslim Cleric: Women Incite Men's Lust with 'satanic Dress' - National - Www.smh.com.au," Australian Breaking News Headlines & World News Online I SMH.com.au, last modified April 23, 2005, http://www.smh.com.au/news/National/Muslim-cleric-women-incite-mens-lust-with-satanic-dress/2005/04/23/1114152362381.html.

"A victim of rape every minute somewhere in the world. Why? No one to blame but herself. She displayed her beauty to the entire world. Strapless, backless, sleeveless, nothing but satanic skirts, slit skirts, translucent blouses, miniskirts, tight jeans: all this to tease man and appeal to his carnal nature."

There are frequent instances of hatred for white Australians, and for Western people, expressed by Muslims in that country. According to a CBN news report in 2009[5], Sheikh Taj Din al-Hilali claimed:

"The most dishonest and unjust people are Western people, and the English in particular. Listen to me, Anglo-Saxons came to Australia in chains, while we Muslims paid our way and came in freedom. We are more Australian than them."

More recently, in 2012, Sheikh Sharif Hussein made a speech describing Australian soldiers as "Crusader pigs" before calling for the death of Hindus and Buddhists[6]. Hussein was, according to the 'Adelaide Now' website, a "leading member of the Adelaide Islamic community" who had been under surveillance by Australian Federal authorities. In 2007, funds from Saudi Arabia to Mr Hussein's mosque were stopped by authorities citing "security concerns".

In 2013, ABC produced a documentary highlighting radical preachers in Australia who were urging young Australians to join jihad, particularly in Syria. Several speakers were filmed supporting Assad's opponents in that country, and backing extreme Islamist groups there. Many of the speeches took place

---

5 "Islam, A Problem In Australia (Islam Prohibits Integration)," YouTube, last modified September 15, 2009, http://www.youtube.com/watch?v=tsiKVc028I0.
6 Andrew Hough and Tony Shepherd, "Adelaide mosque preacher Sheikh Sharif Hussein directs fury at Buddhists, Hindus, Howard and Obama," The Advertiser, August 22, 2013, http://www.adelaidenow.com.au/news/south-australia/adelaide-mosque-preacher-sheikh-sharif-hussein-directs-fury-at-at-buddhists-hindus-howard-and-obama/story-fni6uo1m-1226701605335.

in Al Risalah bookshop in Sydney, described as a "centre of Islamic extremism"[7].

All of this proves that Australia faces the same issues with regard to Islam as other major Western nations. Attitudes among religious leaders to non-Muslims and women are having a very real and damaging effect.

AUSTRALIA'S APPEASEMENT

Free speech is under attack in Australia as it is elsewhere in the democratic world. Evidence for this was provided by marchers in Sydney, who took to the streets to object to the *Innocence of Muslims* film which caused riots across the world. Then Prime Minister Julia Gillard condemned the protests and the placards on display, including those brandished by children. Signs included messages such as "Behead all those who insult the Prophet", "Our dead are in paradise, your dead are in hell" and "Down, down USA"[8]. Some protestors on the day were interviewed by ABC news[9]. Quotes included "Freedom of expression doesn't mean that you can insult people" and "This kind of movie hurts the Muslims so this is not right".

Australia's relationship with Islam became particularly strained in 2014 when a Muslim man, Man Haron Monis, took over the Lindt chocolate café in Sydney and held people hostage over a 16 hour standoff, while the black flag of Islam, proclaiming the Islamic shahada (declaration of faith), was shown in the café's window. Three people were killed, including Monis.

The Lord Mayor of Sydney was quick to defend the city's multiculturalism in the wake of the attack, saying, "We're an

---

7 «Are Young Australian Muslims Being Radicalised on Home Soil?,» ABC News, last modified December 17, 2013, http://www.abc.net.au/news/2013-12-17/are-young-australian-muslims-being-radicalised-on/4724350.

8 «PM Calls Islamic Protest ‹un-Australian›,» NewsComAu, last modified September 17, 2012, http://www.news.com.au/national/police-use-pepper-spray-on-anti-islamic-film-protesters-in-sydney-at-the-us-consulate/story-fndo4bst-1226474744811.

9 «Australian Muslim ‹Your Allowed Freedom of Speech, Within the Limits We Set›,» YouTube, last modified November 22, 2012, http://www.youtube.com/watch?v=o-luLjOXtng.

inclusive multicultural community and we need to deal with this together"[10]. It seems the Mayor was unwilling or unable to recognise that Australia was experiencing Islamic terror, and that lax rules on both migration and criminal behaviour involving Muslims had played their part. Monis had already faced charges of being an accessory to the murder of his ex-wife[11], had been convicted of menace, harassment and causing offence by writing to the families of fallen Australian soldiers and calling them murderers[12], as well as sexual assault. In fact, he was on bail for 40 sexual assaults[13]. Despite all of this, he remained free to walk Australia's streets.

A GLIMMER OF HOPE?

Australia does, however, sometimes reveal a glimmer of hope. For example, the notorious Hizb ut-Tahrir was found guilty by a court of committing gender discrimination at one of its events. Journalist Alison Bevege had attended the event, and having been forced to sit in a women's section, she sued the group for sex discrimination, and won[14].

In 2015, a man was found guilty in Australia's criminal courts of unlawfully procuring sex with a child when he 'married' his 12-year-old daughter in an Islamic ceremony in New South Wales[15]. The following year, Australia would see its first

10 "Live Blog: Siege in Sydney's Martin Place," ABC News, accessed May 5, 2018, http://livenews.abc.net.au/Event/Live_blog_Siege_in_Sydneys_Martin_Place/137139144.

11 AAP, "Murder case against Man Haron Monis and partner weak: magistrate," The Weekend Australian, December 12, 2013, http://www.theaustralian.com.au/news/nation/murder-case-against-man-haron-monis-and-partner-weak-magistrate/story-e6frg6nf-1226781538379.

12 "Sheik Says Letters Were Flowers of Advice," SBS News, last modified September 13, 2013, http://www.sbs.com.au/news/article/2013/09/06/sheik-says-letters-were-flowers-advice.

13 Louise Hall, Paul Bibby, "Sydney Siege Gunman Man Haron Monis Was on Bail for 40 Sexual Assault Charges and Accessory to Murder," The Age, last modified December 15, 2014, http://www.theage.com.au/nsw/sydney-siege-gunman-man-haron-monis-was-on-bail-for-40-sexual-assault-charges-and-accessory-to-murder-20141215-127u1e.html.

14 "Journalist Wins Discrimination Case Against Islamic Extremist Group," Mail Online, last modified March 4, 2016, http://www.dailymail.co.uk/news/article-3476446/Journalist-wins-gender-discrimination-case-against-Islamic-extremist-group-Hizb-ut-Tahir.html.

15 "Father Found Guilty of Procuring 12yo Daughter As 'child bride'," ABC News, last modified April 1, 2015, http://www.abc.net.au/news/2015-04-01/father-found-guilty-procuring-12yo-daughter-unlawful-sexual/6363752.

convictions for the horrendous crime of female genital mutilation. Two women were convicted for carrying out the barbaric act on two separate young girls, also in New South Wales, in 2016[16].

These lights do not glimmer for long and are soon snuffed out. Reports of child marriage, for example, continue to trickle out of Australia, with one report revealing that dozens of girls, some as young as nine, were forced to marry older men in New South Wales[17]. Little was done to prevent it; quite the opposite, in fact. When a Royal Commission into sexual abuse of children was instituted in 2017, Islam was the only religion to escape scrutiny[18].

While child-rape carries on with impunity, Ayaan Hirsi Ali cancelled a trip Down Under because it was deemed unsafe[19]. A petition against her visit read: "Against a backdrop of increasing global Islamophobia, Hirsi-Ali's divisive rhetoric simply serves to increase hostility and hatred towards Muslims." The Muslim girls being forced into a life of sexual and domestic servitude still await a similar petition to protest against their suffering. They may be in for a long wait.

SHARIA AND EXTREMISM IN AUSTRALIA

Sharia law regularly gets the sanitisation treatment in Australia as it does in all Western nations. When Islamic activist Yassmin Abdel-Magied announced to the world that Islam was its "most feminist religion", she was met with incredulity, but the damage had been done. Once again the appalling misogyny of Islam had been denied on national television.

16 "Australia Makes First FGM Convictions," BBC News, last modified November 12, 2015, http://www.bbc.co.uk/news/world-australia-34795203.
17 «Australian Girls As Young As NINE Married off As Child Brides to Men,» Mail Online, last modified September 13, 2017, http://www.dailymail.co.uk/news/article-4878544/Child-brides-Underage-girls-forced-marry-Australia.html.
18 "Islamic Groups Dodge Abuse Inquiry," Herald Sun, Heraldsun.com.au, accessed May 6, 2018 (full article behind pay wall), http://www.heraldsun.com.au/news/national/islamic-groups-have-dodged-scrutiny-by-the-royal-commission-into-institutional-child-sex-abuse/news-story/327a250f5618a2c3a3fdfb1d5d855b83.
19 "Slam Critic Cancels Tour over Security," BBC News, last modified April 3, 2017, http://www.bbc.co.uk/news/world-australia-39475462.

Abdel-Magied claimed that sharia law is "about mercy, about kindness" – something her friends at Hizb ut-Tahrir are also likely to claim. After her appearance on ABC's *Q&A* programme, on which she'd dropped the feminist religion clanger, she wrote to the sharia-supporting, caliphate-seeking HT to ask for advice on how she could have done better[20]. This was after Hizb ut-Tahrir spokesman Uthman Badar had defended child marriage, saying, "Something being illegal according to Western law does not make it immoral". The most feminist religion, indeed.

Other occurrences in Australia worthy of mention are these:

- Government bans on such courts in Australia has not prevented the emergence of sharia bodies providing rulings on family matters including divorce and child custody, as well as financial disputes. A Sheikh in the west of Sydney, who claims to adjudicate on hundreds of sharia divorces per year, was interviewed in a report by *Today Tonight*[21], a current affairs programme. He said that sharia offers a solution to all sorts of issues – he was particularly concerned about women having babies outside of marriage and addressed polygamy favourably. His deep concern was for the "13% extra womans [women] in Australia" who would not be able to find a husband otherwise. It's every Australian woman's right to have a husband, he thought.

The Muslims interviewed by vox pop in the report overwhelmingly expressed a preference for Islamic law over that of democratic Australia. In 2011, the Australian Federation of Islamic Councils submitted a proposal to the Federal Parliament's Committee on Multicultural Affairs requesting that Australian Muslims be allowed to marry, divorce and conduct

20 Andrew Carswell and Alicia Wood, "Radical Islamic group Hizb ut-Tahrir says Australia and the US should be labelled terroritst for their Middle Eastern 'invasions'," The Daily Telegraph, June 24, 2014, https://www.dailytelegraph.com.au/news/radical-islamic-group-hizb-uttahrir-says-australia-and-the-us-should-be-labelled-terrorists-for-their-middle-eastern-invasions/news-story/aa9ab976c44b4863a971cfdf4b89e5cb.
21 "Muslim Sharia Law In Australia," YouTube, last modified July 14, 2011, http://www.youtube.com/watch?v=iN7eQyrDt-U.

financial transactions under sharia law[22]. The proposal argued that all Australians would benefit if Islamic laws were adopted in the mainstream.

- Mohammad Issai Issaka was accused of riot, assaulting police, and resisting arrest during the infamous Sydney riots of 2012. When legal proceedings began, Issaka refused to stand up in court, claiming it was against his religion to do so because the Magistrate was a woman[23]. In the end, a ludicrous 'compromise' was reached "whereby Issaka would walk into the courtroom after the Magistrate and leave before her, so he didn't have to technically stand up for her". This provided another shocking example of the modification of the behaviour of Western women to accommodate Islamic misogyny.
- The Australian National University in 2013 banned any satire of Islam. Admitting they were doing so out of fear, the university authorities ordered the editors of the student newspaper *Woroni* "to pulp a satirical infographic which described a passage from the Koran as a 'rape fantasy'"[24].
- 'Vilification on the grounds of religion' was criminalised in 2016 with Labour and Liberal parties supporting the move[25]. The *Canberra Times* reported that the proposal had been put forward by the Green Party's Shane Rattenbury, who said, "Display of hatred, intoler

---

22 "Muslim Group Wants Sharia Law in Australia," ABC News, last modified May 17, 2011, http://www.abc.net.au/news/2011-05-17/muslim-group-wants-sharia-law-in-australia/2717096.

23 "Muslim Rioter Jailed Despite Apology," Daily Telegraph | We're for Sydney, last modified April 2, 2014, http://www.dailytelegraph.com.au/news/rioter-mohammed-issai-issakas-apology-fails-to-reduce-sentence-for-role-in-hyde-park-riot/news-story/374b68105 506ec36bab653dd08de1efb.

24 Rachel Baxendale, "Australian National University bans Koran satire for fear of violent backlash," The Weekend Australian, last modified May 27, 2013, https://www.theaustralian.com.au/higher-education/uni-bans-koran-satire-for-fear-of-violent-backlash/news-story/de4c41a41a36fd52b0d4a36c701828ae?sv=b531f432be586f1f3ce0af805587265b.

25 Kirsten Lawson, "ACT Parliament Passes Religious Vilification Laws," Canberra Times, last modified August 4, 2016, http://www.canberratimes.com.au/act-news/act-parliament-passes-religious-vilification-laws-20160804-gqlagu.html.

ance and offensive behaviour towards Muslims is one of the biggest intolerance issues in Australia today".

- In December 2017, a man deliberately drove into pedestrians in Melbourne and was subsequently charged with 18 counts of attempted murder. The media quickly claimed that the Afghan immigrant was suffering from a history of drug abuse and mental illness[26]. Prime Minister Malcolm Turnbull assured the public that this was an isolated incident, even though it wasn't. This is the same Malcolm Turnbull who had dined with known Islamists and jihadists[27], and stated that Muslims are Australia's "best allies"[28] a day after the largest ever terror raids had been carried out in the country.

26 Sky News, "Melbourne Car Attack: Driver Charged with 18 Counts of Attempted Murder," Sky News, last modified December 21, 2017, https://news.sky.com/story/19-injured-as-car-hits-crowd-in-melbourne-australia-11179410.
27 Paul Karp, "Malcolm Turnbull Regrets Inviting Homophobic Sheikh to Iftar Dinner," The Guardian, last modified October 26, 2016, https://www.theguardian.com/world/2016/jun/17/malcolm-turnbull-regrets-inviting-homophobic-sheikh-to-iftar-dinner.
28 "Turnbull: Everyday Muslims Are Australia's Best Allies | Daily Mail Online," Mail Online, accessed June 2, 2018, http://www.dailymail.co.uk/video/news/video-1121058/Turnbull-Everyday-Muslims-Australias-best-allies.html.

MUSLIM MAJORITY NATIONS

To TRULY UNDERSTAND the danger of political Islam and sharia, it is imperative we look to countries where Islamists have gained power, and what can happen when they do.

AFGHANISTAN

Afghanistan has undergone a disastrous, and very speedy, transformation in recent decades, resulting in what is arguably the most horrific place in the world to be a woman. Following the withdrawal of the Soviet Union in 1989, a power vacuum ensued and a fractious mess of warlords vied for power.

It is hard to imagine that Afghanistan was ever a place where women were free, but it was. Back in the 1920s, child marriage was banned, as was forced marriage, and women and girls were encouraged to enter education and take off their veils. In the 1970s, women in that country practised medicine, and worked as scientists and teachers. Various photographs from Afghanistan throughout the 20th century show women in universities, in science labs, and even in mini-skirts. Many of today's Afghans would hardly recognise this place, because in the 1990s the Taliban arrived, and Afghanistan reverted to a dark age that is almost indescribable.

The restrictions and punishments listed below were applied to women and girls under Taliban rule (source: The Revolutionary Association of the Women of Afghanistan www.rawa.org):

1. Complete ban on women's work outside the home, which also applies to female teachers, engineers and most professionals. Only a few female doctors and nurses are allowed to work in some hospitals in Kabul

2. Complete ban on women's activity outside the home unless accompanied by a mahram (close male relative such as a father, brother or husband)

3. Ban on women dealing with male shopkeepers

4. Ban on women being treated by male doctors

5. Ban on women studying at schools, universities or any other educational institution

6. Requirement that women wear a long veil (burqa) which covers them from head to toe

7. Whipping, beating and verbal abuse of women not clothed in accordance with Taliban rules, or of women unaccompanied by a mahram

8. Whipping of women in public for having non-covered ankles

9. Public stoning of women accused of having sex outside marriage

10. Ban on the use of cosmetics – many women with painted nails have had fingers cut off

11. Ban on women talking or shaking hands with non-mahram males

12. Ban on women laughing loudly – no stranger should hear a woman's voice

13. Ban on women wearing high heel shoes, which would produce sound while walking – a man must not hear a woman's footsteps

14. Ban on women riding in a taxi without a mahram
15. Ban on women's presence in radio, television or public gatherings of any kind
16. Ban on women playing sports or entering a sport center or club
17. Ban on women riding bicycles or motorcycles, even with their mahrams
18. Ban on women wearing brightly colored clothes. In Taliban terms, these are 'sexually attracting colors'
19. Ban on women gathering for festive occasions such as the Eids, or for any recreational purpose
20. Ban on women washing clothes next to rivers or in a public place
21. Modification of all place names including the word 'women' – for example, 'women's garden' has been renamed 'spring garden'
22. Ban on women appearing on the balconies of their apartments or houses
23. Compulsory painting of all windows, so women cannot be seen from outside their homes
24. Ban on male tailors taking women's measurements or sewing women's clothes
25. Ban on female public baths
26. Ban on males and females traveling on the same bus
27. Ban on flared (wide) pant-legs, even under a burqa
28. Ban on the photographing or filming of women
29. Ban on women's pictures printed in newspapers and books, or hung on the walls of houses and shops

This is the reality at the sharp end of Islam. Men were also placed under severe restrictions by the Taliban: they could not shave or trim their beards; their haircuts were regulated; music and movies were banned; they were forced to pray five times a day; those caught with objectionable literature were executed; and non-Muslims were forced to wear an identifying piece of yellow cloth stitched to their clothing.

THE 'ARAB SPRING'

The first of the 'Arab Spring' countries to overthrow its leader was Tunisia. Its President of 23 years, Zine al-Abidine Ben Ali, was removed and elections were held. The Islamist Ennahda Movement came to power. The party initially promised not to impose sharia, or to push back the rights of women.

A new constitution was drawn up, and pressure from Islamists to include a clause naming women as "complementary" to men caused protests across the country[1]. Tunisian women watched as their formerly secular country looked to be facing a transformation – one that would not be favourable to them.

Tunisia's previous constitution, written in 1956, stated that men and women were equal, introduced civil (as opposed to sharia) marriage and divorce, and banned polygamous marriage. Ennahda member Farida al-Obeidi, Chair of the Constitutional Assembly's Human Rights and Public Freedoms panel, said the wording of the draft constitution was not a backward step for Tunisian women, arguing that "sharing of roles does not mean that women are worth less than men"[2].

This argument is frequently put forward: women's roles are different to men's, and there is no harm in difference. But what characterises this difference? Is it different in that one has all the power and the other none? One can divorce at will while the other needs permission from clerics? One earns money and the other earns none?

Given that thousands of Tunisian women turned out to protest, it is clear that they were not going to be duped by al-Obeidi's verbal trickery. Perhaps it was their secular past, but in early 2014 the country's National Constituent Assembly agreed a new constitution which recognised the equality of men and women. There were still some difficult clauses, however; while the Islamist Ennahda dropped references to Islamic law, the constitution

---

1 "Thousands Rally in Tunisia for Women's Rights," U.S, last modified August 14, 2012, http://www.reuters.com/article/2012/08/14/us-tunisia-women-rights-idUSBRE87C16020120814.
2 "Tunisian Women's Rights Protest," BBC News, last modified August 14, 2012, http://www.bbc.co.uk/news/world-africa-19253289.

still prohibited "attacks on the sacred"[3], which could of course be interpreted as a blasphemy law. Time will tell.

In Egypt, Hosni Mubarak was overthrown and replaced by Mohammed Morsi – a member of the Islamist Muslim Brotherhood. Morsi was President of the ironically named Freedom and Justice Party (FJP) which won the elections following Mubarak's overthrow.

Women and men had stood side-by-side during the revolution, but then a new constitution was devised, and due to the influence of sharia, women in Egypt would find themselves increasingly marginalised and facing very real threats to their basic rights. Even before the drafting of the new Egyptian constitution began, women in Egypt were feeling the harsh changes: beaten and abused by security services; subjected to virginity tests; raped and attacked by groups of men[4].

In November 2012, a new constitution was ratified, and passed a referendum test a month later. There were many reasons to worry, and not just for women. The Protection of Rights clause contained in Article 81 stated that all rights and freedoms shall be "exercised insofar as they do not contradict the principles set out in the Chapter on State and Society in this constitution". The Chapter on State and Society declares, "The state and society shall commit to preserving the true nature of the Egyptian family"[5].

This immediately sets off alarm bells – what precisely does "the true nature of the Egyptian family" mean? We got a strong indication in March 2013 when the Muslim Brotherhood rejected a UN declaration condemning violence against women, insisting that such a thing would lead to the "complete disintegration of society"[6].

---

3 "Tunisia Assembly Passes Constitution," BBC News, last modified January 27, 2014, http://www.bbc.co.uk/news/world-africa-25908340.
4 Paul Danahar, "Revolution 'failing Egyptian Women'," BBC News, last modified July 17, 2012, http://www.bbc.co.uk/news/world-middle-east-18861958.
5 «Egypt: New Constitution Mixed on Support of Rights,» Human Rights Watch, last modified December 5, 2012, http://www.hrw.org/news/2012/11/29/egypt-new-constitution-mixed-support-rights.
6 Patrick Kingsley, "Muslim Brotherhood Backlash Against UN Declarf on Women Rights," The Guardian, last modified December 1, 2017, http://www.theguardian.com/world/2013/mar/15/muslim-brotherhood-backlash-un-womens-rights.

In 2014, London's Henry Jackson Society produced a report[7] 'Marginalising Egyptian Women' which claimed that Morsi's government "helped to create a culture of acceptability surrounding sexual violence against women". The report is worth reading in full, but a particular highlight is the Freedom and Justice Party's attitude to women, and the type of society they seek to create.

Reda el-Hefnawy had been a FJP representative at the UN Human Rights Council. He was asked whose duty it was to protect women from sexual harassment at political rallies, he answered that women should not be mingling with men in the first place[8].

Osama Yehia Abu Salama, a Brotherhood 'family expert', spoke at a seminar aimed at training marriage counsellors. He said that women should be "confined" and controlled by the man of the house[9].

Freedom of speech and religion also took a beating in the new Egypt. Article 44 prohibited the insulting of prophets. In addition, the constitution stated, "No international treaty that contradicts the provisions of this constitution shall be signed."

The Egyptians were in an over-throwing mood, and come 2013, the Muslim Brotherhood's Mohammed Morsi was removed. The Army took power, suspended the constitution, and promised fresh elections[10]. A new constitution was drawn up and there was some cause for relief – it guaranteed freedom of belief and the equality of men and women. The constitution was approved by a referendum, but not until several people had been killed in clashes between secularists and Islamists.

---

7 Emily Dyer, "Marginalising Egyptian Women," The Henry Jackson Society, last modified December 17, 2013, henryjacksonsociety.org/2013/12/17/report-release-marginalising-egyptian-women. /

8 "Shura Council Members Blame Women for Harassment," Daily News Egypt, last modified February 11, 2013, http://www.dailynewsegypt.com/2013/02/11/shura-council-members-blame-women-for-harassment.

9 David D. Kirkpatrick and Mayy El Sheikh, "Muslim Brotherhood's Words on Women Stir Liberal Fears," The New York Times - Breaking News, World News & Multimedia, last modified March 14, 2013, http://www.nytimes.com/2013/03/15/world/middleeast/muslim-brotherhoods-words-on-women-stir-liberal-fears.html.

10 "Army Ousts Egypt's President Morsi," BBC News, last modified July 4, 2013, http://www.bbc.co.uk/news/world-middle-east-23173794.

Abdel Fattah el-Sisi was elected President of Egypt in May 2014. Morsi's Freedom and Justice Party was banned from participating in the election.

When we're considering the Arab Spring, and how quickly a society can transform under Islamist influence, it is hard not to contemplate previous revolutions in the Middle East. I am thinking specifically of Iran.

In 1979, the people of Iran overthrew Shah Mohammed Reza Pahlavi. The demonstrations against the Shah had begun in 1977 and ended in January 1979, when the Ayatollah Khomeini transformed the nation into today's Islamic Republic of Iran.

In the Islamic Republic, veiling is enforced and a strict dress code applies to the country's women. Blasphemy and apostasy carry the death penalty, and adultery is punished by way of death by stoning. The intricacies of life under the Shah are beyond the scope of this book, but there are some points that should be mentioned – particularly with regard to women's rights and religious freedoms.

According to Monique Girgis, who wrote 'Women in pre-revolutionary, revolutionary, and post-revolutionary Iran'[11] in 1996, life was very different in many respects for Iranian women prior to the establishment of the Islamic Republic. For example, rather than impose veiling like the Ayatollah, under the Shah Iran took active steps to unveil women. The Family Protections Act was introduced in 1967, with a revised version in 1975. Of great significance, this legislation imposed a minimum marriage age (20 for men, 18 for women), and disallowed polygamy unless a husband obtained the permission of the first wife, or the courts. The usual justification for a second wife was that the first was unable to give birth. Divorce laws were also reformed and men could no longer divorce their wives arbitrarily, but via the courts only. As Girgis's study points out, these were hardly sufficient in the cause of genuine gender equality, but they were certainly a step in the right direction, and were markedly superior to the situation that exists today.

---

11 Monique Girgis, "Iran Chamber Society: Iranian Society: Women in Pre-revolutionary, Revolutionary and Post-revolutionary Iran [Chapter One]," Iran Chamber Society, 1996, accessed May 7, 2018, http://www.iranchamber.com/society/articles/women_prepost_revolutionary_iran1.php.

What exists today in Iran, thanks to sharia and an Islamist government, is a nation where adultery, homosexuality, apostasy, and blasphemy carry the death penalty.

ELSEWHERE

Indonesia is home to the largest Muslim population in the world and is often used as an example of how Muslim-majority society can exist in peace and secular prosperity. However, in recent years, sharia law has gained a foothold in Indonesia – particularly on the island of Aceh – and the rights of women have suffered.

Sharia religious police first appeared on the streets of Aceh in 2006[12]. Since then, Islamic dress codes have been enforced, men and women prohibited from mixing[13], people lashed for drinking alcohol[14], and death by stoning has been adopted as punishment for adultery[15]. The prominent human rights organisation Human Rights Watch released a report in 2010 documenting the rise of sharia on some Indonesian islands, and concluded that "the laws, and their selective enforcement, are an invitation to abuse"[16].

In late 2013, the Sultan of Brunei[17] decided to impose death by stoning as punishment for adultery. Introducing sharia law, Hassanal Bolkiah, one of the world's richest men, said that the new laws should be regarded as special guidance from God:

---

12 "BBC NEWS | Asia-Pacific | Aceh Wary over New Sharia Police," Home - BBC News, last modified December 8, 2006, http://news.bbc.co.uk/1/hi/world/asia-pacific/6220256. stm.

13 "Indonesia Islamic Laws 'abusive'," BBC News, last modified December 1, 2010, http://www.bbc.co.uk/news/world-asia-pacific-11883781.

14 Karishma Vaswani, "Five Flogged by Indonesian Police," BBC News, last modified August 6, 2010, http://www.bbc.co.uk/news/world-asia-pacific-10890137.

15 "BBC NEWS | Asia-Pacific | Aceh Passes Adultery Stoning Law," Home - BBC News, accessed June 2, 2018, http://news.bbc.co.uk/1/hi/world/asia-pacific/8254631.stm.

16 "Indonesia: Local Sharia Laws Violate Rights in Aceh," Human Rights Watch, last modified April 17, 2015, http://www.hrw.org/news/2010/11/29/indonesia-local-sharia-laws-violate-rights-aceh.

17 David Eimer and Colin Freeman, "Brunei Introduces Death by Stoning Under New Islamic Laws," Telegraph.co.uk, last modified October 22, 2013, http://www.telegraph.co.uk/news/worldnews/asia/brunei/10395702/Brunei-introduces-death-by-stoning-under-new-Islamic-laws.html.

"By the grace of Allah, with the coming into effect of this legislation, our duty to Allah is therefore being fulfilled."

The truth is – as Afghanistan, Egypt and Iran have shown – religious tyranny can come to power very rapidly. There are vast numbers of Islamists in the world who dream of creating societies in the West similar to the one suffered by the Afghan people under the Taliban, or by people in Saudi Arabia or Iran. We can only fight this by identifying it. We can only identify it with honesty, but Western populations are being lied to by our leaders, while feminists and human rights groups stick their fingers in their ears. This too must be identified if we are to stand any chance of defending our freedom.

NINETEEN EIGHTY-FOUR

TWO PLUS TWO MAKE FOUR

"Freedom is the freedom to say that two plus two make four."

—George Orwell

In perhaps his most famous work, British author George Orwell masterfully depicted a futuristic nightmare in which all thoughts, words, and actions are regulated and policed by an uber-powerful state. With the exception of the 'proles' (the common man or woman), people are monitored 24 hours a day by 'Big Brother' – primarily via two-way 'telescreens' – and any hint of dissent is severely punished. Even a suspect facial expression will attract the attentions of the state.

Winston Smith, the book's main character, is employed at the Records Department where he rewrites history to suit the propaganda of the rulers, to the extent that objective truth no longer exists. What is true is determined by the powerful, and the powerless are forced to believe it, irrespective of what they see with their eyes or feel in their hearts. A person who insists that the truth is something other than that espoused by 'The Party' will be guilty of an offence and punished by the thought police.

The penalty is death.

I wrote earlier in this book about the Austrian politician Susanne Winter, who faced charges of incitement and degradation of religious symbols for stating that Mohammed had married a six-year-old child. She claimed that *"in today's system"*[1] Mohammed would have been considered a paedophile. She was convicted and fined €24,000, as well as handed a three month suspended prison sentence. It seemed not to matter to the Austrian court that marrying a six-year-old, and consummating the marriage when the girl reaches the age of nine, is entirely consistent with widely-held Islamic belief. Indeed, many Islamic states – including Yemen and Saudi Arabia – either have no minimum age for marriage, or set that age at nine in line with Mohammed's example.

In Saudi Arabia, the Grand Mufti (again, not a fringe extremist), Sheikh Abdul Aziz Al-Sheikh, said in 2009, "It is incorrect to say that it's not permitted to marry off girls who are 15 and younger"[2].

Similarly, a second Saudi judge, Sheikh Habib Abdallah al-Habib, refused to annul the marriage of an eight-year-old girl to a 47-year-old man (a marriage allegedly arranged by her father in settlement of a debt) and stated, "We should know that Shariah law has not brought injustice to women."

In 2011, a member of Saudi Arabia's highest religious council, Dr Salih bin Fawzan, issued a fatwa (religious ruling) and declared that girls could be married "even if they are in the cradle"[3].

In Yemen, attempts to raise the age of marriage for girls was dismissed as "un-Islamic"[4] by clerics, and as a result, child marriage remains widespread in that country.

1 Soeren Kern, "Free Speech Found Guilty by Europe," Gatestone Institute, last modified April 23, 2012, http://www.gatestoneinstitute.org/3026/lars-hedegaard-acquitted.
2 "Top Saudi Cleric: OK for Young Girls to Wed - CNN.com," CNN International - Breaking News, US News, World News and Video, last modified January 17, 2009, http://edition.cnn.com/2009/WORLD/meast/01/17/saudi.child.marriage.
3 "Saudi Arabia's Top Religious Leader Okays Pedophilia," Fellowship of the Minds, last modified January 4, 2015, https://fellowshipoftheminds.com/2015/01/04/saudi-arabias-top-religious-leader-okays-pedophilia/comment-page-1/.
4 "YEMEN: Islamic Lawmaker Decries Child Marriage Ban As Part of 'Western Agenda'," accessed May 8, 2018, http://latimesblogs.latimes.com/babylonbeyond/2010/04/yemen-fierce-opposition-to-child-marriage-ban-persists-among-conservatives.html.

In Britain in 2013, an undercover investigation revealed that several major mosques across the country were willing to marry young girls against their will[5], although there was no evidence of the forced marriage of girls as young as nine. At the Al-Quba Mosque and Shah Poran Islamic Education Centre in Manchester, clerics told a reporter, posing as a mother, that the girl's silence indicated her consent to marriage.

In the same programme, a reporter posing as an older brother approached a major UK mosque in Birmingham asking one of its representatives to marry his 14-year-old sister to a 20-year-old man. He was told, "In Islamic law she is OK to get married because she will be the age of maturity."

The mosque's representative acknowledges that the age of sexual consent and marriage in the UK is 16, but on hidden camera he states:

> "Obviously, you take Islam as priority over the law of the land. But then we do consider the law of the land, but then we've got to look at what Islam says, and that's why I've got the right from a mufti; they say do it. If anyone, any authority finds out…then what are you going to do?"

The reporter asks if it is OK for the young girl to live with her new husband following the marriage, and is told:

> "She's married, she's married. By sharia, grace of God, she's legal to get married and there's nothing against that. We're doing it because it's OK through Islam, but then you've got the kaffirs, the law, the English people, you know, [saying] that…you can't get married twice, but, by the grace of God, we can get married four times. Obviously, Islam has made it easy for us. They don't understand, that's the only problem."

The reaction to this programme from Islamic organisations in Britain was very telling. A spokesman for the mosque responded, saying:

---

5 "UK Imams Agree to Perform Underage Marriages," ITV News, accessed May 7, 2018, http://www.itv.com/news/2013-10-06/uk-imams-agree-to-perform-underage-marriages/.

*"Though Islamic sharia law allows marriages in special
circumstances in the Muslim world when girls reach puberty,
with the consent of the girls and parents concerned, we do
not live in a Muslim country, so we do not practise that."*

It is important to recognise that there was no condemnation
of the marriages based on the health or well-being, or indeed the
basic human rights, of the girls themselves, merely on the basis
that the UK is not a Muslim country.

Ibrahim Mogra of the Muslim Council of Britain, who makes
regular appearances on British television and is widely accepted
as a moderate voice, stated:

*"UK law does not allow the marriage of underage girls
and that's all that matters to us here. In this country, it is
illegal, it is forbidden, and no imam should be allowed to
conduct the marriage of an underage child[6]."*

Again, there is a notable lack of condemnation of underage
marriage *per se.*

It is, of course, important to address the theological justifica-
tions within Islam for the practice of child marriage, given that
it is frequently argued that child marriage in Islamic states is a
cultural rather than religious matter.

The religious justification for child marriage comes from the
ahadith, which are the sayings and actions of Mohammed and,
together with the Koran and Islamic jurisprudence, form the
principles of sharia law. These are the ahadith which pronounce
the marriage of Mohammed to Aisha:

"A'isha (Allah be pleased with her) reported: 'Allah's
Messenger (may peace be upon him) married me when I
was six years old, and I was admitted to his house at the
age of nine'."

Sahih Muslim 8:3309

---

6 "Clerics at 18 Mosques Are Caught Agreeing to Marry off Girls of 14," Mail Online,
last modified October 7, 2013, http://www.dailymail.co.uk/news/article-2447720/
Clerics-18-mosques-caught-agreeing-marry-girls-14-Four-imams-investigated-undercover-
operation.html.

"'The Apostle of Allah married me when I was seven years old. [The narrator Sulaiman said, 'Or six years.'] He had intercourse with me when I was nine years old.'"

Abu Dawud 2:2116

"Abu Bakr married ['A'ishah] *to him when she was* [only] *six years old."*

Al-Tabari, Vol. 9, pp. 129-130

In early 2016, an attempt was made in Pakistan to ban child marriage[7]. The legislation was shot down by the Council of Islamic Ideology, a body that advises whether proposed legislation is compatible with sharia. It did not succeed because not only was it dubbed un-Islamic, it was even decreed to be "blasphemous". Blasphemy, of course, is punishable with the death penalty.

The UN Committee on the Rights of the Child has condemned Iran for rising numbers of child brides there in recent years[8] and politely asked it to raise its marriage age from nine years old.

Given all of this, isn't it the case that Susanne Winter was accurately observing widely held Islamic belief? Isn't it then the case that she was prosecuted for telling the truth? It is not relevant that there is some dispute within Islam as to the age of Aisha; the fact is that the above ahadith exist, and are overwhelmingly accepted – therefore Winter's claims are true.

The American author Robert Spencer was barred from Britain because his words were, according to then Home Secretary Theresa May, "not conducive to the public good". Spencer is an expert on Islam, and one of the facts he has stated many times is that Islam sanctions wife-beating. He has been heavily criticised for this, and was taken to task (apparently) by an imam

7 Maryam Usman, "Bill Aiming to Ban Child Marriages Shot Down," The Express Tribune, last modified January 16, 2016, http://tribune.com.pk/story/1027742/settled-matter-bill-aiming-to-ban-child-marriages-shot-down. /
8 Jack Moore, "U.N. Condemns Iran for Increase in Child Brides As Young As 10 Years Old," Newsweek, February 5, 2016, http://europe.newsweek.com/un-condemns-iran-increase-child-brides-young-10-423435.

on BBC radio who insisted that this claim was untrue[9]. On the programme, Spencer named the relevant verse of the Koran, Sura 4:34:

> "*Men have authority over women because God has made the one superior to the other, and because they spend their wealth to maintain them. Good women are obedient. They guard their unseen parts because God has guarded them. As for those* [from] *whom you fear disobedience, admonish them and send them to beds apart and beat them. Then if they obey you, take no further action against them. Surely God is most high.*"

Spencer also quoted several other passages from the Koran which he found objectionable.

In response to this, Imam Yunus Dudhwala avoided the issue by arguing that the real question was whether the presence of Spencer and Geller in the UK would be "helpful".

He then labelled Spencer "an extremist", but could not repudiate any of Spender's Koranic quotes. The extent of his riposte was to allege that Spencer was quoting out of context, and when asked to expand on this by the presenter, he claimed that the supremacist and war-like verses quoted by Spencer were relevant only to the age of jihad 1,400 years ago. This is inconsistent, however, with the widely-held belief that the Koran is the direct and infallible word of God, applicable to all times and places.

Dudhwala went on to claim that all are equal in the eyes of God, as revealed in the Koran, and as evidence of this, he quoted the following:

> "*Whoever takes a life, any life, whether it's Muslim or non-Muslim, it is like taking the life of every single human being.*"

---

9 "Robert Spencer Knows More About Islam Than East London Imam on BBC Radio Interview," YouTube, last modified January 12, 2015, https://www.youtube.com/watch?v=-XYmZ3T6c6s.

It appears that Dudhwala was somewhat confused, because here is what the Koran actually says.

Koran 5:32:

> "We ordained for the Children of Israel that if anyone slew a person – **unless it be in retaliation for murder or for spreading mischief in the land** – it would be as if he slew all mankind: and if anyone saved a life, it would be as if he saved the life of all humanity."

When challenged as to why he was unable to counter Spencer's quotes, the imam replied that he had not been prepared to answer such questions, and remarkably added that Spencer was at an advantage in this debate because "this is his field".

What are we to learn from this episode? Quite simply this: Robert Spencer has been barred from Britain for accurately quoting passages from the Koran. The truth, according to the UK government, is "not conducive to the public good".

Freedom is the freedom to say that sex with children is paedophilia.

THE THOUGHT POLICE

> "It is intolerable to us that an erroneous thought should exist anywhere in the world."
>
> George Orwell

In Pakistan, blasphemy is a criminal offence carrying the death penalty. This, I must emphasise, is the law of the land and not the ranting of a fringe extremist who – to quote Christopher Hitchens – "is standing on a street corner selling pencils from a cup".

Section 295-C of the Pakistani Criminal Code states:

> "Use of derogatory remarks, etc., in respect of the Holy Prophet. Whoever by words, either spoken or written or

by visible representation, or by any imputation, innuendo, or insinuation, directly or indirectly, defiles the sacred name of the Holy Prophet Mohammed (PBUH) shall be punished with death, or imprisonment for life, and shall also be liable to fine."

Between 1986 and 2010, a total of 1,274 people were charged with blasphemy in Pakistan[10]. Some of the more infamous cases in recent years include that of Asia Bibi, a Christian woman accused of blasphemy by her neighbours (who had reportedly refused to drink the water she carried because she was a Christian) and sentenced to death by Judge Muhammed Naveed Iqbal in November 2011.

In Saudi Arabia, where religion and government are as one, apostasy (leaving Islam) carries the death penalty. Again, this is the law of the land. In 2013, a man was beheaded when charges of sorcery and adultery were upheld by the country's senior courts[11]. In the same year, a Saudi preacher was handed a sentence of eight years for raping and murdering his daughter. He was also ordered to pay 'blood money' to her mother. Despite the regular use of the death penalty in Saudi Arabia, it did not apply in this case because, according to rights groups, a father cannot be executed for murdering his wives or children under Islamic law[12].

In Iran, also an Islamic state governed by sharia law, the penalty of death by stoning is applied. Amnesty International produced a document[13] detailing the specifications of the penalty. Article 104 of the Penal Code reads:

"The size of the stone used in stoning shall not be too large to kill the convict by one or two throws and at the same time shall not be too small to be called a stone."

10 "Timeline: Accused Under the Blasphemy Law," DAWN.COM, last modified August 18, 2013, http://dawn.com/news/750512/timeline-accused-under-the-blasphemy-law.
11 «Saudi Man is Executed for Sorcery,» BBC News, last modified June 19, 2012, http://www.bbc.co.uk/news/world-middle-east-18503550.
12 "Saudi Celebrity Cleric Who Raped and Murdered His Daughter, Five, Claimed He Injured Her Because He Doubted She Was a Virgin," Mail Online, last modified February 13, 2013, http://www.dailymail.co.uk/news/article-2277437/Saudi-celebrity-cleric-raped-murdered-daughter-claimed-injured-doubted-virgin.html.
13 Amnesty International, "Iran - End executions by stoning," Home | Amnesty International, published January 2008, accessed May 25, 2018, https://www.amnesty.org/download/Documents/56000/mde130012008en.pdf.

I must stress again, this is the law of the land, not the work of fringe extremists.

In Afghanistan, women are routinely jailed for being raped[14]. In the United Arab Emirates, where the so-called 'moderate' Dubai is capital, two women (an Australian and a Norwegian)[15] were given longer sentences than their convicted rapists for the crime of 'adultery'. The 'moderate' Muslim Council of Britain's Suhaib Hasan has called for similar punishments to be applied in the UK.

Taking all of the above into account, and a lot more besides, let me ask you a question: do you fear Islam as a political force? If you do, then you are irrational, you are a bigot, and you are a racist. Welcome to Islamophobia.

How does a state set about controlling a person's thoughts? It begins with controlling their words, and then does the same with their fears. State propaganda will convince people that their words and fears are not only irrational, but immoral. It will convince people that the evidence they see before them is not actually there; it is simply their bigotry that is the problem.

If a person continues to insist that they have every right to fear stonings or child marriage, they will be told that they are on a par with the apartheid regime of South Africa, or the Ku Klux Klan in the American Deep South. This cements the notion that their thoughts and fears are wicked, and they will become confused.

The state will then create laws to enable it to crack down on thoughts and fears, and those who speak out of turn will be silenced by legislation. This legislation will apply to those who tell objective truths and to those expressing opinions based on the evidence they can see. Examples of people prosecuted for expressing opinions include the elected politician Geert Wilders in the Netherlands and Lars Hedegaard in Denmark.

In *Nineteen Eighty-Four*, Winston Smith is eventually captured by the Thought Police and brought to the Ministry of

---

14 Caroline Wyatt, "Fears over Violence Against Afghan Women," BBC News, last modified January 14, 2012, http://www.bbc.co.uk/news/world-south-asia-16543036.
15 Amena Bakr, "Woman Jailed in Dubai After Reporting Rape Hopes to Warn Others," Reuters - World News, last modified July 21, 2013, http://www.reuters.com/article/2013/07/21/us-emirates-courts-norway-idUSBRE96K0AK20130721.

Love to be tortured. His torturers make it clear that it is not enough for him to pretend he believes in and supports the dictates of the ruling Party; he must *actually feel* this. Outward submission must become inward submission.

This is chillingly described as follows:

> "*We are not content with negative obedience, nor even with the most abject submission. When finally you surrender to us, it must be of your own free will.*"

In late October 2013, 'A European Framework National Statute for the Promotion of Tolerance' was presented to the European Parliament for consideration[16]. The homogenisation of Europe, its peoples, its politics, and its views, was to advance with full steam. The aim of this proposal was to create a Europe-wide hate crime, and force citizens of European nation-states to be obediently tolerant. 'Tolerance', it stated, means:

> "*Respect for and acceptance of the expression, preservation and development of the distinct identity of a group.*"

Groups, as is probably obvious, include religious groups.

Pay close attention to the words 'respect for'. You will be forced to respect the expression of the identity of a group, whether or not you actually respect this expression, or even *ought* to respect it. In short, you *will* like it, whether you like or not.

What if the identity of a group is expressed through the imposition of blasphemy rules, as in the case of Islam? You are then, in effect, being told to respect the fact that you are not allowed to criticise a religion, regardless of its doctrine or its practices.

The legislation does, at least on the surface, contain some reassuring elements. An explanatory note, for example, stating that tolerance "does not denote acceptance of such practices as

---

16 "A European Framework National Statute for the Promotion of Tolerance," European Parliament, Europarl.europa.eu, accessed May 8, 2018, http://www.europarl.europa.eu/meetdocs/2009_2014/documents/libe/dv/11_revframework_statute_/11_revframework_statute_en.pdf.

female circumcision, forced marriage, polygamy, or any form of exploitation or domination of women" sounds positive.

Here is another one:

> *"Tolerance is a two-way street. Members of a group who wish to benefit from tolerance must show it to society at large, as well as to members of other groups and to dissidents or other members of their own group...Foreign migrants, for their part, must adhere to the principle of coexistence of diverse groups within a single society."*

These are welcome clauses, but are they cancelled out by this?

> *"Members of vulnerable and disadvantaged groups are entitled to a special protection."*

This clause is later explained as meaning:

> *"The special protection provided...may imply a preferential treatment. Strictly speaking, this preferential treatment goes beyond mere respect and acceptance."*

How is this to be interpreted?

I do not ask the reader to come to conclusions, merely to consider the legislation overall. Should any group be subject to preferential treatment? What groups are likely to be covered by such protections, and how might this protection manifest given the propensity of authorities to avoid charges of Islamophobia?

The main cause for alarm is, to my mind, application of the legislation to education and the media. The proposals require that all education, from elementary school to university, promotes "a climate of tolerance as regards the qualities and cultures of others". The same demand is made of the media, both publicly and privately owned, which is required to "devote a prescribed percentage of their programmes to promoting a climate of tolerance".

To demonstrate the mind-control potential of this kind of legislation, the following passage is the final one I will examine:

*"Juveniles convicted of committing crimes listed...
will be required to undergo a rehabilitation programme
designed to instil in them a culture of tolerance."*

Anyone who isn't horror-struck by the use of the word 'rehabilitation' does not fully understand the concept of totalitarianism.

The European Council on Tolerance and Reconciliation is still pushing its ideas into legislatures around Europe. It did so in the British House of Commons in October 2015[17].

THE UNITED NATIONS

Let me turn back to the United Nations now and examine its record on controlling people's views on matters pertaining to Islam.

The European proposal above applies to children and young people who are to be 'rehabilitated' until they demonstrate the required level of tolerance. In a press release by the then UN Secretary General Kofi Annan in 2004, the word 'unlearn' was used. We must, he said, "unlearn" Islamophobia.

You can read the press release in full here http://www.un.org/News/Press/docs/2004/sgsm9637.doc.htm

Here are some notable passages:

*"Islam's tenets are frequently distorted and taken out
of context, with particular acts or practices being taken to
represent or to symbolize a rich and complex faith. Some
claim that Islam is incompatible with democracy, or irrevo-
cably hostile to modernity and the rights of women. And in
too many circles, disparaging remarks about Muslims are
allowed to pass without censure, with the result that prejudice acquires a veneer of acceptability."*

But what if Islam's tenets are not taken out of context? What if they are taken in the correct context? What if we discuss child

---

17 "The European Council On Tolerance And Reconciliation - Ectr News," The European Council On Tolerance And Reconciliation - Home, accessed May 8, 2018, http://ectr.eu/ectr-news/ectr-presentation-in-the-house-of-commons-in-london.

marriage, or apostasy? What if we tell the truth? This passage assumes that none of the negative baggage attached to Islam is actually based on fact, but what if it is, and provably so?

The obligatory conflating of objection to Islam and racism predictably appears in a later paragraph:

> "*United Nations special rapporteurs continue to monitor the exercise and infringements of this right* [freedom of religion], *and to recommend ways to combat Islamophobia and other forms of racism and intolerance.*"

Another one reads:

> "*Any strategy to combat Islamophobia must depend heavily on education – not just about Islam, but about all religions and traditions, so that myths and lies can be seen for what they are.*"

Here you can see the similarities to the European proposal. Yet again, the assumption is that all negative views about Islam are false, based not on truth but on prejudice. Again, people are being told that what they see with their own eyes is distorted or misleading. It implies that it is people's own fault if they feel fear about Islam.

Another paragraph:

> "*An honest look at Islamophobia must also acknowledge the policy context. The historical experience of Muslims includes colonialism and domination by the West, either direct or indirect. Resentment is fed by the unresolved conflicts in the Middle East, by the situation in Chechnya, and by atrocities committed against Muslims in the former Yugoslavia. The reaction to such events can be visceral, bringing an almost personal sense of affront.*"

The presumption here is that because there are global political issues involving Muslim majority societies, there can be no critique or criticism of Islam itself; discussion of any negative aspects of the religion must be avoided. But there is no connection between legitimate objections to elements of Islam and wider political matters.

We must not, and should not, be prevented from condemning misogynistic aspects of sharia because of global political complexities. However, this is one of the most common defences I hear when I am reprimanded for criticising Islam: "You've got to put it into context"; "Islamic societies were colonised"; "The United States invaded Iraq"; etc. The reasoning seems to be that because the United States invaded Iraq, for example, Muslim men must be allowed to beat their wives, and Islamic societies must be permitted to enslave women generally.

Here is another one:

> *"Efforts to combat Islamophobia must also contend with the question of terrorism and violence carried out in the name of Islam. Islam should not be judged by the acts of extremists who deliberately target and kill civilians. The few give a bad name to the many, and this is unfair."*

This is about the only semi-reasonable statement in the document. Of course it is a small minority of Muslims who are involved in terrorism, but terrorism is not what many of us are concerned about. Our anxieties have everything to do with misogyny, blasphemy laws, child marriage, and all of the other things I have mentioned. These do not feature in the UN press release.

In 2013, Turkish Prime Minister Recep Tayyip Erdoğan described Islamophobia as a "crime against humanity" at the official opening of the fifth UN Alliance of Civilizations Global Forum[18]. This is the same Recep Tayyip Erdoğan who has stated that he does not believe in equality between men and women, and that women should not be in political power because this is "against human nature"[19]. In other words, he is a man who

---

18 "PM Erdo'an: Islamophobia is a Crime Against Humanity," DailySabah, last modified September 12, 2013, https://www.dailysabah.com/turkey/2013/09/12/pm-erdogan-islamophobia-is-a-crime-against-humanity.

19 SPIEGEL ONLINE, "Erdogan the Misogynist: Turkish Prime Minister Assaults Women's Rights - International," SPIEGEL ONLINE, last modified June 19, 2012, http://www.spiegel.de/international/europe/turkish-prime-minister-erdogan-targets-women-s-rights-a-839568.html.

expresses the very things that worry people about Islam, and then claims these worries constitute a "crime against humanity".

What a topsy-turvy world we live in.

Turkey, once the most free and secular of Muslim-majority states, has taken a sinister turn under Mr Erdoğan's leadership. For example, a renowned pianist, Fazil Say, was handed a 10-month prison sentence (suspended) in Istanbul having been convicted of offending Islam and insulting Muslims. He had retweeted this message:

"I am not sure if you have also realised it, but if there's a louse, a non-entity, a lowlife, a thief or a fool, it's always an Allah-ist[20]*."*

Erdoğan has overseen a serious backslide for women in Turkey as the country is increasingly Islamised. In 2014, a minister in his government suggested that women should not laugh in public[21], and activists are worried that this kind of rhetoric will become more acute if Islamists increase their grip on power[22]. Erdo an has even openly condemned the concept of a moderate Islam when Saudi Arabia (of all places) promised to modernise[23].

It is of the utmost importance to those in pursuit of global blasphemy laws that words (therefore language) are redefined and manipulated. What is 'extreme' in one context is deemed to be a 'right' in another. Criticism of the human rights abuses committed in the name of Islam is itself deemed to be a human rights abuse. The purpose of this is to twist morality and water down concrete notions of right and wrong. The result is confusion; people who no longer understand their own thoughts or fears. A powerful and oppressive elite to whom it is intolerable that an erroneous thought should exist anywhere in the world can thus control such people.

---

20 "Turkish Pianist Guilty over Insults," BBC News, last modified April 15, 2013, http://www.bbc.co.uk/news/world-europe-22151212.
21 Constanze Letsch, "Turkish Women Defy Deputy PM with Laughter," The Guardian, last modified November 30, 2017, http://www.theguardian.com/world/2014/jul/30/turkish-women-defy-deputy-pm-laughter.
22 "'No Other Government Has Been So Radical Against Women'," HuffPost, last modified April 18, 2014, http://www.huffingtonpost.com/2014/04/18/turkey-womens-rights_n_5153013.html.
23 "Erdogan Rejects 'moderate Islam' as a Western Tool to Weaken Muslims," RT International, November 11, 2017, https://www.rt.com/news/409532-erdogan-rejects-moderate-islam/.

THE ANTI-SEX LEAGUE

WHILE IT IS true that constraints are, perhaps rightly, placed on sexual practices in most of the world's societies, it is also true that a person cannot be truly free if they do not have authority over their personal or intimate affairs. People must be free to start or end private relationships, leave a marriage of their own volition, and enter into consenting sexual relationships of their choice.

It is fascinating to make a comparison between sexual and intimate relationships in Islamic societies and those in Western societies. In Islamic nations, sexuality is fiercely restricted and regulated by robust state laws. These laws manifest in ways that are often barbaric and brutal, and the party who carries the heavier burden is the female. Sexuality, marriage, and intimacy are governed by religion via the state. As Islamism expands globally, so do ideas about the control of sexuality, and so does the barbaric treatment of women and girls, without which such control could not be enforced.

The author and historian Daniel Pipes once wrote that the "deepest differences between Muslims and Westerners concern not politics but sexuality"[1].

---

1 Daniel Pipes, "Strange Sex Stories from the Muslim World," Daniel Pipes, last modified December 29, 2004, http://www.danielpipes.org/blog/2004/12/strange-sex-stories-from-the-muslim-world.

Here are some examples.

SAUDI ARABIA

In Saudi Arabia, a woman must have a male 'guardian'. This man has almost complete dominion over her life, including marriage and divorce. Under sharia law, women do not have the right to divorce without permission (either from their husband or powerful clergy in the sharia court). Women are also expected to seek permission to work, travel, educate themselves, or even undergo medical treatment. Under sharia, women have few child-custody rights, except those granted by the father or clergy, and can lose their children altogether, once the children reach a certain age, if the father so demands.

The control of a woman's sexuality is central to the control of the woman overall. This system is bound up in a concept of honour. The idea is that a man's honour is tied to how much he can control 'his' women, in particular her sexuality. If a woman behaves in a way which is deemed to be sexually improper, her guardian is expected to punish her to restore the honour he has lost. This can, and often does, mean killing her. For example, a young woman was murdered by her father in 2008 for speaking to a man on Facebook. Clerics responded by demanding that Facebook be banned[2].

To control sex in Saudi Arabia, the genders are strictly segregated. Women can only work in places or areas where they will not come into contact with men. They are also forced to wear the burqa or niqab to cover themselves entirely, including their faces. Restaurants are segregated, with family sections that allow accompanied women, and separate areas for men. Even homes often have a separate women's quarter known as a *harim*. Women are not permitted to leave home without the permission of a guardian (but through practicality this sometimes happens). Women were not allowed to drive until recently, and even using public transport is discouraged.

---

2 "Facebook Girl Beaten and Shot Dead by Her Father for Talking Online," Mail Online, last modified March 31, 2008, http://www.dailymail.co.uk/news/article-550569/Facebook-girl-beaten-shot-dead-father-talking-online.html.

In 2011, Manal al-Sharif posted a video of herself driving on YouTube[3] and Facebook. Two years later, a group of women got behind the wheel and took to the streets in protest at the ban on women driving[4]. Saudi 'scholars' offered their esteemed opinion as to why women shouldn't drive, and it all came down to one thing: sex. Kamal Subhi, who presented a report to the country's legislative assembly in 2011, warned that women driving not only meant the "end of virginity", but would also increase prostitution, pornography, homosexuality and divorce[5]. In 2013, Sheikh Saleh al-Lohaidan warned that the consequences of this decadence (women driving cars) would be catastrophic because of "negative physiological impacts, as functional and physiological medical studies show that it automatically affects the ovaries and pushes the pelvis upwards"[6]. The obsession with controlling sex could not be more obvious, or insane.

Some Saudi women, while objecting to the freedom of other women, also revealed a sex obsession within their reasoning. One woman said in a survey:

> "Female driving will destroy family life because it will give husbands a chance to know other women who (as drivers) will be free and without guardians[7]."

As Margaret Attwood wrote in her superb novel *The Handmaid's Tale*, the oppression of women cannot succeed without the complicity of women.

The Women To Drive Movement, as it was known, finally saw some success in late 2017. The Saudi King issued a Royal

3 "Manal Al Sharif Driving in Saudi Arabia (with English Subtitles)," YouTube, last modified May 27, 2011, https://www.youtube.com/watch?v=sowNSH_W2r0.

4 "Dozens of Saudi Arabian Women Drive Cars on Day of Protest Against Ban," The Guardian, last modified August 8, 2017, http://www.theguardian.com/world/2013/oct/26/saudi-arabia-woman-driving-car-ban.

5 Sebastian Usher, "Saudi Cleric in Virginity Warning," BBC News, last modified December 2, 2011, http://www.bbc.co.uk/news/world-middle-east-16011926.

6 "Cleric Says Driving Risk to Ovaries," BBC News, last modified September 29, 2013, http://www.bbc.co.uk/news/world-middle-east-24323934.

7 Ahmed Abdel-Raheem, "Word to the West: Many Saudi Women Oppose Lifting the Driving Ban | Ahmed Abdel-Raheem," The Guardian, last modified July 14, 2017, http://www.theguardian.com/commentisfree/2013/nov/02/saudi-protest-driving-ban-not-popular.

Decree that drivers' licences should be issued to women, without the permission of the guardian[8].

PAKISTAN

In the Islamic Republic of Pakistan, sexuality is strictly governed. Like in Saudi Arabia, sex before marriage is a crime. Pakistan is particularly notorious for the infamous Hudood Ordinance which was introduced in 1979 by the military leader Muhammad Zia-ul-Haq as part of his attempts to Islamise the country.

The Hudood Ordinance included laws against *zina* (adultery) and *zina bil-jabr* (rape). Under these rules, if a woman alleges she has been raped, she must provide four male Muslim witnesses to the fact. If she cannot do this – which is highly likely – she may find herself charged with adultery.

In 2002, an example of this brutal injustice was aptly demonstrated by the sharia courts of Pakistan. Zafran Bibi reported that she had been raped. She became pregnant as a result. She was then sentenced to death by stoning.

She found herself in a rather difficult spot: the judge told her that in accusing her brother-in-law of raping her, she had confessed to her crime. Furthermore, in refusing to disown her child, she reinforced her guilt. This, said the judge, was proof that she had not been raped.

A *New York Times* report on this case in 2002 claimed that the Hudood laws were applied to "all forms of adultery, whether the offense is committed with or without the consent of the parties"[9]. In other words, there is little difference between rape and adultery, and in both cases, women are severely punished. The aim is to immerse the sexual act in fear and loathing; adultery or pre-marital sex are thus equal in morality terms to rape – if not even worse.

---

8 Martin Chulov, "Saudi Arabia to Allow Women to Obtain Driving Licences," The Guardian, last modified November 27, 2017, https://www.theguardian.com/world/2017/sep/26/saudi-arabias-king-issues-order-allowing-women-to-drive.

9 Seth Mydans, «In Pakistan, Rape Victims Are the ‹Criminals›,» New York Times, May 17, 2002, www.nytimes.com/2002/05/17/international/asia/17RAPE.html.

According to a report in 2003, around 80% of the women in prison in Pakistan were there because they had failed to provide four male Muslim witnesses to their rape[10].

AFGHANISTAN

Afghanistan is another country where the sex act is strictly contained, and where around half of the women in prison have been jailed for being victims of rape[11]. In 2012, a young woman, Gulnaz, was convicted of "adultery by force" and sentenced to 12 years in prison when she claimed she had been raped by a family member. She was eventually freed when she agreed to marry her rapist[12].

In the eyes of the wider Afghan society, Gulnaz had become damaged goods – no longer a virgin and therefore a source of dishonour. Honour could only be restored if she married her rapist. She was also a single mother as a result of the rape, and that too would be intolerable.

Keep in mind what Gulnaz's life would now be like: she would become a domestic and sexual slave to a man who had raped her – for life. She would have no divorce rights because sharia law does not afford unilateral divorce rights to women without permission.

Women in Afghanistan (and elsewhere in the Islamic world) face many threats, marriage slavery being chief among them. Women are sometimes traded or handed over in marriage as settlement of a debt. Nazir Ahmad settled his US$165 debt in Jalalabad by marrying his 16-year-old daughter to the son of the lender[13]. According to the Revolutionary Association of the Women of Afghanistan, the vast majority of Afghan women are

10 "Women and Religious Minorities Under the Hudood Laws in Pakistan — Asian Human Rights Commission," Asian Human Rights Commission, last modified June 3, 2004, http://www.humanrights.asia/resources/journals-magazines/article2/0303/women-and-religious-minorities-under-the-hudood-laws-in-pakistan.
11 "Sharp Rise in Jail Terms for Afghan Rape and Abuse Victims," Telegraph.co.uk, last modified May 21, 2013, http://www.telegraph.co.uk/news/worldnews/asia/afghanistan/10070377/Sharp-rise-in-jail-terms-for-Afghan-rape-and-abuse-victims.html.
12 Jeremy Kelly, "Afghan Woman to Be Freed from Jail After Agreeing to Marry Rapist," The Guardian, last modified December 1, 2017, http://www.theguardian.com/world/2011/dec/01/afghan-woman-freed-marry-rapist.
13 "Afghan Girls Traded for Debts, Blood Feuds - USATODAY.com," USA TODAY: Latest World and US News - USATODAY.com, last modified 10, 2007, http://usatoday30.usatoday.com/news/world/2007-07-09-afghan-girls_N.htm?POE=cl.

married without their consent. Many young women commit suicide to escape this fate – often by setting themselves alight[14].

IRAN

Iran is no better. Here, sex outside of marriage is a crime carrying a punishment of 100 lashes. Adultery is punished with death by stoning.

Stoning became an oft-used punishment in Iran following the installation of Islamic sharia law in 1979. In a famous case, Sakineh Mohammadi Ashtiani was sentenced to death by stoning for adultery in 2006. This was changed to hanging following an international outcry. In March 2014, Mohammad-Javad Larijani, the Islamic regime's Secretary General for Human Rights, announced that Sakineh Ashtiani had been pardoned due to good behaviour[15].

Like in other Islamic states, homosexuality carries the death penalty in Iran. In 2012, four men – identified by the Human Rights Activist News Agency in Iran as Saadat Arefi, Vahid Akbari, Javid Akbari and Houshmand Akbari – were sentenced to be hanged following a guilty verdict for sodomy which had been approved by high court judges[16]. Ayatollah Abdollah Java-di-Amoli, an influential cleric and an Islamic 'scholar' based in the city of Qom, referred to homosexuals as "inferior to dogs and pigs"[17], and the country's then President, Mahmoud Ahmadinejad, famously told a New York audience that there

---

14 "Afghan Women Set Themselves On Fire To Escape Abusive Marriages « RAWA News," Revolutionary Association of the Women of Afghanistan (RAWA), last modified July 12, 2010, http://www.rawa.org/temp/runews/2010/07/12/afghan-women-set-themselves-on-fire-to-escape-abusive-marriages.html.
15 Hugh Tomlinson, "Ashtiani Freed After 9 Years on Death Row," The Times & The Sunday Times, last modified March 19, 2014, https://www.thetimes.co.uk/article/ashtiani-freed-after-9-years-on-death-row-5gk8c3nnds7.
16 "Iran to Execute 4 Men Convicted of Sodomy," The Jerusalem Post | JPost.com, last modified May 17, 2012, http://www.jpost.com/International/Iran-to-execute-4-men-convicted-of-sodomy.
17 Saeed Kamali Dehghan, "Homosexuals Are Inferior to Dogs and Pigs, Says Iranian Cleric," The Guardian, last modified April 18, 2012, http://www.theguardian.com/world/iran-blog/2012/apr/18/iran-cleric-condemns-homosexuality.

were no homosexuals in Iran[18].

So hated is homosexuality in Iran that people who are 'guilty' can be forced to undergo sex changes[19].

The Iranian Islamic state doesn't like sex much at all, at least outside of its strict guidelines. The Iranian regime chooses to fill its people with fear, and presents sex as a deeply immoral act. Cleric Hojjat ol-eslam Kazem Sediq, while leading a Friday prayer in Tehran, told worshippers that women who do not dress modestly are the cause of earthquakes. The only way to avoid being "buried under the rubble" was to follow Islam's sexual codes more strictly[20]."

This is a particularly effective bit of cruelty in Iran – a country which has lost thousands of people to earthquakes.

The strict and cruel regulation of sexuality in Islamic states unequivocally demonstrates the totalitarian nature of those states, and Islam provides the required authority. In *Nineteen Eighty-Four*, sex is also controlled by the totalitarian state, and the anti-sex league exists to demonise sexuality and regulate intimacy.

Totalitarian leadership seeks to control the strongest and most powerful of human emotions: love; sex; the passion of one human being for another. If it does so, it can utilise that passion and energy for its own ends, including – of course – waging war against its enemies.

18 "'We Don't Have Any Gays in Iran,' Iranian President Tells Ivy League Audience," Mail Online, last modified September 25, 2007, http://www.dailymail.co.uk/news/article-483746/We-dont-gays-Iran-Iranian-president-tells-Ivy-League-audience.html.
19 "Iran's Thriving Sex-Change Operations Industry," HuffPost, last modified January 23, 2014, https://www.huffingtonpost.com/2012/06/04/iran-sex-change-operation_n_1568604.html.
20 BBC News, "Iranian Cleric Blames Quakes on Promiscuous Women," Home - BBC News, last modified April 20, 2010, http://news.bbc.co.uk/1/hi/8631775.stm.

HOPE LIES WITH THE PROLES

"If there is hope, it lies with the proles."

George Orwell

IN *NINETEEN EIGHTY-FOUR*, George Orwell introduces us to the proles, who could best be described as the ordinary majority, or the working class. Orwell argues that true power lies in the hands of the proles; the only problem is that they do not realise it. While freedom of speech continues to be eroded, the likelihood that they will realise it moves further and further away.

If the ordinary majority is represented by the proles, who is it that represents The Party in our world? It is, of course, the elitist establishment, represented in the UK by the House of Commons, as well as the media and legal and financial elite.

The House of Commons, the elected chamber of the UK Parliament, is dominated by four political parties: the Conservative Party, the Labour Party, the Scottish National Party, and the Liberal Democrats. Despite ostensibly being opposed to each other, on matters involving Islam, they are entirely inseparable.

There is much evidence of the ever-increasing gap between The Party and the proles in the United Kingdom: the unnecessarily complex and exclusive language used in politics, as well as the class system that hand-picks most of our politicians from Oxford and Cambridge, two universities overwhelmingly occupied by the wealthy and privileged. They graduate and often go straight into one government office or another, then comfortably slot into the House of Commons as MPs.

Many politicians have little idea about the lives of the majority of people they represent. They don't know what it is to experience the daily slog of manual outdoor labour, or stand behind a supermarket cash register hour after hour on minimum wage. They don't know what it means to watch helplessly while the rich put energy prices up, or wealthy economists talk about how much their evening meal will cost.

Nowhere, however, is the gap between Party and prole so starkly illustrated than with the following two matters: Islam and immigration. These two issues prove beyond doubt that the Government of Britain, and the political parties which officially oppose it, are not in the slightest bit interested in the thoughts or opinions of the voting majority.

Take the burqa. Despite polls showing that a clear majority want it banned[1], not a single party will make it a manifesto pledge (with the exception of UKIP in 2017, but this was soon dropped). Indeed, they do the opposite; they go out of their way to make it clear that such a proposal is not, and never will be, on the table. This is proof positive that the will of the majority in this 21st Century democracy is now subject to what is or isn't offensive to Islam.

The deliberate sanitisation of Islam by all major political parties illustrates their thinking – they believe that the public is incapable of examining the evidence and coming to its own conclusion. They believe, in other words, that the voting public is completely stupid.

Following the brutal slaughter of a young British soldier on the streets of London by religious men who stated clearly that they had carried out the killing upon the orders of the

---

1 "YouGov | Two Thirds Brits Want Burqa Ban," YouGov: What the World Thinks, accessed May 8, 2018, http://yougov.co.uk/news/2011/04/14/two-thirds-brits-want-burqa-ban/.

Koran (a detail that did not appear in the mainstream news), then-Prime Minister David Cameron made this extraordinary statement:

> *"There is nothing in Islam that justifies this truly dreadful act."*

The indomitable Lord Pearson of Rannoch did not let Mr Cameron's words pass without comment, and in November 2013, he asked the following question in the House of Lords:

> *"What was the basis for the statement by the Prime Minister on 3 June that 'There is nothing in Islam that justifies acts of terror'?"*

Of course, he didn't receive much of an answer. Baroness Warsi (who resigned in 2014 to protest the fact that the government was not sufficiently anti-Israel) responded to Lord Pearson. In addition to the mandatory whataboutery, Warsi[2] went on to say the following:

> *"As many noble Lords have said in this debate, Islam, like all world religions, neither supports, nor advocates, nor condones terrorism. I am saying that the values of al-Qaeda and like-minded terrorists are not only contrary to what we as a country stand for, they are a distortion of the Islamic tradition itself. Al-Qaeda's ideology is fundamentally at odds with both classical and contemporary Islamic jurisprudence. That is why the majority of Muslims across the globe reject their ideology."*

When pushed by Lord Pearson to address the slaughter of Judeo-Christians by Muslims around the world, particularly the Middle East and North Africa, Warsi replied that such killers did "not follow any faith".

---

2 "Cranmer: Baroness Warsi, Are These People Muslims?," Cranmer (blog), last modified November 25, 2013, http://archbishop-cranmer.blogspot.co.uk/2013/11/baroness-warsi-are-these-people-muslims.html.

What was perhaps the most disturbing comment came from Lord Triesman of the Labour Party:

> "...*in introducing this debate, the noble Lord* [Pearson] *talked about the 'dark side' and birth rates of people who are, obviously, not quite as good as us; people stirring up hate and 'red hot' people striving against us; people who we will finally see looking down the barrel of a gun at us; the plight of Christians, and so on. These are all characterisations which, candidly, should have no place in the debates in this country and our Parliament*[3]*.*"
> The response? "Hear, hear!"

Lord Triesman had therefore decided that even *raising questions* on Islam has 'no place' in Britain's Parliament, and many of the Lords agreed.

THE EDL

The English Defence League (EDL) was formed by Stephen Yaxley Lennon in 2009. He immediately changed his name to Tommy Robinson to protect his identity, and it is by this name that he is known. He formed the organisation following a 'protest' by the Islamist group Al-Muhajiroun against British soldiers returning from Iraq in Robinson's home town of Luton. The group had verbally abused returning soldiers and labelled them murderers.

Although the EDL had no formal membership structure, it became associated with various unsavoury types and became broadly thought of as a far-Right racist group. Tommy Robinson has acknowledged that there were problems with some who had attached themselves to the EDL. Indeed, he left the organisation, citing just that reason. It is evident, however, that the EDL was demonised by a selective and dishonest mainstream media.

---

3 "Lords Hansard Text For 19 Nov 2013 (pt 0001)," United Kingdom Parliament Home Page, accessed May 8, 2018, http://www.publications.parliament.uk/pa/ld201314/ldhansrd/text/131119-gc0001.htm#13111956000150.

Let's start with the violence that sometimes occurred at EDL rallies. At a demonstration in Manchester in 2009, 'ugly scenes' were described by reporter Mat Trewern from BBC Radio Manchester[4]:

> *"At one point, earlier on, when it became extremely tense, members of the UAF [Unite Against Fascism] tried to break the police line between the two groups, which in turn angered the EDL members."*

In Bolton, Greater Manchester, in 2010, a further clash was reported between the EDL and UAF. Seventy-four arrests were made – 55 of them from supporters of UAF and only nine from the EDL[5]. Weyman Bennett, joint secretary of UAF, and fellow Left Winger Martin Smith were arrested on suspicion of conspiracy to commit violent disorder[6].

Not long afterwards, a group calling itself Justice4Bolton was set up to call on the police to drop the charges against the UAF supporters who had been arrested. The initiation meeting was addressed by Member of Parliament Yasmin Qureshi and Bolton Trades Union Council Secretary Martin Challender.

Challender said, "It is important that we reserve the right to protest[7]." But isn't that what the EDL was doing?

There are some examples of violence attributed to EDL supporters:

- Eight EDL supporters arrested for throwing bottles at police in Oldham in 2010[8].

---

4 BBC NEWS | UK | England | Manchester | "Dozens Arrested During Protests," Home - BBC News, last modified October 10, 2009, http://news.bbc.co.uk/1/hi/8300431.stm.

5 74 Arrests in Demo Clash,» BelfastTelegraph.co.uk, last modified March 21, 2010, http://www.belfasttelegraph.co.uk/breakingnews/breakingnews_ukandireland/74-arrests-in-demo-clash-28524766.html.

6 "Dozens Arrested As English Defence League and Anti-fascists Clash in Violent Street Protests," Mail Online, last modified March 21, 2010, http://www.dailymail.co.uk/news/article-1259409/Police-attack-right-wing-group-anti-fascists-clash-violent-street-protests.html#ixzz0vBHaB3Av.

7 "Meeting over Rally Arrests," The Bolton News, last modified July 6, 2010, http://www.theboltonnews.co.uk/news/8256031.Meeting_over_rally_arrests/.

8 "Eight Arrested at EDL Gathering," BBC News, last modified September 12, 2010, http://www.bbc.co.uk/news/uk-england-manchester-11275810.

- Sixty EDL supporters arrested in London for throwing fire-crackers and bottles in 2011[9].
- It is fair to say, then, that both UAF and the EDL have some nasty characters among their support base, but here are some differences:
- The EDL does not associate with jihadis and Islamists and those who seek to destroy Britain and replace its democratic order with religious tyranny. The UAF, however, frequently does just this. One of UAF's vice chairs, for example, was Azad Ali. Ali has been a spokesman for the sharia-advocating Islamic Forum of Europe, which wants to move the UK from "ignorance to Islam"[10].
- The EDL has been denounced by pretty much everyone in power, while UAF counts mainstream politicians as members and supporters[11]. Public figures who support UAF include the former Mayor of London Ken Livingstone, numerous MPs, and interestingly, members of the sharia-supporting Muslim Council of Britain.

In Birmingham in 2010, Prime Minister David Cameron made the following statement:

> *"The EDL are terrible people. We would always keep these groups under review, and if we needed to ban them, we would ban them, or any groups which incite hatred[12]."*

So let's get this straight. There are violent clashes between two groups of protestors on a regular basis: the English Defence

9 "Sixty Arrests As EDL Members Clash with Police Including 44 Pulled off a Coach That Had Stopped Outside a Mosque," Mail Online, last modified September 9, 2011, http://www.dailymail.co.uk/news/article-2033322/The-chilling-pictures-English-Defence-League-members-posing-arsenal-deadly-weapons.html.
10 Andrew Gilligan, "IFE: Not Harmless Democrats | Andrew Gilligan," The Guardian, last modified September 15, 2017, https://www.theguardian.com/commentisfree/belief/2010/mar/04/islamic-forum-europe-dispatches-gilligan.
11 «Founding Signatories»,» Unite Against Fascism, accessed May 9, 2018, http://uaf.org.uk/about/founding-signatories/.
12 Jasbir Authi, "David Cameron makes dash to West Midlands," BirminghamMail, last modified October 24, 2012, http://www.birminghammail.co.uk/news/local-news/david-cameron-makes-dash-to-west-124267.

League and Unite Against Fascism. The Prime Minister, on the campaign trail, states that *one* of these groups is comprised of "terrible people", but says nothing about the other. The group he doesn't mention, UAF, causes more violence than the EDL, as police have confirmed[13]. Why then is the EDL comprised of terrible people but UAF is not?

Simple. The EDL doesn't like Islam.

The English Defence League, for all its faults, achieved something very important. It raised the issue of Islam in the place where it most needed to be raised – among ordinary people. It spoke out for the vast numbers living on housing estates the length and breadth of this land who are seeing unprecedented transformations in the towns and cities they grew up in. It got working-class people thinking and talking about democracy, freedom of speech, and secularism. It spoke of the threats to the identity of ordinary English people. It spoke of the hidden and unpunished crimes across vast suburban areas: gang-rape of white English girls (covered up by local authorities); the disappearance of young English girls under burqas; and countless other issues which had until then been completely ignored.

If Britain is to defeat Islamism, it will be necessary to replace the current political establishment, and this can only be done with the people's vote. Our leaders are far too busy silencing critics of Islam to confront the problems it causes. The Government courts Saudi money and allows British mosques to preach hatred of Britain and its citizens. The European Union, of which we are unfortunate enough still to be a member despite voting to leave, is coming up with plans to 'rehabilitate' Islamophobes. British and European leadership is incompetent on this matter, as is Western leadership generally.

The only way Islamism will be defeated, or even confronted, is through the power of the people. We must use our vote and our right to stand for political office in order to unseat complicit MPs. Britain was reminded of this power when it voted to leave the European Union in June 2016. The United States of America was reminded when it voted for Donald Trump.

If there is hope – it lies with the proles.

---

13 Viv Smith, "Police: 'The English Defence League is not the problem'," *Socialist Worker*, accessed May 8, 2018, www.socialistworker.co.uk/art.php?id=22944.

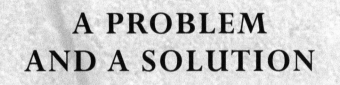

A PROBLEM
AND A SOLUTION

INTERNATIONALISM

THE ATLANTIC CHARTER

"The President of the United States and the Prime Minister, Mr Churchill, representing HM Government in the United Kingdom, being met together, deem it right to make known certain common principles in the national policies of their respective countries on which they base their hopes for a better future for the world.

"Their countries seek no aggrandisement, territorial or other.

"They desire to see no territorial changes that do not accord with the freely expressed wishes of the peoples concerned.

"They respect the right of all peoples to choose the form of Government under which they will live; and they wish to see sovereign rights and self-government restored to those who have been forcibly deprived of them.

"They will endeavour, with due respect for their existing obligations, to further enjoyment by all states, great or small, victor or vanquished, of access, on equal terms, to

the trade and to the raw materials of the world which are needed for their economic prosperity.

"They desire to bring about the fullest collaboration between all nations in the economic field, with the object of securing for all improved labour standards, economic advancement, and social security.

"After the final destruction of Nazi tyranny, they hope to see established a peace which will afford to all nations the means of dwelling in safety within their own boundaries, and which will afford assurance that all the men in all the lands may live out their lives in freedom from fear and want.

"Such a peace should enable all men to traverse the high seas and oceans without hindrance.

"They believe all of the nations of the world, for realistic as well as spiritual reasons, must come to the abandonment of the use of force. Since no future peace can be maintained if land, sea, or air armaments continue to be employed by nations which threaten, or may threaten aggression outside of their frontiers, they believe, pending the establishment of a wider and permanent system of general security, that the disarmament of such nations is essential. They will likewise aid and encourage all other practicable measures which will lighten for peace-loving peoples the crushing burden of armament[14]."

The Atlantic Charter, above, is one of the most interesting examples of the powerful growth of internationalism over the last century or so. Internationalism can be mild, meaning cooperation between nations, or extreme, effectively amounting to borderlessness.

The latter is that path we have taken.

---

14 NATO, "'The Atlantic Charter' - Declaration of Principles Issued by the President of the United States and the Prime Minister of the United Kingdom," NATO, last modified October 1, 2009, http://www.nato.int/cps/en/natohq/official_texts_16912.htm.

THE UNITED NATIONS CHARTER

In 1945, representatives of 50 countries met in San Francisco to draw up the United Nations Charter. It was signed on 26 June by the 50 countries present, with Poland becoming the 51st signatory soon afterwards. The Charter was subsequently signed by China, France, the Soviet Union, the UK, and the USA, and the United Nations officially came into existence on 24 October 1945. United Nations Day is (apparently) celebrated on 24 October each year[15].

Here are its purposes and principles:

- *"To maintain international peace and security, and to that end: to take effective collective measures for the prevention and removal of threats to the peace, and for the suppression of acts of aggression or other breaches of the peace, and to bring about by peaceful means, and in conformity with the principles of justice and international law, adjustment or settlement of international disputes or situations which might lead to a breach of the peace;*
- *To develop friendly relations among nations based on respect for the principle of equal rights and self-determination of peoples, and to take other appropriate measures to strengthen universal peace;*
- *To achieve international co-operation in solving international problems of an economic, social, cultural, or humanitarian character, and in promoting and encouraging respect for human rights and for fundamental freedoms for all without distinction as to race, sex, language, or religion; and*
- *To be a centre for harmonizing the actions of nations in the attainment of these common ends."*

It all sounds wonderful, but it raises important questions, and those questions are left unanswered.

---

15 "History of the United Nations," United Nations, last modified April 26, 2017, http://www.un.org/en/sections/history/history-united-nations/index.html.

Some examples:

"To take effective collective measures for the prevention and removal of threats to the peace." What if we don't agree on what constitutes a threat to the peace, and what if it threatens my country more than yours?

"To achieve international co-operation in solving problems of an economic, social, cultural, or humanitarian character, and in promoting and encouraging respect for human rights and for fundamental freedoms for all without distinction as to race, sex, language, or religion." This one is the real issue. Not all countries believe in freedoms for all, and they won't sign up to these principles, so what then?

The answer isn't in the document.

If a country doesn't subscribe to the founding principles of the UN; in fact, if a country firmly rejects them, that country is still more than welcome to join. Why? Because the UN believes in the equality of nations, and as such, a country's government, no matter how barbaric, will be treated as if it is a legitimate member of the club. The principles therefore mean nothing.

THE UN DECLARATION OF HUMAN RIGHTS

In 1948, the General Assembly of the United Nations (its primary decision-making body) adopted the UN Declaration of Human Rights[16] (UNDHR). It wasn't a treaty in its own right, but part of its intent was to clarify the meaning of 'fundamental freedoms' and 'human rights' in the binding UN Charter.

Here are some of the articles of the Declaration of Human Rights.

> *"Article 1. All human beings are born free and equal in dignity and rights. They are endowed with reason and conscience and should act towards one another in a spirit of brotherhood.*
>
> *Article 2. Everyone is entitled to all the rights and*

---

16 "Universal Declaration of Human Rights," United Nations, last modified May 16, 2018, http://www.un.org/en/universal-declaration-human-rights/.

freedoms set forth in this Declaration, without distinction of any kind, such as race, colour, sex, language, religion, political or other opinion, national or social origin, property, birth or other status. Furthermore, no distinction shall be made on the basis of the political, jurisdictional or international status of the country or territory to which a person belongs, whether it be independent, trust, non-self-governing or under any other limitation of sovereignty.

Article 3. Everyone has the right to life, liberty and security of person.

Article 4. No one shall be held in slavery or servitude; slavery and the slave trade shall be prohibited in all their forms.

Article 5. No one shall be subjected to torture or to cruel, inhuman or degrading treatment or punishment.

Article 7. *All are equal before the law and are entitled without any discrimination to equal protection of the law. All are entitled to equal protection against any discrimination in violation of this Declaration and against any incitement to such discrimination.*

Article 8.

(1) Everyone has the right to seek and to enjoy in other countries asylum from persecution.

(2) This right may not be invoked in the case of prosecutions genuinely arising from non-political crimes or from acts contrary to the purposes and principles of the United Nations.

Article 16.

(1) Men and women of full age, without any limitation due to race, nationality or religion, have the right to marry and to found a family. They are entitled to equal rights as to marriage, during marriage and at its dissolution.

(2) Marriage shall be entered into only with the free and full consent of the intending spouses.

(3) The family is the natural and fundamental group unit of society and is entitled to protection by society and the state."

In 2013, the Kingdom of Saudi Arabia was elected to the board responsible for putting into action the above principles. With this in mind, let's have a look at these articles again.

Article 1 – "All human beings are born free and equal in dignity and rights". In sharia countries, the female is officially the property of the male.

Article 2 – "Everyone is entitled to all the rights and freedoms set forth in this Declaration". Oh dear. We know that women are chattel, but in sharia societies, Muslims and non-Muslims do not have equal rights either. A non-Muslim's testimony in court is worth less than a Muslim's, for example.

Article 3 – "Everyone has the right to life, liberty and security of person". The liberty or security of person does not apply to women, gays, atheists, or secularists in any society where sharia law calls the shots – including those sitting at the UN.

Article 4 – "No one shall be held in slavery or servitude; slavery and the slave trade shall be prohibited in all their forms". Dr Charles Jacobs wrote in *Arutz Sheva* in 2013:

> *"One might think American student activists would be upset about Mauritania, the West African country with the largest population of black slaves in the world – estimates range from 100,000 to more than a half-million. In Mauritania, slaves are used for labor, sex and breeding. The wholly owned property of their masters, they are passed down through generations, given as wedding gifts or exchanged for camels, trucks, guns or money[17]."*

Article 5 – "No one shall be subjected to torture or to cruel, inhuman or degrading treatment or punishment". Death by stoning for adultery or homosexuality; amputation for theft; punishment of rape victims. Need I say more?

Article 7 – "All are equal before the law and are entitled without any discrimination to equal protection of the law".

---

17 Charles Jacobs, "Arabs Have Black Slaves - Today," Israel National News, last modified March 29, 2013, http://www.israelnationalnews.com/Articles/Article. aspx/13067.

Women are worth less than men, non-Muslims are worth less than Muslims. That is sharia, everywhere it is practised.

Article 8 – (1) "Everyone has the right to seek and to enjoy in other countries asylum from persecution". One assumes, then, that the receiving country has a right to know whether a migrant is in fact genuinely fleeing persecution. Has the UN ever suggested that the West should make sure, as per the UNDHR, that all asylum seekers are persecuted? No, I don't believe it has.

Article 16 – (1) "Men and women of full age, without any limitation due to race, nationality or religion, have the right to marry and to found a family. They are entitled to equal rights as to marriage, during marriage and at its dissolution". In every single country in the world that practises sharia law, men and women of full age do not have equal rights as to marriage, during marriage or at its dissolution.

Article 16 – (2) "Marriage shall be entered into only with the free and full consent of the intending spouses". Legal child marriage is widespread across the Muslim world. Forced marriage also. Needless to say, much of it is carried out in countries that are members of the UN.

Article 16 – (3) "The family is the natural and fundamental group unit of society and is entitled to protection by society and the state." It depends. Does it have to subscribe to points one and two, or will it be considered worthy of protection by the state in any case?

THE BIRTH OF THE EUROPEAN UNION

The global zeitgeist of the 20th century aspired to international cooperation, and this was particularly the case following the end of the Second World War. The foundations of the UN were believed by many to be the antidote to the cause of the war, which was broadly believed to be nationalism. Nationalism, therefore, would become a political position that was consistently and stealthily condemned. It provided fertile ground for the seeds of European integration to be sewn.

The European Coal and Steel Community was established in 1951 to create a common market and neutralise competition between member states, and included France, Belgium, West Germany, Italy, the Netherlands and Luxembourg. The idea of it was to make further wars between European countries 'materially impossible'. The Schuman Declaration[18] of 9 May 1950 proposed the new organisation, making it French government policy.

The Schuman Declaration states:

> "*Europe will not be made all at once, or according to a single plan. It will be built through concrete achievements which first create a de facto solidarity. The coming together of the nations of Europe requires the elimination of the age-old opposition of France and Germany.*
>
> "*By pooling basic production and by instituting a new High Authority, whose decisions will bind France, Germany and other member countries, this proposal will lead to the realization of the first concrete foundation of a European federation indispensable to the preservation of peace.*"

Schuman was also clear that European federalism would not happen at once, but by stealth – and that is exactly what has happened.

The European Union has evolved over decades through new treaties, regulations and directives, and binding decisions of the European Court of Justice. All have steered Europeans in one direction – towards greater integration. National sovereignty has been all but wiped out as law after law, which cannot be overturned by popular vote, are imposed from without, and governments seek EU permission to act in their own national interest. This makes the election of national governments something close to futile. What say does a population really have if those it elects subsequently seek authority from those it did not?

---

18 "The Schuman Declaration - 9 May 1950 - European Commission," European Union, last modified October 24, 2017, https://europa.eu/european-union/about-eu/symbols/europe-day/schuman-declaration_en.

David Cameron, for example, had to plead with EU leaders in 2016 to allow him to alter the social welfare rules in Britain[19], a ploy he hoped would see off the threat of Brexit (British exit from the EU). Some of his 'demands' included the ability to decide how much newly arrived migrants should receive in welfare benefits in the UK. He also wanted to stop paying child support to the children of migrants who were not even living in Britain. He was given neither (not wholly, at least).

The European Union was sold to the people as a common market, and that was indeed its foundation, but it is a common market that comes with a sting in the tail: the free movement of people. To listen to Europhiles, one would assume it was entirely impossible to have common trade with another country without having an open border to each other's populations. Countries all over the world make trade deals all the time, almost always without the respective countries opening their borders.

In summary, over a short period during the 20th century, two major international bodies came into being. One would go on to become the EU and aim to bring about a federal Europe. The other, the United Nations, sought to bring the world together to end war. Internationalism had arrived.

But there is something peculiar about this new global world. This 'something' is called ideology; politics has simply become a competition between ideologies – the winner gets to put theirs in to effect.

Is there an ideological aim to rid the world of the Europe we know? If there were, it would probably look a lot like what has taken place since the end of the Second World War.

---

19 Alice Foster, "EU Referendum 2016: What Are the Full Details of Cameron's Deal? All the Key Points," Express.co.uk, last modified June 23, 2016, http://www.express.co.uk/news/politics/645777/EU-referendum-David-Cameron-Brexit-EU-deal-European-Union-Brussels-emergency-break-UK.

WHAT TO DO ABOUT IT

BEFORE I START on this rather controversial chapter, let me clarify a couple of points. I fully acknowledge that Europeans come in all colours. I know that many non-white Europeans are patriotic and loyal to their countries. I know that all citizens of European countries are equal in terms of rights and responsibilities. However, I make no apologies for recognising that Europe has indigenous peoples, and that these peoples have white skin. In multi-ethnic Europe, though, white people are denied a voice in the public sphere if it is from a white person's perspective, while ethnic, religious and racial minorities are encouraged to address issues from their specific perspectives. Contempt for white people is widespread, and this is fuelling the destruction of Western society.

If I were to try to wipe out Europe, this is how I would do it:

1. Mass migration. Have you noticed that in the new globalised world, most human traffic seems to be heading in a certain direction? If we are blending the world, bringing down borders and amalgamating cultures, why isn't there mass migration between China and Japan? Why isn't there mass migration between France and Germany? The fact is that globalism features one kind of movement only – from the developing world to the West.

Why might this be? If a 'persecuted person' (I put this in quote marks because most of the people arriving in Europe are *not* being persecuted) claims asylum in a safe country, why do so many end up in the West? There are safe countries elsewhere, are there not?

In September 2015, *Breitbart* reported[1] that five of the wealthiest Muslim countries had taken no Syrian refugees at all. The countries had claimed that doing so would open them up to the risk of terrorism.

The report states:

> *"Although the oil-rich countries have handed over aid money, Britain has donated more than Saudi Arabia, the United Arab Emirates and Qatar combined."*

These countries were not, however, widely condemned by politicians or media for their 'racist' standpoint.

At the height of the US presidential election campaign, the UN's High Commissioner for Human Rights condemned Republican nominee Donald Trump's views as "deeply unsettling and disturbing"[2]. Zeid Ra'ad al-Hussein said he was concerned about "the focus on vulnerable communities in a way that suggests that they may well be deprived of their human rights". Donald Trump simply said he would control America's borders and put American interests first. There was nothing to suggest he was a threat to people's human rights.

The UN is not shy about making demands on the West to accommodate the rest of the world. Its special rapporteur on the human rights of migrants said[3] in 2015 that "rich countries"

---

1 Breitbart News, "Muslim Countries Refuse to Take A Single Syrian Refugee, Cite Risk of Exposure to Terrorism," Breitbart, last modified September 5, 2015, http://www.breitbart.com/london/2015/09/05/gulf-states-refuse-to-take-a-single-syrian-refugee-say-doing-so-exposes-them-to-risk-of-terrorism/.
2 "Trump Danger to World, Says UN Official," BBC News, last modified October 12, 2016, http://www.bbc.co.uk/news/election-us-2016-37628345.
3 Gabrielle Jackson, «UN Expert: Rich Countries Must Take in 1 Million Refugees to Stop Boat Deaths,» The Guardian, last modified April 14, 2018, https://www.theguardian.com/world/2015/apr/22/un-urges-wealthy-countries-to-take-one-million-syrian-refugees-in-next-five-years.

(who *can* he mean?) should take a million people from Syria and elsewhere. François Crépeau reportedly said that Europe was creating a market for smugglers by not providing "any official mechanism" for people to leave their countries. But isn't this kind of message from officials likely to boost the people-smuggling trade, letting the world believe that Europe can, and will, accommodate anybody fleeing from anything?

2. Degrade, insult, and demonise the indigenous people. Here is a dictionary definition of the word 'indigenous': "naturally existing in a place or country rather than arriving from another place".

The UN claims it doesn't have a definition of indigenous, but offers this as a suggestion:

> *"Indigenous communities, peoples and nations are those which, having a historical continuity with pre-invasion and pre-colonial societies that developed on their territories, consider themselves distinct from other sectors of the societies now prevailing on those territories, or parts of them. They form at present non-dominant sectors of society and are determined to preserve, develop and transmit to future generations their ancestral territories, and their ethnic identity, as the basis of their continued existence as peoples, in accordance with their own cultural patterns, social institutions and legal system."*

According to the UN, the status of 'indigenous' is reserved for "non-dominant" groups, thereby carefully excluding native Europeans in European societies. This is significant because if Europeans want to "preserve, develop and transmit to future generations their ancestral territories, and their ethnic identity, as the basis of their continued existence as peoples, in accordance with their own cultural patterns, social institutions and legal system", they can't, because they are 'dominant'.

There is no greater example of the denigration of the indigenous people of Europe than the hysterical hatred and fear of the word 'white'. The very word 'white', or discussion of an issue pertinent to white people, is actively and fiercely quashed.

Vilification of European peoples and cultures can be found in the concept and application of multiculturalism itself. Multi-culturalism sends transparent messages to the newly arrived migrant:

- You are welcome in our country, but our culture is worthless so don't bother joining it.
- Your culture is superior by virtue of the fact that it is not ours – this remains the case regardless of the practices of your culture.

Here is part of an article I wrote in late 2016 entitled 'Leftism is a Mental Illness':

> Described as a "national spokeswoman of the Left-wing youth movement Solid", Selin Gören was attacked by three men in Mannheim and *"forced to perform a sex act"*. When she went to the police, she lied about the identity of her attackers, claiming they spoke German when in fact they had been speaking "Arabic or Farsi". She did this because she didn't want to encourage racism.
>
> A male Norwegian politician, who was raped by a migrant[4] in his home, revealed how he felt guilty that his rapist was to be deported back to his native Somalia because he may face hardship there. His concern for a convicted rapist was therefore greater than his concern for himself or his fellow Norwegians. This brings me to another recognisable and recognised personality disorder trait: hatred of one's own ethnic group. This one is partic-ularly widespread within the Left-wing movement.
>
> Anti-white sentiment is common among Left Wingers, including among white activists. This is perfectly illustrated in an English anti-Englishness that won't, for example,

---

4 "Male Norwegian Politician Raped by Asylum Seeker Felt Guilty," Mail Online, last modified April 7, 2016, http://www.dailymail.co.uk/news/article-3528236/Male-Norwegian-politician-raped-asylum-seeker-says-feels-GUILTY-attacker-deported-man-suffer-Somalia.html.

celebrate the country's national day because a city is too 'multicultural'[5] and it wouldn't be feasible to celebrate all the cultures. The idea that English culture should have a special place in England doesn't appear to be entertained.

3. Lie, lie, and lie again. The most striking aspect of the migrant crisis has been just how many obvious lies have been told. When refugees began to arrive in Britain in late 2016, we were repeatedly told, as though it were true, that they were in fact children. It was perfectly clear that many of those coming across the English Channel from Calais were not children.

Take this example from the *Daily Mail*. The *Mail* had itself reported on a 21-year-old who had passed himself off as 12[6], but only a couple of days later, it published another article on the issue and repeatedly referred to the migrants as 'children'[7]. Furthermore, fleeing war in Syria was the consistently repeated justification for it all, despite the fact that EU statisticians claimed only one in five[8] of those arriving were actually from Syria.

We also are repeatedly told that the migrants are in fact 'refugees' or 'asylum seekers' without any reference to what those terms actually mean. The word 'refugee' is a legal term and is defined by several treaties. But even though vast numbers of people arriving in Europe do not fit the definition, they are treated as if they do.

That we need countless migrants for economic reasons is another lie. There are millions of unemployed people in Europe, but we are told we must import people from the third world in order to be able to function. If there is a shortage of workers in

---

5 Zoie O'Brien, "Anger As Council Officials Say UK City is 'too Multicultural? to Celebrate St George's Day," Express.co.uk, last modified April 26, 2016, https://www.express.co.uk/news/uk/663922/Anger-as-council-officials-say-UK-city-is-too-multicultural-to-celebrate-St-George-s-Day.

6 "'12-year-old' in Foster Care Was Actually 21-year-old Jihadi," Mail Online, last modified October 24, 2016, http://www.dailymail.co.uk/news/article-3863392/Foster-mother-discovers-12-year-old-Afghan-refugee-orphan-cared-21-year-old-jihadi.html.

7 "We Can't Cope with More Migrants, Councils Tell Theresa May," Mail Online, last modified October 26, 2016, http://www.dailymail.co.uk/news/article-3872758/We-t-cope-migrants-councils-tell-Town-halls-warn-families-face-increased-tax-bills-pay-influx.html.

8 "'Only 1 in 5 Migrants Are from Syria'," Metro, last modified September 19, 2015, http://metro.co.uk/2015/09/19/eu-statisticians-claim-only-1-in-5-migrants-are-from-syria-5398412.

Germany, for example, why are jobs there not being filled by people from Greece or Spain, where youth employment is sky high? Statistics have revealed that 99% of those who arrived during the influx to Germany remained unemployed a year later[9]. This was despite Chancellor Merkel's demands that companies hire more migrants, which inevitably means prioritising migrants over Germans. It also means that jobs will be given to people who are entirely unqualified to do them.

THE SOLUTION?

I am often asked for my solutions to these problems – to the Islamisation of the West and the weakness that facilitates it. I will conclude by providing just a few (these refer in the main to the UK, but could be applicable in any Western nation).

1. Restore accountable government via nation-state sovereignty. International bodies should be disbanded and sovereignty restored to nation-states. Only when this occurs can the people truly hold governments to account for their actions. If held accountable, governments are far more likely to act in the interests of their own people. International cooperation should be promoted, but it cannot morph into a situation where one country is not able to stand independently and defend itself from threats.

2. Reform education. Education at all levels must change; it should teach a high standard of mathematics, sciences, languages, and accurate history. Children should be taught about their own country positively, and learn of its achievements in the world.

3. Apply the law equally to all. This is one of the most important steps we can take as it is the answer to countless problems. If the law were applied to all people equally, harmful

---

9 Oli Smith, "Merkel's Open-door Policy Hits German Economy As 99% of Migrants STILL Don't Have a Job," Express.co.uk, last modified September 15, 2016, https://www.express.co.uk/news/world/710927/million-migrants-Germany-unemployed-Merkel-open-door-policy.

Islamic practices would soon be brought under control. Those who found it unbearable not to mutilate their daughters, for example, may leave the country; others would simply discontinue this criminal practice (especially if deportation were the punishment).

We must also rid ourselves of religious tribunals. All marriages, divorces, child custody cases, and domestic violence cases should be dealt with under one set of laws only – those enacted by the UK's elected legislature. We must alter charity legislation to ensure that 'charities' like the Islamic Sharia Council cannot exploit their status to impose political control.

Laws are nothing if they are not enforced. We must enforce the law of the land with no fear or bias, and no consideration as to the race or religion of the perpetrator or the victim of a crime. Finally, if force is required to close down sharia courts, then force is what will be used.

4. Control immigration and deport criminals. If a migrant commits a violent crime against anyone in the host country, they should be deported on a permanent basis. Expulsion should also serve as punishment for breaching immigration laws themselves. All decisions as to immigration, whether asylum, economic, or otherwise, must be made with the best interests of the host population in mind. Deportation must also be included in the list of punishments for those who commit FGM or child marriage. This is the only punishment that will work.

It is vital, therefore, that all who enter a country can prove who they are and where they have come from. We must not accept migrants that we are unable to expel.

5. Investigate mosques for incitement to violence and prosecute the culprits using existing laws. Those who are not British citizens should be deported and those who are should go to jail. There is plenty of evidence in the public domain, including in this book, about what is being said in many mosques across Britain. Much of this meets the definition of criminal incitement.

These are some of the vital steps I believe should be taken as a matter of urgency; any sane society would be doing these things already. However, these changes will only occur when the people of Europe realise their power and the lies they have been told. As mainstream journalists are not delivering the truth, we must promote alternative media and challenge mainstream lies using every method available to us.

We need to rediscover the nation-states that bind us and focus on the good that they offer. Believing in ourselves and our countries is all that will prompt us to defend them. If we hate ourselves, why would we come to our own defence? Westerners are the proud tenants of a wonderful place, but we must keep it wonderful so that the next generations of Westerners can enjoy it as well.

Above all, we must use our democracies in order to save them. Brexit showed us just what a democratic vote can do, and we can do it again and again until we achieve change. We must, however, have somebody to vote for. Those who are concerned about the content of this book must step up and be counted. We must stop being afraid. If we do not confront what frightens us now, the future will be far more frightening for us all.

CONCLUSION

THE 21ˢᵀ CENTURY Western world faces an enormous battle. It is a matter of fact that a violent totalitarian religious ideology is growing in power in every corner of the world – that ideology is based on the religion of Islam, and it has widespread support. I am not referring to Islamic terrorism; I'm referring to sharia law.

The Western world has established many great democracies, and people within them urgently need to understand the danger these democracies are in. Women in particular are under threat. Those who care about freedom need to alert themselves, and fast. A society where speech is regulated is a society of fear, where one lives in the isolation of keeping one's opinions to one's self at all times, or where disagreement can lead to death. It is a society of misery. It is also a society that is slow to change because people fear speaking out.

Governments throughout the world, whether through ignorance or denial or political positioning, are assisting in the rise of political Islam. They have legislated to condemn criticism of Islam, and gone out of their way to defend it whenever an Islamic terror attack takes place. They are directly aiding the advancement of the Islamist ideology, and the United Nations is helping.

Islam is not a tiny minority of extremists that can be ignored; it is a powerful movement that rules several countries and is seeking to rule more. It is intent on global domination, and is now firmly ensconced in the Western world.

Western leaders must realise that it is the ideology of Islam that has to be confronted. Whether sharia arrives by the bomb or the ballot box, sharia will be the result. It's sharia we have to oppose.

International bodies like the United Nations must exclude and isolate countries that don't adhere to the values the UN is intended to protect. Saudi Arabia has no place on a human rights council; it is an insult to human rights.

Democratic states must start walking the walk. It is time to step up and defend our beliefs and our values, cease apologising and relativising, and stop pretending that brutal tyranny is just another 'culture'.

This is not a clash between equally moral positions; it is a battle between freedom and oppression, compassion and barbarism, civilised behaviour and violence. We need to decide what side we are on, and fight for that side to win.

Lightning Source UK Ltd.
Milton Keynes UK
UKHW01n1424090718
325438UK00003B/32/P